THE JAZZ LIFE OF

Dr. Billy Taylor

INDIANA UNIVERSITY PRESS   *Bloomington & Indianapolis*

THE
JAZZ
LIFE
OF
Dr. Billy Taylor

DR. BILLY TAYLOR
with
TERESA L. REED

This book is a publication of

INDIANA UNIVERSITY PRESS
Office of Scholarly Publishing
Herman B Wells Library 350
1320 East 10th Street
Bloomington, Indiana 47405 USA

iupress.indiana.edu

Telephone orders   800-842-6796
Fax orders   812-855-7931

∞ The paper used in this publication
meets the minimum requirements of
the American National Standard for
Information Sciences-Permanence of
Paper for Printed Library Materials,
ANSI Z39.48-1992.

Manufactured in the
United States of America

Library of Congress
Cataloging-in-Publication Data

Taylor, Billy, 1921–2010, author.
  The jazz life of Dr. Billy Taylor /
Dr. Billy Taylor with Teresa L. Reed.
    pages cm
  Includes bibliographical references,
index, and discography.
  ISBN 978-0-253-00909-8 (cloth : alkaline
paper) — ISBN 978-0-253-00917-3 (e-book)
  1. Taylor, Billy, 1921–2010. 2. Jazz musi-
cians—United States—Biography. I.
Reed, Teresa L., [date–] author. II. Title.
  ML417.T24A3 2013
  781.65092—dc23
  [B]

                                    2012047536

1 2 3 4 5   18 17 16 15 14 13

TO THOSE WHO TEACH MUSIC

Jazz is America's classical music.

Contents

Introduction

On a frigid December evening, I left my room at Le Parker Meridian and decided to walk the five blocks to the place where Dr. Billy Taylor left his heart. That place, that era, and that magic were so deeply ingrained in his being that his stories about 52nd Street came alive in my own mind, transporting me to the reality of something that I could feel and hear even though its sights and sounds had already vanished well before I was born. I weaved my way through Manhattan's bustling throngs, its street vendors, showgoers, tourists, subway catchers, and fashionable canines, each exhaling hurried breaths of cold, steamy air from faces set like flint in their respective forward-moving directions. Swimming against this current of future-facing pedestrians, I was looking to arrive at a place in the past. Dr. Taylor's 52nd Street was nearing the golden anniversary of its swan song. But I had the faith of an archeologist. The history made on 52nd Street was too significant, too world-changing to have vanished altogether. Some evidence of its glory days must still survive.

Swing Street. A ten-minute walk brought me to the corner of 52nd and 6th Streets, where, in a nearly frostbitten state, I turned in the direction where the Onyx Club, the Famous Door, the Hickory House, and the Three Deuces had been in the 1930s and 1940s. Of course, there were different buildings in the places where these clubs once stood, but I imagined myself tracing the footsteps of a twenty-two-year-old Bill Taylor, perhaps even walking on the same pavement that brought him, more than six decades earlier, to this very spot as he headed to the Three Deuces for his audition on an equally frigid night.

A single edifice on 52nd Street survives from that era: Club 21. It was always known as a speakeasy-turned-swanky-restaurant more than as a jazz club. Owned during the 1940s by Sherman Billingsley, 21 was unique in that it stood out as one of the very few establishments on that block that remained closed to African Americans even though most of the surrounding jazz clubs were already integrated and regularly hosting both racially mixed bands and clientele. But at least it was still standing and had not gone the sad way of its peer institutions. Perhaps it contained the ghosts of patrons who stopped here for steak and lobster before heading to the Onyx Club for drinks and a late-night set of Dizzy Gillespie. If only its walls could talk.

When I began working with Dr. Taylor in 2006, I quickly learned that 52nd Street was the physical address, the geographical landmark, the spiritual mecca in his life that made all the difference. Whether we were covering his boyhood on Flagler Place, or his college days at Virginia State, or his work on the *David Frost Show,* our conversations always seemed to veer around to that most sacred of memories, a beautiful time in jazz history when musicians enjoyed a unique sort of kinship. In Dr. Taylor's day, the flashing lights and foot-tapping excitement of these clubs on 52nd Street beckoned loudly to lovers of great jazz as well as to up-and-coming musicians. These clubs offered a showcase of legendary jazz performances, all contained within the short distance of a few city blocks. This was also a musical boot camp, a place where master musicians presided over the jam sessions that trained and toughened the newcomers, a place where battered and bruised egos could go to the club next door and hear the likes of Billie Holiday, Teddy Wilson, and Erroll Garner long enough to lick their wounds and gain enough inspiration and confidence to go back to the next jam session and try it again.

Approaching Club 21, I decided to ask the doorman if he knew anything about 52nd Street's former glory days as a jazz hub. There were few patrons coming in for dinner that night, so he kindly took the time to converse with me about the restaurant's intriguing past as a speakeasy back in the era of Prohibition. He told me all about Club 21's secret cellars and hidden doorways and about the legendary gangsters who dined there; but he had no information at all to offer about the jazz of that era.

After approaching several others who appeared to be employed at the various establishments on the block, it became clear to me that, save for the single sign that bore its nickname—Swing Street—few of today's pedestrians who hurried along this corridor had any idea that they were treading on sacred jazz ground.

My hope sank. I was saddened by this collective loss of cultural memory, saddened by this great city's failure to properly preserve the status and distinction of this place that changed America forever. And for the first time, I really understood with my heart more than with my head the near desperation with which Dr. Taylor told and retold his story of coming of age at the time and on the street where the path led from swing to bebop, the street where young Bill Taylor was transformed—musically, spiritually, and creatively—into the Billy Taylor that millions have come to know and love.

Dr. Taylor was in his mid-eighties when we began our collaboration. Although he had supposedly retired from public life some time earlier, the fact is that he remained incredibly busy, incredibly engaged, still traveling, still performing, and still planning up until the very last ounce of his health gave way. Most of our conversations were by phone, and during our talks, each of which lasted for between one and two hours, it was typical for him to pause several times in order to answer a seemingly endless stream of calls that were coming in on a separate line. Caught between the tension of the work that he loved and the story that needed to soon find its place on paper, the ostensibly retired Dr. Taylor was a master at avoiding cadences. He was arranging meetings, answering requests for interviews, setting up rehearsals and performances, confirming campus visits, and accepting awards the entire time that he was working on his memoir, determined to use every moment to the fullest, refusing to speculate on which of those moments might be among the last.

No single volume—not even one authored by Dr. Taylor himself—can contain a completely detailed accounting of all of his performances, awards, or achievements. The richness and breadth of Dr. Taylor's contribution to jazz is simply too daunting to capture in one monograph. Even if this were possible, it would be out of character for Dr. Taylor to go on and on about his own accolades. This simply was not his way of doing things. Instead, his manner was to pay homage to those who shaped and influenced him, to shine the spotlight on history's forgotten jazz heroes, and to educate, encourage, and advise the next generation.

I sought to guide Dr. Taylor through a series of conversations about his life that could then be converted into a readable narrative, one that retained the integrity of his life story and the essence of his voice. Admittedly, I was star-struck during those first phone calls, fully aware that I was speaking to a major figure, terrified of saying the wrong thing, of asking the wrong question, of wasting his time. I had a rigid, businesslike focus on the task at hand. By contrast, Dr. Taylor was relaxed and good-natured, decidedly unfazed by his own greatness, and never in too much of a hurry to ask me about my day, my work, my students, and the mundane happenings of my life. Over time, he put me at such ease that my businesslike shell dissolved in the warmth of his kindness, and what began as a collaboration between a jazz legend and an anonymous ghostwriter evolved into the affection that one has for her cherished surrogate grandfather. On many occasions, the objectives I planned for our working sessions were compromised when Dr. Taylor wanted to just talk—not about this autobiography—but about the weather in New York, or the event he'd been to the night before, or the drink he tried at Starbucks, or a remodeling project under way at his house that was taking too long. He wanted to talk about Teddi and how pretty she was to him after all these years, about an outing with his daughter and son-in-law, about some exercises I should try for my own developing jazz piano technique, or about some students he'd heard at "Jazz in July" at University of Massachusetts–Amherst. He wanted to talk about his brother, Rudy, about his upcoming visit back home to Washington, D.C., about an appointment with the dentist. I eventually forgot that he was famous and I found myself scolding him for delayed attention to some physical symptom; and he forgot that I was his ghostwriter and found himself giving me marital advice and telling me what he *really* thought of the presidential election.

Dr. Taylor left behind a large body of writings, quotations, and printed and recorded interviews. Those who have heard or read these documents may find that, on occasion, Dr. Taylor has told more than one version of the same story. He noted the fallibility of memory and had a healthy sense of humor about the inconsistencies that can result from this most human of flaws. The anecdotes and stories conveyed here are presented as Dr. Taylor related them to me, and his wonderful, incomparable spirit emerges as a constant, transcending any variations in the narrative of his life's work.

During the entire time that we worked together, I met with him in person only twice. And on that second and last occasion, I am so glad that I obeyed my impulse before we departed. As we said goodbye, I embraced him and looked into those gentle, wise, and elderly eyes sparkling from behind those extraordinarily thick and ornate glasses, and I said, "I love you, Dr. Taylor."

Dr. Taylor wanted to tell his life story, but more importantly, he wanted to tell that story as a lesson in jazz, an accounting of the great African American experience that birthed and cradled America's Classical Music. Those who knew him best may find certain parts of his personal story conspicuously absent, and that was his wish. Every life includes pain, hardship, and struggle; Dr. Taylor, however, was obsessed with creative energy, with the beauty and dynamism of life's possibilities. Whenever he spoke of struggle, it was always in terms of that which had been—or could be—overcome.

Our last working session was scheduled for July 21, 2010, just days before his eighty-ninth birthday. If something came up that caused him to unexpectedly miss our appointment, he'd usually call me back within a day or two to reschedule our phone meeting. This time, however, was different. His phone call never came. Immediately, I missed him, and I still do.

I am deeply indebted to some very special people who supported my effort to bring Dr. Taylor's memoir to fruition. My thanks to James McBride, to Kim Taylor-Thompson, to Lloyd Pinchback, to Janet Haggerty, to Tom Benediktson, to Isaiah Feken, and to my colleague Dr. Daniel Arthurs; my very, very sincere thanks to Dr. Larry Ridley for spending many unselfish hours reading the manuscript, for offering extremely helpful feedback, for decorating our work with his infectious sense of humor, and for sharing heartwarming anecdotes about his friendship with Dr. Taylor along the way. Thanks, of course, to Raina Polivka at Indiana University Press, and thanks, as always, to my patient and long-suffering husband, James, for his unwavering support through this entire process.

Dr. Taylor never returned my phone call, but I knew him well enough to safely assume that only the most pressing of circumstances would cause him to miss our scheduled appointment. Indeed, he'd gotten a call to jam, a call to sit in with Dizzy, and Art, with Duke, and Mary Lou, with Ben and Bird and with all the greats of 52nd Street who were waiting, waiting, waiting for him to come and take his turn. Never one to refuse a good gig, he answered their call and left me here to finish his last, great tribute to America's Classical Music.

> Play on, Dr. Taylor.
> No jealousy here.
> *Teresa Reed*
> *April 12, 2012*

Chronology of the Life of

WILLIAM EDWARD TAYLOR JR.

JULY 24, 1921
Born in Greenville, North Carolina

1926
Taylor Family moved to Washington, D.C.

CA. 1928
Began piano lessons with Mrs. Elmira Streets

1938
Graduated from Dunbar High School; enrolled at Virginia State College

1942
Graduated with bachelor of science degree in music from Virginia State College

1942–1943
Spent approximately one year back in Washington, D.C., after graduating from Virginia State; worked for the government and freelanced around the city

1943
Moved to New York; began working at the Three Deuces on 52nd Street

1944
Toured with Eddie South Trio

1945
Performed with the Cozy Cole Quintet in Billy Rose's *The Seven Lively Arts;* released first recordings

1946
Performed with Slam Stewart's Trio

JUNE 22, 1946
Married Theodora Castion

1946
Toured Europe with the Don Redman Orchestra

1949
Published *Billy Taylor's Basic Bebop Instruction* (Hansen)

1949–1951
Worked as house pianist at Birdland

1951
Played in an early trio with Charles Mingus and Marquis Foster; many later trios would follow in a forthcoming period of prolific recording

1953
Honored in *Down Beat*'s International Jazz Critics Poll as "Best New Star Pianist"

1958
Became musical director for *The Subject Is Jazz;* was the first African American music director on television

1959–1962
Worked as disc jockey with New York's WLIB

1962–1964
Worked as disc jockey with New York's WNEW

1964
Joined Harlem Cultural Council; along with Daphne Arnstein, founded Jazzmobile; released "I Wish I Knew How It Would Feel to Be Free" (recording on Capitol label completed in late 1963)

1964–1969
Worked as disc jockey and program director of New York's WLIB

1968
Appointed to the New York Cultural Council

APRIL 29, 1969
Attended Seventieth Birthday Celebration for Duke Ellington at the White House during the Nixon administration

1969–1972
Musical director for the *David Frost Show*

1970
Named to New York State Commission on Cultural Resources by Governor Nelson Rockefeller

1970
Joined David Frost at the White House and played piano for President Richard Nixon's Christmas reception

1971
Partnered with Inner City Broadcasting to purchase WLIB

1972
Appointed to the National Council on the Arts by President Nixon

1973
Premiered *Suite for Jazz Piano and Orchestra* with Utah Symphony Orchestra at Mormon Tabernacle in Salt Lake City

OCTOBER 9, 1973
Performed at White House State Dinner for President Richard Nixon

FEBRUARY 5, 1975
Performed at White House State Dinner for President Gerald R. Ford. Trio included Larry Ridley on bass, Bobby Thomas on drums

1975
Completed doctoral degree at the University of Massachusetts–Amherst; joined ASCAP Board of Directors

1977–1982
Hosted National Public Radio's *Jazz Alive!*

JUNE 18, 1978
Along with a host of jazz greats, attended President Jimmy Carter's "Jazz at the White House" festival

1981
Became jazz correspondent for Charles Kuralt's *CBS Sunday Morning*

1983
Published *Jazz Piano: A Jazz History* (W. C. Brown)

1983
Won an Emmy Award for his feature on Quincy Jones on *CBS Sunday Morning*

1984
Awarded *Down Beat* magazine's Lifetime Achievement Award

1986
Received the New York Mayor's Arts Award

1988
Named a Jazz Master by the National
Endowment for the Arts

1992
Awarded a National Medal of Arts by
President George Bush

1994
Named the artistic advisor and spokesman
on jazz at the John F. Kennedy Center for
the Performing Arts in Washington, D.C.

SEPTEMBER 1998
Attended President Bill Clinton's Millennium Lecture on Jazz at the White House

1999
Published *The Billy Taylor Collection*
(Hal Leonard Publishing)

NOVEMBER 2000
Attended President Bill Clinton's dinner
celebrating the two hundredth anniversary of the White House

2003
Received the keys to the city of Greenville,
North Carolina, where a street and jazz
festival were named in his honor

JUNE 2004
Performed at the White House for Presi-
dent George Bush's commemoration of
Black Music Month

2005
Announced retirement from public
performance

DECEMBER 28, 2010
Spoke with Fats

THE
JAZZ
LIFE
OF

Dr. Billy Taylor

ONE

Beginnings

1921–1938

THE SEDUCTIVE POWER OF JAZZ resides in its distinctive sway, its particular saunter, its gait, its *swing*. The genealogy of that swing begins in West Africa, where a primal pulse spawned the ritual drumming, call-and-response singing, and orisha-possessed dancing that were the musical and spiritual life's blood of its people. Like an endless vine with roots planted firmly in the soil of its African origin, that dynamic Mother Pulse stretched the length of the Atlantic Ocean and was carried as precious cargo in the musical memories and bodies of the enslaved and scattered people who became the Diaspora. Wherever these enslaved people landed, their African heartbeat, their fertile musical Mother Pulse, generated seedlings, new musical forms specific to their new environments but still identifiably African. In the Caribbean, these seedlings matured in forms like junkanoo, mambo, mento, and reggae. In the United States, the transplanted Africans injected the creative pulse of their homeland into their field hollers, work songs, spirituals, blues, and jazz. When the slave law silenced their drumming, the Mother Pulse persisted nonetheless, emerging as the body rhythms of the ring shout and the juba-pattin' on the plantations, the handclaps of the black church, the vocal percussion of the quartet, the syncopation of ragtime, jazz, the backbeat of R & B, and the beat-boxing of the South Bronx. Songs from their African homeland emerged in new African American melodies that essentially use the five notes of the pentatonic scale; the hollers, guttural tones, and bent notes of the blues and black gospel; the flatted thirds and sevenths of jazz.

In jazz, the African heartbeat, the Mother Pulse of the homeland, is alive and well in its *swing*, the distinctive rhythms of black bandsmen and piano thumpers whose sound emerged in places like New Orleans, Charleston, Kansas City, Houston, Dallas, Fort Worth, various locations in Oklahoma, Chicago, and St. Louis. In the early 1900s, this *swing* was the musical embodiment of the defiance that African Americans were once forbidden to express in their words or with their actions. In the racially segregated world of yesteryear, where lines were drawn and boundaries were fixed, jazz was bold and free and transcended the metronomic regularity of the European bar line. For African Americans in the early 1900s, the *swing* in jazz was the equivalent of a head held high with shoulders erect, chest out, and a clenched, pulsating fist waving in the air. The *swing* in jazz was a dead-on, eyeball-to-eyeball stare between black and white America. That gait, that lilt, that *swing* spoke volumes in pride, love, longing, struggle, history, and hope. And just as there is no wet without water, there is no jazz without its *swing*. Call it interesting, call it creative, even call it beautiful; but don't call it jazz unless it swings. The *swing* is the essence that connects jazz to its creative roots, to Duke, to Art Tatum, to "Satchmo," to Basie, to Dizzy and Charlie Parker, to Mary Lou, and to all the other great masters who birthed, cradled, and lifted this music into the world. I know because I was there. Duke was right: *"It don't mean a thing if it ain't got that swing."*

The *swing* in jazz symbolizes the life stories of those who created and championed it. My part of this story begins at a time when all of black America was panting, out of breath from running away from the past and racing full steam ahead toward the promise of the future. I was born in Greenville, North Carolina, in the hot, steamy summer of 1921. My birth year represents both the best of times and the worst of times for African Americans. With souls set afire by the likes of Garvey and Du Bois, young African Americans, including my own parents, were eager to define new possibilities for themselves as well as for our entire race. They wanted to purge from their lives every single vestige of the miserable slave past, and they wanted to live, instead, in a brand-new consciousness of possibility. It was in 1921 that Eubie Blake and Noble Sissle produced their long-running musical *Shuffle Along*, the first Broadway hit production to feature an entirely African American cast. It was in 1921 that Harry Pace established the first black-owned and -operated record company, Pace Phonograph. During that year, the African American Baptist Church published its time-honored collection of sacred songs, the *Gospel Pearls*. As that generation pined for a new day, 1921 also saw a revival of the Ku Klux Klan's venomous campaign of white supremacy, especially in the South. And this racist oppression helped bring about the Great Migration, a period in the 1910s and 1920s during which more than a million African Americans left the cotton and tobacco fields of the sweltering and oppressive "Jim Crow" South for better opportunities in the North. For us, 1921 was a year when eyes both bright and dim were fixed on historically pivotal prizes.

My earliest memories are of the places we lived in the South, first in Greenville, and later, in Raleigh, North Carolina. I remember that Greenville was a pleasant country town with tall cornfields and the Tarr River nearby. My father, Dr. William E. Taylor Sr., was a dentist, and his best friend was a doctor. The two of them decided to set up offices together and begin practicing in Greenville. My mother, Antoinette Bacon Taylor, was a Washington, D.C., native and a graduate of Howard University's Miner Teachers College. She started her career in one of the small, rural, segregated schools in the Greenville area. For people like my parents, a little town like Greenville was filled with contradictions. On one hand, Greenville might have been the perfect place for two young, educated African American professionals, a place with a desperate need for those who were qualified to serve and enhance the community. On the other hand, however, Greenville, like most southern towns, struggled beneath the weight of those unfortunate times. In many ways, the South of the 1920s was little improved over what it had been during slavery. Too many southern African Americans were impoverished, barely literate sharecroppers, people who labored in cotton and tobacco fields from sunup to sundown and who lived in constant fear of burning crosses and lynch mobs. Their lives were focused on survival, and to a great extent, surviving in the South was a matter of "knowing your place." Keeping African Americans in their "place" was a major function of the educational system in a town like Greenville, where, at that time, racial segregation was both pervasive and blatant. White schools were well funded, well equipped, well staffed, and exclusively for white children.

African Americans, by contrast, struggled to provide education for their children. Black schools in the South, if not in churches or in private homes, were often little dirt-floor country shacks, single rooms crowded with eager children of all ages. With very little money and few resources, many of these schools typically operated five or six months of the year. In many cases, the subjects taught to southern black children only reinforced the presumption that they were inferior and therefore could look forward only to a life of servitude, sharecropping, or other manual labor. My mother's brief teaching experience in Greenville was one reason that she convinced my father that we should consider living in a larger town. We soon moved to Raleigh, where I recall that there were more children for me to play with and our home there was just across from Shaw University. Founded just after the Civil War, Shaw was the oldest African American college in the South. Living in the slightly more urban town of Raleigh must have given my parents an opportunity to enjoy more culture and recreation, since I distinctly remember chasing tennis balls when my father played there with other athletically minded friends. I was told that I actually attended kindergarten in Raleigh, but I don't remember that at all. What I do remember, however, is being at a dance and seeing a small jazz band perform. I especially remember the drummer. He was a real showman and did all kinds of magical and funny things with his drumsticks while the people danced around the band.

Raleigh was much bigger and better than Greenville, but still too far south for my mother's taste. So they decided that we would join the great northward migration and move back to Washington, D.C. It was perhaps fortunate that I was big for my age, since this enabled my mother to enroll me in grade school in Washington, D.C., when I was only five years old. Even at that young age, I recall the wonder and intrigue of being in the nation's capitol, a place so beautiful that it seemed to be a majestic sandstone and marble wonderland. The president and I lived in the same city!

And that is exactly how my parents wanted me to feel—carefree, safe, and full of optimism and bright-eyed wonder. They didn't want me to know, for example, that at the same time I started school in this fascinating new city of mine, the curious people of Washington were lining the streets for a parade, not in honor of some visiting dignitary from a foreign nation, but to marvel at a spectacle of another kind. On September 13, 1926, thousands of men in their white robes and pointed white hoods stretched the expanse of Pennsylvania Avenue. Bearing their American flags and arranged in formation, they marched triumphantly, some of their number creating the shape of a large letter K at the front as the dome of the nation's capitol stood in the background.

Our parents wanted to shelter us from scenes like these; so they fashioned for us a self-sustaining community, a city within this city, a section of Washington, D.C., away from this marble wonderland. My boyhood Washington, D.C., was an entire universe of its own—rich, vast, vibrant, noisy, and colorful. It was an African American world in which I could go anywhere and become anything I wanted; and yet, it was all entirely within the distance of a short walk from my home.

In this urban hamlet bursting with vitality, history, and hope were the ties that bound us all together. Whether on the playground or at Sunday school, at the barbershop, at the drugstore, or at the theatre, I felt a certain kinship to those around me. At every turn, there were stories of our achievements and constant talk of progress from adults who lavished us with good advice and older folks who nurtured us with well-spun tales, hot-buttered grits, fried okra, sweet potato pie, and hearty laughter. We were wealthy in Henry O. Tanner's art, in Claude McKay's poetry, and in James Weldon Johnson's literature; and we were filthy rich in music, so culturally affluent, in fact, that it was unnecessary to venture beyond the boundaries set for us. Segregation fused all of the ingredients of our creativity into one magnificent stew, the power, flavor, and intensity of which pervaded everything around us. Segregation hid us from the rest of the world but saturated us in our own splendor.

Howard University, the Howard Theatre, my grandfather's Florida Avenue Baptist Church, and everything from grocery stores to cafés and delis, from schools to movie houses, were all within minutes of my doorstep. A young boy like me could get a sandwich at any one of several cafeterias lining U Street, places where you could count on good food, the latest gossip, and reminders to stay out of trouble. I could stroll to catch a movie at one of several theatres—the Lincoln Theatre, the Republic Theatre, the Booker T. Theatre, and the Howard Theatre—all within walking distance and just a few blocks away from each other. I could play with the other kids at the 12th Street YMCA, or see our local Negro Leagues stars, the Homestead Grays, play baseball at Griffith Stadium.

My grandfather's church was adjacent to the fence around Griffith Stadium. For my father, who was the choir director at his church, the temptation of baseball proved irresistible. There was one particular occasion when my grandfather's inspired preaching moved the hearts of the faithful, and as is customary in the black Baptist tradition, the sanctuary soon filled with the joyful sounds and exclamations of the Spirit. My father, however, filled with love of sport, took advantage of the situation: We all looked up to notice that, during the rousing of the congregation by the Holy Spirit, my father had abandoned his musical post, and my uncle was directing the choir in his place. My father had slipped out the back door of the church to go to the game!

Interestingly, even though Griffith Stadium was in the heart of the black community, it happened to be the only ballpark in Washington, D.C., at that time. It was host to both the Negro Leagues teams and the Washington Senators, a major-league team. Therefore, it was absolutely normal for white baseball fans to come into my neighborhood on game days. Yet I was forbidden to cross into the white neighborhood on any day, one of the many oddities of segregation.

My neighborhood showcased the gamut of who we were, from street sweepers and domestic workers, to professional and well-heeled society people who dressed in their finery and attended elegant dances at the Lincoln Colonnade, and sophisticated banquets and other affairs at the Whitelaw Hotel, or at the Dunbar Hotel. Thanks to segregation, almost every establishment in my neighborhood—from Scurlock Photography Studios, to Freedmen's Hospital, to the *Afro-American Newspaper*—was black-owned. For a young African American boy like me, the black community of Washington, D.C., in the 1920s and 1930s was but an extension of the house where I lived, a place where friends and neighbors felt more like cousins, where the grown-ups were variations of my own parents, and where the places across the street or around the corner felt every bit as safe and embracing as my own living room.

I grew up surrounded by role models, and I came of age under the protective and reassuring gaze of relatives and neighbors who expected great things from my generation. After all, it was the age of the "New

Negro," of W. E. B. Du Bois, of the "Talented Tenth." African Americans were abuzz with the notion of advancing the race. And while history records that there was a renaissance under way in Harlem, there was an equally significant artistic and cultural movement among our people during this same period in my hometown.

African Americans in Washington took race progress very seriously, a fact that becomes clear when considering the number of luminaries that lived in the very neighborhood where I grew up. Well before I came on the scene, Washington, D.C., already boasted a rich heritage of African American achievement. The eminent poet Paul Laurence Dunbar was a Washingtonian who lived on U Street beginning in 1898, and it is for him that my *alma mater*, Dunbar High School, was named. The incomparable Duke Ellington was born in Washington, D.C., in 1899 and returned there frequently to perform. Dr. Charles Drew, the inventor of the blood bank, was born there in 1904 and was a graduate of Dunbar High. Harlem Renaissance legends Langston Hughes and Alain Locke both lived for a time in Washington and had connections to Howard University, as did historian Carter G. Woodson, who taught there beginning in the late 1910s. Much later, in the 1930s, Thurgood Marshall lived just a few doors up the hill from me on Fairmont Street, just two blocks west of Howard University. He would become the first African American justice on the Supreme Court. To be African American in Washington, D.C., in the 1920s and 1930s was to be in the epicenter of progress and pride, pride fueled by the awareness that the colorful, noisy, wonderful world in which we lived was of our own making.

My family was full of musicians—cousins, aunts, and uncles who sang beautifully and played various instruments. My father was a remarkable man who was not only a dentist, but was also a four-letter athlete, a great singer, and the choir director at my grandfather's Florida Avenue Baptist Church. He was known throughout the community for both his musical leadership and his riveting baritone solos. Our first house in Washington, D.C., was on Flagler Place, just two blocks south of Howard University. There were times when my dad's choir came to our house to rehearse for some special occasion, for Christmas, for Easter, or for some other religious gathering. There were also several different instruments around our house, including a baritone horn and a C melody saxophone. I am not sure how we acquired those instruments, and I don't know exactly who might have played them, but I suspect that my father may have taken them up at various times in his life. In addition to the horn and saxophone, we had a player piano, and I remember placing my tiny fingers on the keys in many eager yet futile attempts to match the nimble, rapid motions of the invisible virtuoso.

Like many on his side of the family, my dad was European-classically trained and took music very seriously. All of my father's siblings and cousins sang, but my father's youngest brother, Percy, was the only one who came close to being a professional musician. My uncle Percy studied at Juilliard and served for many years as the church organist. My father's sister, my aunt Marjorie, was also a fine organist and sometimes substituted for Uncle Percy. My uncle Julian was a wonderful singer and, like my grandfather, became a highly respected Baptist minister.

Although European-classical training was important in my father's family, two of his brothers were very interested in jazz. Both my uncle Clinton and my uncle Robert were amateur jazz pianists, and both played stride piano, which was the popular style of the day. They both influenced me greatly, but neither ever played professionally. My uncle Clinton pursued a career in art and eventually became head of the Art Department at A&T College. Uncle Robert also pursued other interests, but he was the uncle that I admired most of all, and his style of playing was the one I most tried to emulate.

Although a soft-spoken man, my grandfather, the Reverend William Andrew Taylor, also sang. He took his greatest pride, however, in the musical accomplishments of his children. When the Taylor children were younger, they had a family singing group that performed concerts periodically at the church. Once older, however, they each went their separate ways, as children typically do. There were rare instances that my father and his brothers and sisters reunited to sing, but this happened only at my grandfather's insistence and on certain special family occasions. They reluctantly complied, although I'm sure that both Uncle Bob and Uncle Clinton would have much preferred to be somewhere else listening to or playing jazz.

The Taylor family's musical talent extended to my generation. My cousin Maureen Taylor Brent was also my classmate at Lucretia Mott

Elementary School. She had a very lovely voice that she undoubtedly inherited from her father, my uncle Julian. Maureen sang in various school
programs but decided to marry and raise a family rather than pursue
singing seriously.

On my father's side of the family, music was a calling, something
to be studied and mastered. On my mother's side, music was equally
important but approached quite differently. Although I was close to all
of my cousins, I was especially close to those on my mother's side. I
have vague memories of my mother's father, but I recall that he worked
on the railroads earlier in his life but was blind during his later years.
The reigning matriarch of the Bacon family was my mother's mother,
Mary Bacon. Every Sunday after church, our routine was to visit with
the Bacon relatives. We'd go to my grandmother's house and to visit my
aunt Alcinda, my cousins Antoinette and Chauncey, and two cousins
both named Russell, one Russell Bacon and the other, Russell Lyles.
Both my grandmother and my aunt Alcinda had pianos in their homes,
and my mother's brother, my uncle Nathaniel, played by ear. Although
he played some stride piano, his style was more pop-oriented, as he enjoyed the kinds of things you'd hear on the radio. When we visited my
grandmother on Sundays, it was common for my uncle Nathaniel to sit
at the piano and start in on some tune, impromptu family performances
that we all enjoyed. Or if we visited Aunt Alcinda, we'd hear her husband, Russell Lyles, playing light classical pieces, along with the kinds of
popular songs heard on the radio. So I had the benefit of both my father's
classical approach to music and the more relaxed, recreational approach
that was typical on my mother's side. Looking back, I can see that both
of these perspectives gave me a very balanced foundation.

Radio also immersed me in good music. I remember that in the
summertime when we weren't in school, I could turn on the radio in
the morning or in the afternoon and hear, "Ladies and gentlemen, from
the Savoy Ballroom in Harlem, New York City, here's the Count Basie
Band!" Man, was that exciting! In the 1930s, radio carried great performances by Ella Fitzgerald, Chick Webb, Billie Holiday, Cab Calloway,
and many others from the Savoy and from the Apollo Theatre. We loved
hearing broadcasts of *Amateur Night at the Apollo*, which showcased
debut performances of many artists who are now numbered among the

all-time greats. There were also radio broadcasts from the Cotton Club and from the Grand Terrace in Chicago. Even the Mills Brothers and Don Redman had radio shows for a time. But we were especially excited about listening to performances from the Savoy and from the Apollo not just for the great music, but also because we knew that these two places were integrated. The Cotton Club employed African American musicians, singers, and dancers, but none were allowed there as patrons. Even if you were a wealthy African American and could afford to go there, you could not walk into the Cotton Club, sit at a table, and order a drink. At the Savoy and at the Apollo, however, blacks and whites enjoyed the dancing and the music together, and we knew this and were fascinated by it and proud of it.

Because of my family's love for music, I found support and encouragement at every turn. Whether trying some tune at the piano or strumming something on the guitar, I always had a ready audience of relatives there to cheer me on. I admired both my uncle Clinton and my uncle Bob, but Uncle Clinton was older and already away in college studying art by the time I was old enough to begin learning the piano. I remember that he had a nice light touch at the keyboard, and I often wonder what else I might have gleaned from him had I been able to spend more time with him.

I spent lots of time with Uncle Bob (Robert Lee Taylor), however, and in my estimation, he was the coolest, hippest guy around. A street-savvy fellow with eclectic interests, Uncle Bob was an athlete, had worked as a newspaperman, was employed for a time by the government, was a community activist, and also spent time in the army. Uncle Bob also worked at the Y, so he knew everyone in the neighborhood and everyone knew him. His style of playing was reminiscent of Fats Waller and Art Tatum, and I admired him greatly. I pestered him for lessons, and in response, he gave me records to listen to from his collection. I remember that one of the recordings he gave to me was called "The Shout," by Art Tatum. It was not one of Tatum's hit records, but I remember that it was very fast stride piano, much too heavy for me at the time. Uncle Bob said to me, "I had to teach myself, so you're going to have to listen and learn on your own." Every now and then, however, he'd show me a lick or two. In one sense, those records were Uncle Bob's way of keeping his bothersome young nephew occupied and out of the way. In another sense, however, those recordings were like gifts of gold and became cornerstones in my own development as a musician.

There was a record store called Waxy Maxy's that was right down the street from my father's dental office. The owner was a friend of my father's and was very kind to me. He'd let me come into the shop and grab any record I wanted off the shelf and he'd allow me to listen for free. I spent hours there, and I'm sure my fingerprints and clumsy grip ruined a few of the records that he would have liked to sell. But he never made a fuss about it, and I got to listen to lots of great music.

Although my father tolerated my admiration for Uncle Bob and his piano skills, he certainly would have preferred that my primary musical inspiration come from elsewhere. In those days, upstanding African Americans revered Bach, Beethoven, and Mozart, the European masters of the time-honored classical canon. During that period, there was a general assumption that European classical music could effect moral and social uplift, could elevate the spirit and refine human character. It was even common for popular magazines of the day to carry articles by respected scholars on the social virtues of European classical music. By contrast, jazz was considered mere "good-time music," and, although appreciated and enjoyed, it was not to be taken seriously. In my neighborhood, however, opportunities to enjoy good music were plentiful, and regardless of the preference, be it for classical or for jazz, there was musical fare to suit every taste. After all, we were but a stone's throw away from both Howard University and the Howard Theatre, where artist recitals, concerts, and theatrical productions were ongoing. World-class performers associated with Howard University include opera singer Madame Lillian Evanti, who was a Howard graduate; concert baritone Todd Duncan; and pianist Hazel Harrison, the latter two of whom were both on the faculty of the Howard Music Department and enjoyed rich and varied performing careers. Alongside the ample supply of classical music in my community, jazz giants like Duke Ellington, Cab Calloway, Claude Hopkins, Earl Hines, and Jimmy Lunceford were appearing regularly at the Howard Theatre and at nightclubs like the Crystal Caverns and the Republic Garden.

The Howard Theatre featured a variety of entertainment. Very early on, I saw black comedians working at the Howard Theatre in "blackface."

This may seem strange, since "blackface" comedy came out of the minstrel show, which was very degrading to African Americans. However, at that time, Vaudeville had adopted many aspects of minstrelsy, and anyone who wanted to get into show business—black or white—had to conform to the custom of the day; the norm at that time was for comedians to perform in "blackface." But the African Americans who were in "blackface" at the Howard Theatre did routines that reversed the typical storyline, where the black guy was always the butt of the joke. Instead, the skits always ended with the black guy coming out ahead, always winning. Still, there were some who found the very sight of "blackface" to be offensive.

My father valued discipline and achievement, and so in order to ensure my learning to play the piano *correctly*, he arranged for me to have lessons with a local piano teacher, Mrs. Elmira Streets. I was around seven or eight years old when I started lessons with Mrs. Streets, and I'm sure it didn't take her long to realize that I had little interest in scales, arpeggios, and Hanon exercises. Very early on, I discovered my ability to reproduce melodies just by hearing them, so I hated to practice! Whenever Mrs. Streets played a piece, I could render it immediately by ear without ever actually looking at the notes on the page. At that time, it was much more fun to improvise and play by ear than it was to develop the discipline of reading music. If I practiced at all, it was only during those times that my mother was literally standing over me, forcing me to play what was written on the page. She wasn't a musician, but she was a schoolteacher, and she understood that repetition was essential to practicing. And she also had a good enough ear to be able to tell whether I was making logical music or just stumbling along or fooling around.

"That doesn't sound right," she'd say. "Do it again." And so I would submit to the torture and do it again, and again, and again until my mother was satisfied. But my mother couldn't stand watch over me all the time. So week after week, I came to my lesson having done the least amount of practicing possible.

Eventually, my parents enlisted Mrs. Streets to give piano lessons to my brother Rudolph, whose attitude was the exact opposite of mine. One day, she approached my father and said, "Dr. Taylor, both of your sons are musically gifted. Now, the younger one, he's the one you should really invest in. He takes his time, practices his lessons carefully, works hard, and always comes to my studio well prepared. So give him all the support and encouragement you can. As for that older one, I'm afraid he'll never amount to much of anything. You can forget about him. He'll never be much of a musician."

Piano teachers would often feature their students in piano recitals held either in their living rooms or in a church or a community hall. During these recitals, each student would come to the stage and play a piece that had been studied in the lessons. I liked being onstage, so when there was a recital coming up, I'd suddenly get serious about my lessons and I'd learn my piece in time for the big performance. This really angered my teacher: "Now, why on earth can't you show that kind of hard work and dedication every week?" she'd ask.

I replied, "I don't have a concert every week."

To her credit, Mrs. Streets was long-suffering. As I look back on those early years, I realize that she was indeed a very good teacher, and I am indebted to her for imparting to me the fundamentals of music. I regret, however, that I didn't apply myself more in those lessons. Although Hanon exercises seemed hopelessly irrelevant to my dream of playing jazz and emulating the ever-cool Uncle Bob, I realize now how much time I could have saved by working harder with Mrs. Streets.

On one hand, I disliked conventional piano lessons, since what Mrs. Streets taught—endless scales, arpeggios, finger exercises, and sight-reading—seemed of little use to me. On the other hand, however, I had an insatiable appetite for playing the piano, and it was to my advantage that opportunities to experiment, to listen, and to learn were always plentiful. Although my four years of lessons with Mrs. Streets were comparatively unproductive, I remained committed to jazz piano and played at dances, at parties, in assembly hall—anywhere there was a piano. Of course, I was young, unprepared, and pretty awful back then, but I was driven and determined to improve in my own way.

In those days, it cost 15 cents to go to the movies if you went to one of the earlier shows, and the price went up to 35 cents if you wanted to go to a later show. So I would collect and sell Coke and ginger ale bottles back to the grocery store and earn enough pocket change to go to the movies. Sometimes, some pretty big names would come to the theatres to play the organ or the piano during the intermission of the movie.

Shep Allen was the manager of the Howard Theatre, and he was a good friend of my family. He knew that I was interested in music, so he allowed me to come to the theatre and stay as long as I wanted. I'd buy a ticket to the noon show, but for the price of that one ticket, I'd stay all day. Between features, I'd slump down in my chair in an attempt to make myself invisible. But I wasn't fooling anyone. They didn't turn on the house lights or clear everyone out between features, but they knew I was there getting lots of free entertainment. They didn't seem to mind.

For young hopeful musicians, the proving ground was the Howard Theatre's Amateur Night Contest. These contests were started as part of an effort to revitalize the legendary theatre after it suffered from the financial collapse of 1929. For some years after the stock market crash, the Howard Theatre was dormant except for a brief period when it was used as a church. In the early 1930s, Shep Allen got the idea to reopen the Howard both with big-name acts and with Amateur Night contests that invited participation from local talent.

I wanted so badly to play in the hip style of Fats Waller, Art Tatum, and Uncle Bob, but there was no one who gave regular lessons in jazz. There was a gentleman named Louis Brown, a ragtime pianist who worked at the Howard Theatre. Since I was a regular there and he knew of my interest in music, he stole away a few minutes whenever he could to show me some things at the piano. But since he was on the job, he was always in a hurry. I once asked him about Fats Waller, and his response was to play for me the quickest version of "Handful of Keys" I'd ever heard.

"See, it goes like this," and seemingly within seconds, the speed-of-light demonstration was over and Mr. Brown was scurrying back to his duties at the theatre. His fingers moved so rapidly that all I could see was a blur, and the notes went by too quickly for me to glean much from his demonstration except that it made me realize how badly I needed to practice!

It was in the early 1930s, and I was around eleven years old when I went to the Lincoln Theatre to see Fats Waller. I'd heard him play at the Howard Theatre with his own show, and he was one of my idols. At eleven years of age, however, my young mind had no way to comprehend just how accomplished he was. By the early 1930s, Fats Waller had already composed and recorded prolifically, and had already performed at

Carnegie Hall and on the radio; by the mid-1930s, he would also appear in film and would tour Europe. He was not only an entertaining singer and a master stride pianist, but his use of the pipe organ for jazz was also completely unique at that time. Fats Waller was one of the rare African American jazz artists to record with white musicians during the days of segregation. Even more rare was the fact that the group consisting of Fats Waller, Gene Krupa, Eddie Condon, and Jack Teagarden was called "Fats Waller and His Buddies." It was nearly unheard-of for an African American working alongside whites to get this sort of top billing in those days.

He'd recently been booked for a week's engagement playing the organ at the Lincoln Theatre between motion pictures, but to me, he was much more than the entr'acte. Forget the movie—he was the main event! I entered the theatre and got as close to the organ as I could, close enough to see his enormous hands and acrobatic fingers commanding the keys, his feet dancing majestically across the floor pedals. He was gargantuan, and I was transfixed by the sight of his dexterity, mesmerized by his music. He was a genius.

As soon as the show was over, I rushed backstage—heart pounding, palms sweating, breath trembling—to meet him. There he was, standing just a few feet away engaged in a conversation. Perhaps it was his burly stature, or the severe look of his dauntingly thick eyebrows, or maybe it was his august presence, but whatever the case, I simply froze. Paralyzed with awe, I stood there like a statue as he walked right past me, close enough for me to feel the brush of air from his movement. And there went the only chance I'd ever have in my life to speak to the one and only Fats Waller, a man whose historical significance would extend into the next millennium. That missed opportunity taught me the importance of seizing the moment, of swallowing my fear, of speaking up and introducing myself to great artists whenever there was a chance to do so.

Although I never spoke to Fats Waller, watching him play and standing for that brief moment in the path of his shadow would affect me forever. I was too young to know that his name would be hailed in history books for all of posterity. Yet deep down I realized that the privilege of standing near him carried with it a mandate for my destiny, a charge to pursue my fullest musical potential. Having witnessed at close range the mastery of Fats Waller, I knew that mediocrity could never be an option.

It was around the time of my encounter with Fats Waller that I played my first paid gig. I made 50 cents playing at the Republic Garden on U Street, just a short walk from my house. There was an older guy there who was supposed to play, but he had some kind of emergency and couldn't fulfill the gig. So he knew that I played piano and, in desperation, called on me to take his place, which I was very happy to do although I was underage and had no business there in the first place. My parents learned about my gig after the fact, and in retrospect, I marvel at how tolerant they were. I was much older when I learned that Uncle Bob's connections on the street were to thank for the fact that I had entered the club scene at so young an age but had managed to stay out of trouble.

The people in my community were also nurturing and supportive, and in a number of ways they indulged my drive to play the piano. As I was getting a little older, my father insisted that I do something constructive to earn some pocket change for myself. So I got a paper route delivering the *Afro American,* a weekly newspaper published out of Baltimore and read widely throughout my neighborhood. As I delivered the *Afro American* door-to-door, it was often the case that there'd be a piano in my customer's parlor, and I was more than happy to regale the patrons on my route with impromptu performances. I also quickly learned that playing the piano was an easy way to attract pretty girls, since if you were any good, they'd often be interested enough to come and sit beside you on the piano bench!

My youthful eagerness to make music sometimes impaired my judgment, but fortunately, family members were willing to smooth things over for me whenever I was in danger of getting myself into trouble. My aunt Alcinda, my mother's older sister, was always a ready advocate for me. Each Sunday, my brother and I enjoyed stopping by for a taste of her delicious, soulful cuisine, particularly her homemade, hot buttered soft dinner rolls. Aunt Alcinda was a fabulous cook, and it was somewhat to my mother's chagrin that it was her food that we often preferred. It was Aunt Alcinda who came to my rescue when I took the bold step of purchasing a guitar without my mother's permission. In those days, parents maintained tight control over what their children did, where they went, who they saw, what they earned, and what they spent. So I had taken a very foolish risk, indeed! Aunt Alcinda spoke to my mother on my behalf and was somehow able to convince her to forego the punishment that was due me. In addition to Aunt Alcinda, I had a beautiful older cousin, Antoinette Lyles (named after my mother), who taught me to dance, and another older cousin, Russell Bacon, who stood up for me. Although I enjoyed going to football and baseball games, I was never interested in the rough-and-tumble contact sport that attracts most young boys. I much preferred to be at the piano, and my mother often had to make me go outdoors. I would have been in danger had Russell not come to my rescue when I was threatened by some of the neighborhood ruffians.

While my family was very tolerant of my obsession with jazz piano, the members of my grandfather's church were less understanding. In those days, good Christian people drew a very rigid line between God's music and the Devil's. But in my community, God's music and the Devil's music were very close neighbors. If you walked out of the front door of my grandfather's church on Florida Avenue and went about a half block to your left, you were looking at the Howard Theatre, which, for many of the church people, was a den of iniquity. But there were more people drawn to that den of iniquity than to my grandfather's church, so when the older folks voiced their disapproval of my activities, the Reverend Taylor, in his own soft-spoken yet dignified manner, simply defended my right to indulge in the music of my generation.

When I was thirteen years old, I got special permission from my mother to play at one of the local clubs, and this was the first gig that paid a significant amount of money. One of the musicians came to my house to ask my mother if I could cover for him while he took another gig at a different establishment. He assured my mother that the musicians were all gentlemen, that I'd be taken care of, and that there wasn't a thing to worry about. He was very convincing, so my mother agreed. But as soon as I got in the guy's car, he lit up and began smoking weed! Soon, the car was filled with this horrible smell, and even though this was in the dead of winter, I rolled down the window so that I could breathe. When I arrived at the club, I was immediately exposed to the seedier side of nightlife. This was a run-down old dive, and if my mother had known where this guy had taken me, she would have been mortified. I went to the little room where the musicians were waiting, and my eyes nearly popped out of my head as the women backstage, with no proper dressing room, passed freely in front of me wearing fewer clothes and exposing more skin than I'd ever seen before. I was at the age where I enjoyed looking at girls' ankles, but this was a real shock! I was big for my age, so no one thought a thing about my being there. They just laughed at my obvious embarrassment and carried on, virtually in the nude, as though everything was normal. I made 5 dollars that night, a large amount of money for a boy my age. Despite the great pay and my new fascination with females, I am glad that I never returned to that club again. And my mother never found out about the naked women or the marijuana.

One of the ironies of segregation was that it stymied certain opportunities at the same time that it fostered others. On one hand, segregation placed unfair constraints on African Americans who were eminently qualified to shine on the world stage. Performers and scholars who could have easily rivaled the world's best were shut out of the venues and opportunities afforded to whites. As a boy, I could never understand the invisible fence that kept me from passing freely from one part of town to the other. It made no sense to me at all that I was safe on U Street, but suddenly unsafe on F Street, where I was forbidden to go to the theatres there in the downtown section. Nobody could explain to my satisfaction why I was not permitted to go to the National Theatre, or to shop in certain stores like Julius Garfinkel's, or to eat a sandwich at Woolworth's. I was African American—we were called "colored" back then—but this was neither a crime nor a contagious disease. Although it made no sense to me whatsoever, neither I nor my peers ever dared to challenge those constrictions. Our elders wouldn't allow it.

As irrational as it was, segregation also meant that the African American community received the full benefit of what our artists, intellectuals, and other luminaries had to offer. When I was growing up in D.C., African American children could go to one of three high schools, each of which had a distinct reputation. Cardoza High School was known for its emphasis on business; Armstrong High School (Duke Ellington's alma mater), was known for the visual and manual arts; and Dunbar High School had a reputation for its academic emphasis.

Dunbar had a very interesting history. It opened in 1870 and was actually the first and oldest high school for blacks in the country. Its humble beginnings were in the basement of the Fifteenth Street Presbyterian Church until it moved to M Street. For a time, therefore, it was known simply as the "M Street High School." It was considered during my day to be the best African American high school in the United States. If you attended Dunbar, you were automatically expected to go to college.

As I recall my coming-of-age, it seems ludicrous that there were five teachers with doctorates on the faculty of Dunbar when I was a student there. Teachers who could have easily achieved tenure at Yale, or at Harvard, or at any other Ivy League institution had to settle instead for teaching high school simply because of their race. We heard stories about their accomplishments all the time, and even though they could not break through the barrier of segregation, they inspired us. The first three African American women in the country to earn doctorates were all connected to Dunbar High School. Sadie Tanner Mossell was a graduate of Dunbar, and she was the first African American woman with a PhD, which she earned from the University of Pennsylvania in 1921. Georgiana Simpson was the second black woman to earn a PhD, and after receiving her doctorate from the University of Chicago, also in 1921, her only option for many years was to return to Washington, D.C., and teach at Dunbar before she was eventually offered a college professorship. Eva Dykes, the third African American female to receive a PhD, graduated with her doctorate from Radcliffe, also in 1921, and taught at Dunbar for several years before getting a college post. Carter G. Woodson, who was only the second African American to earn a doctorate from Harvard, taught French, English, and history at Dunbar High before rising to national prominence. The list of notable African Americans who graduated from or taught at Dunbar High School is too long to recount. Their faith in the power of education was remarkable, considering that segregation confined most of them to high-school teaching even though they were qualified to do much more.

It was to my great advantage, however, that such stellar role models were close at hand. These were dedicated teachers whose very lives were invested in the success of their students, teachers who cultivated our minds and challenged us to dream big, teachers who deeply believed in what was possible for us even though the possibilities and opportunities in their own lives had been curtailed. While the children of our community enjoyed a certain oblivion to the world beyond our neighborhood, these brilliant men and women knew the harsh realities of the larger society and the indignities of racism in ways that we did not. Accomplished professionals with advanced degrees, they knew how it felt to be the constant object of condescension, how it felt to be insulted, ordered around like children, and flippantly called "boy," "gal," and worse. They knew in ways we did not the dire consequences of an ill-timed glance or a defiant gesture. Yet they had unwavering confidence in the power of education, and they instructed us with a passion bordering on desperation, and with prophetic eyes that saw well into the future. They were compelled to prepare us for a day that they could see only with their faith.

One such teacher was Henry Grant. I first came to know Mr. Grant at Shaw Junior High. He was teaching at Dunbar by the time I enrolled there for high school. Mr. Grant noticed my diehard attraction to the piano. Once the long-suffering Mrs. Streets had finally come to the end of her patience with me, I explored the possibility of playing other instruments, including the saxophone and the guitar. I was playing saxophone in the school orchestra when Mr. Grant noticed my habitual tendency to practice and experiment at the piano. Mr. Grant kept an eye on me and decided to mentor and encourage me in ways that always inspired me to learn more and become better. Rather than using heavy-handed discipline, Mr. Grant taught in a way that was subtle, yet effective. For example, there were the compliments he'd give me for being creative, or there was the time that he showed me what a tenth was and taught me how to extend my hand to reach this interval on the keyboard. While he encouraged my creativity, he also had me studying compositions by Debussy and Bach. One of the things that Henry Grant did to get our attention was have us listen to Debussy études and Duke Ellington together so that we could compare the similarities between their use of harmony. He would also write jazz harmonizations and arrangements of traditional Christmas songs. A gentle taskmaster and a wise and understanding man, Mr. Grant used patience and encouragement to help build my dream of playing jazz piano.

Mr. Grant's encouragement was one reason that I abandoned the saxophone to concentrate on piano. The other reason was my schoolmate

Frank Wess. In high school, I had the privilege of sitting next to Frank in the school orchestra, and he was so incredible that he was intimidating. In fact, I would say that he was almost as good a saxophonist as a teenager as when he played as an adult. I knew there was no way I could ever become his equal on saxophone, so I decided to devote myself entirely to piano, with the intention that I would become as good on my instrument as Frank Wess was on his.

Although very accessible to his students, Mr. Grant was also a giant in his own right. Several jazz masters, including Duke Ellington and Frank Wess, link their success to Henry Grant's early tutelage. He was one of the intellectuals of that period who was wise enough to recognize early on that African American music had something unique and distinctive to offer apart from the European classical tradition. Furthermore, he was the kind of teacher who encouraged his students to pursue excellence in both jazz *and* classical music without sacrificing one to the other. Mr. Grant lived on T Street and came from an important musical background himself. He was the son of the singer Henry Fleet Grant, who many believe was the first African American high school music teacher in Washington, D.C. Mr. Grant attended Livingston College in North Carolina, as well as New York University. He was a composer, choir director, pianist, and organizer of concerts and music festivals in the Washington, D.C., area.

In 1919, Mr. Grant helped to organize the National Association of Negro Musicians (NANM), which was formed to advance achievement and excellence among African American musical artists. Interestingly, he was the only high school teacher among the charter group of the NANM. He was also the chairman when more than 200 black musicians met in Chicago to establish that organization. In the early 1920s, he also served as editor of its journal, *The Negro Musician*. Other charter members were noted composers and performers like Nathaniel Dett, Clarence Cameron White, and Cleota Collins. The NANM held an annual convention, conducted workshops, showcased new talent, and gave scholarships. In 1921, Marian Anderson became the first recipient of an NANM scholarship, and subsequent scholarship recipients include national figures like composers William Levi Dawson and Florence Price, singer Grace Bumbry, and pianist Leon Bates. Nearly a century after its birth, the National Association of Negro Musicians is still going strong, and I'm grateful that one of its founders was the teacher who showed me how a jazz musician uses the tenth at the keyboard and so much more beyond that.

At Dunbar, we took great joy in recounting the achievements of our alumni, and every soul in my neighborhood knew and celebrated James Reese Europe! Born in Alabama to a father who was a former slave, James Reese Europe's family moved to Washington, D.C., where he and his siblings attended Dunbar when it was still called the "M Street High School." Europe eventually went to New York, where, as early as 1910, he created the Clef Club Orchestra, which also served as a musicians' union and talent agency for black players. Europe was an innovator and eventually became an international figure and one of the most important architects of African American music in the twentieth century. As the director of the Clef Club Orchestra, he added banjos and mandolins to the conventional symphonic instruments and led the way in playing a style of music that was first called "syncopated dance music," an ances- tor to what would be later known as *jazz*. In the 1920s, white artists took most of the credit for jazz, and Paul Whiteman proclaimed himself the "King of Jazz" despite the music's African American roots. And when Whiteman introduced Gershwin's highly popular *Rhapsody in Blue* in 1924, the public had no reason to question his claim. But African Ameri- can artists were performing jazz in concert more than a decade before the premiere of *Rhapsody in Blue*. On May 1, 1912, James Reese Europe gave the first-ever jazz concert at Carnegie Hall. Though rarely cited in history books, the sold-out performance was enthusiastically received by critics and the public alike. It was during World War I that Jim Europe, with his 369th "Hellfighters" Army Band, won fame overseas, especially in France, where his band was commissioned to play for soldiers on leave in Aix-les-Bains in 1918. Europe was thus largely responsible for introduc- ing the French to the sound of African American music. While serving overseas, he wrote letters to his family back in Washington in which he expressed amazement at the freedom and respect he enjoyed in France as compared to the segregation that was common in the United States. What he conveyed in those letters must have had a profound effect on his sister and my teacher, Mary Lorraine Europe.

While her brother had achieved international acclaim, Mary Europe received her degree in music from Howard University and was known and regarded in Washington, D.C., as a fine pianist and organist who was not only in demand locally, but was the accompanist of choice for renowned artists such as Harry T. Burleigh, Roland Hayes, Clarence Cameron White, and violinist Joseph Douglass, the grandson of Frederick Douglass. She was also the accompanist for the Coleridge Taylor Choral Society and played at performances where Samuel Coleridge Taylor himself conducted. By the time I enrolled at Dunbar High School, Ms. Europe was a pillar of the institution, having been there already for more than thirty years.

Ms. Europe was a very proud woman who instilled in us a respect and appreciation for the achievements of our people. On one particular occasion, some boys in the school hallway were rough-housing in the typical way that boys do to prove their masculinity. The disturbance caught Ms. Europe's attention, and she corrected the unruly boys by teaching them a lesson.

She used the example of Roland Hayes to instruct these boys about the real meaning of manhood, telling them this story: Roland Hayes was born in Georgia, the son of former slaves. When his father died, he was forced to quit school to help support his family. He worked hard in an iron foundry, and when he was able to resume his education much later, he endured the embarrassment of attending classes with students who were much younger than he was. Roland had a beautiful singing voice and was determined that he would somehow get the training he needed to pursue a career in music. He continued to work hard and save his money until he could hire a tutor. As he studied, practiced, and prepared himself, he continued to support himself by working at various jobs. After years of struggle, Roland Hayes became the first African American male concert singer to win international acclaim. He eventually began performing throughout Europe. It was during a performance in Germany in 1927 that Hayes was greeted by a particularly hostile audience. Hayes got up to sing, only to be ridiculed by hecklers. Refusing to be unnerved by the inhospitable crowd, Hayes just stood there, defiantly waiting for the boos and hisses to subside. He then signaled to his accompanist, who started playing Schubert's "Du bist die Ruh," one of the favorite songs of the

German people. As Hayes started to sing, the hostility evaporated and the people were simply overcome by the exquisite beauty of his voice.

"There he was," said Ms. Europe, "in a foreign country facing a hostile crowd, and he stood before them without flinching. That's what it means to be a *real* man."

Hearing the story that Ms. Europe told us about genuine manhood is one reason that Roland Hayes became one of my heroes. The faculty arranged for him to speak to us in assembly, and when he did, we knew that he was royalty as he imparted to us the virtues of hard work and determination. When we heard him sing, we all understood the true extent of his greatness, and how his voice could hypnotize a crowd and transform their hatred into humble appreciation.

Another one of my heroes was Paul Robeson, the singer, actor, athlete, and activist whose many varied achievements seemed to place him well ahead of his time. When I was around fourteen or fifteen, the faculty at Dunbar High School arranged for Mr. Robeson to come and meet with the students in an assembly. When I first laid eyes on him, I was overwhelmed, as he was bigger than life in every sense of the word. This prodigious, statuesque, yet most gracious gentleman spoke to us about the importance of staying in school and pursuing higher education. He explained to us that the possibilities for achievement were endless so long as we committed ourselves to study and hard work. His message was thoroughly inspiring, and his deep, rich, thunderous voice fascinated me. When Mr. Robeson laughed, his voice echoed with such power that it filled every corner of the space where he stood. When I saw him in movies, his regality on screen was to me every bit as genuine as it had been in person.

Another famous graduate of Dunbar High School who inspired me musically was George Walker. He was younger than me but graduated from high school at the age of fourteen, and therefore actually finished ahead of me. A pianist, he was also only fourteen when he gave his first public recital, on the campus of Howard University. He went on to have a very distinguished career as a pianist and composer, eventually studying in Paris with Nadia Boulanger and writing commissions for the New York Philharmonic, the Cleveland Orchestra, the Boston Symphony, and many other orchestras. While we were in high school, I admired

George for his technique and his dedication. But he was clearly headed in the direction of European classical music; my heart was always in jazz.

As I was a teenager interested in music, it was only natural that my circle of friends came to include other boys with the same interest. Three of my best buddies back then were John Malachi, Rob Harley, and Horace Preston. John Malachi was a pianist a little older than I whose playing I really admired. As a teenager, John was already playing with the older musicians, and for a time, he even had a band of his own. Rob Harley was my age and played on about the same level as I did. And Horace Preston was a good friend and classmate whose fans included, of all people, my mother. On more than one occasion, my mother mentioned how much she preferred Horace's "nice light touch" to what she called my "banging" on the keys. That "banging," however, was my zeal and exertion, my vigorous and heartfelt attempt to make my music *swing* the way that I knew jazz was supposed to. With time, my "banging" conformed to the natural curvature of the distinctive rhythm that I wanted to capture, but it wasn't so easy at first.

One day, John, Rob, and Horace invited me to go and listen to an old-fashioned guy named Jelly Roll Morton. I would have much preferred to hear some of the hip, younger lions, but my friends convinced me, so I went along. Jelly Roll had recently bought an interest in one of the clubs on U Street, the Jungle Inn, which was just a couple of doors down from the Lincoln Theatre. He was in Washington both to perform and to do some recordings for the Library of Congress. We arrived at the club and took our seats at a table near the piano. The room was quite small, so we were directly in his view when he came out to play. Having been told that the four of us were young musicians, he simply turned to us and sneered to his partner, "Man, those ain't nothing but kids!" He then sat at the piano, turned to us, and said, "You punks can't play like this." He then started to play, and I noticed that the sounds he was producing on the piano were that of an entire New Orleans band! I could hear the clarinet line in his right hand, the trombone line in his left hand, and everything in between. As if that weren't enough, he was playing in keys like E and A. Although I'd mastered all of the keys, for jazz, those were keys that I tended to avoid at that time. He captivated us all from the first tune, and we soon conceded that his assessment of us was right. So we respectfully paid attention. I'm not sure what my buddies were thinking, but it seemed as though Jelly Roll could see the consternation on my face, which only provoked him to show off even more! Jelly Roll Morton was an innovator, and in many respects, he laid the groundwork for later developments in jazz. Having witnessed his performance that day, I have always felt that history treated him unfairly. Much has been made about his arrogance, his involvement in gambling and prostitution, and his life on the so-called wrong side of the tracks. But he impressed me that day as a remarkable composer and virtuoso pianist who had rightfully earned his place as one of the important architects of jazz even though he never really got credit for being the pioneer that he was. Understandably, this embittered him. I am hopeful that students and scholars of jazz will continue taking another look at Jelly Roll Morton in order to set the record straight.

Jelly Roll Morton really inspired me to shift my practicing into high gear. After working very hard and playing every chance that I could both as a soloist and with various small groups around Washington, D.C., I finally felt ready for my first major musical rite of passage: the Amateur Night Contest at the Howard Theatre.

I may have been a little cocky when I made my first solo attempt at Amateur Night. But I took my music very seriously and I practiced constantly and was therefore very eager to display my skill on the night of my first big performance. From backstage, I peeped around the curtain to look at the sea of people, all dressed to the nines and waiting to cheer and applaud, or to heckle if the occasion required it. Some of the earlier acts of the evening were okay, and others were quite good.

The act before me went on, and the stagehand alerted me that I was next. I'd never met this girl before, but I'll always remember the moment she started to play the piano. She was better than okay, better than good. To my utter dismay, she was spectacular! I suddenly felt my bravado weakening, and I started to second-guess the piece that I'd prepared, which now seemed too simple, almost elementary. So when my name was announced, I went onstage with a spontaneous change of plans. Instead of playing the piece that I'd prepared, I decided on the spot to do "Honeysuckle Rose," one of Fats Waller's most popular tunes.

I placed my fingers on the keys, and before long, it was as if I was in a speeding car with no driver. In my head, I could hear the sounds I wanted to make, but my intentions went one way and my fingers went another! I was in over my head. Not the outcome I expected. I was very disappointed in myself for making such a foolish and impulsive decision. My performance was sloppy and embarrassing, and I am sure that if there was any applause at all, it was to hurry me off the stage to make room for the next act. For the moment, I was defeated on what seemed like the most important evening of my young life.

Thankfully, that defeat was short-lived. The beauty of apparent failure is that it is the best teacher one can ever have. That experience motivated me to regroup, to try it again. I mustered my determination, and with my mission in clear view, I returned to the trenches. I remembered the story of Roland Hayes. I remembered the shadow of Fats Waller and the unspoken mandate. I practiced for hours, day and night, night and day, anticipating the chance for redemption. I'd stood in his shadow, and although I had been too afraid to speak to him, he was speaking to me every single day. Mediocrity was not an option.

It was in 1936 that I entered the Amateur Night contest again, and this time, I won! On that glorious night, Lucky Millender's band was playing at the Howard, and his pianist at that time was Billy Kyle, a very exciting musician who, for me, ranked alongside some of the great legends. Although he was featured regularly on the radio with John Kirby's small combo and with many big bands, and although he was a big influence on me, Bud Powell, and many others, history never gave Billy Kyle the attention he was due. The prize for winning Amateur Night included the opportunity for me to come back during the next show and play with Lucky Millender's band. Although I was elated to have won, I wasn't too thrilled about the prospect of filling Billy Kyle's very large and well-worn shoes. I didn't really feel that I'd measure up to Kyle, but my performance with Millender's band was due to take place almost immediately after the contest ended, so I was determined to give it my best shot. I was extremely nervous about all of this, but Kyle was kind enough to come over and chat with me backstage before the show, *which would be broadcast live on the radio!* He was a generous man and took the time to compliment my playing and give me a few pointers. The broadcast was a success. Little did I know that Billy Kyle's influence on my life would go far beyond the prize for winning Amateur Night. Years later, when Kyle was very busy as a first-call pianist, he recommended me for various recording gigs. Although he could have simply declined these gigs without another thought, he instead recommended me by name to get the kind of recording work that, in those days, was not easy to come by. When he did, I reminded him of the master class that he gave me that night at the Howard Theatre after I'd won the Amateur Night competition.

Winning this contest was a very affirming milestone in my young life as a performer, and it placed me in great company. Other winners of the Howard Theatre's Amateur Night contests include Ella Fitzgerald, Bill "Ink Spots" Kenny, and Billy Eckstine.

I have always had enormous respect for women in jazz, and this respect may well have been born when a girl both outplayed me and inspired me the night of my first unsuccessful attempt to win the Amateur Night contest. It embarrasses me that I can't recall her name, since hers is one of many names of accomplished female jazz artists whose work has faded into obscurity because of gender bias. Perhaps the humiliation of the moment prevented me from taking note of who she was. To this day, however, I respect her for her musicianship and for teaching me a lesson that I've never forgotten.

My small and embracing world had a seemingly endless supply of creativity and inspiration. In 1936, however, the broader world forced its way into our awareness. There was a man in Germany named Adolph Hitler whose bigotry and hatred for Jews was quite blatant. He espoused a view of white supremacy that was even more extreme than segregation in America. The Olympic Games were held in Berlin that year, and one of our track stars, Jesse Owens, would be there to compete. Because he was African American, we knew that Owens would be in hostile territory, so we waited anxiously to hear the news of his performance. When he won four gold medals, the newspapers carried the story, noting how visibly stunned Hitler was that Owens had so clearly and beautifully challenged his misguided notions about race.

Although racial tensions kept people divided both at home and abroad, there was something that I witnessed in my neighborhood that was a definite sign of things to come. Waxy Maxy's record store was frequented by two brothers who were obviously not from our neighborhood, and who were neither white nor African American. They'd ride to the front of the record store in a large, chauffeured automobile, politely greet the manager, and then proceed straight to the back of the store to bargain with him for old jazz records, which they considered to be more valuable than the others. One of them would say, "How much would you take for this Jelly Roll Morton record?" and the owner would say, "Twenty-five cents." The men, who I later learned were the sons of the Turkish ambassador, would reply, "We'll give you seventeen cents," and the bargaining would continue from there. I now understand that their bargaining was in keeping with Middle Eastern tradition, which seemed strange to me at the time. These two Turkish brothers with the fascination for African American music were Ahmet and Nesuhi Ertegun. Much later, in the 1940s, Ahmet, along with Herb Abramson, founded Atlantic Records, the label that introduced rhythm-and-blues greats Ruth Brown and Ray Charles to the world. In their own way, the Erteguns defied segregation to frequent our neighborhood and patronize our music. They also produced jazz concerts that featured racially mixed groups, shocking the Washington D.C., establishment and delighting their friends. Later, Ahmet and Nesuhi defied segregation again by recording and promoting the African American artists whose music not only became a soundtrack for the 1950s, but inspired the races to sing and dance together.

From childhood through my teen years, I had the pleasure of learning to play the music that I loved, music that I hoped would become my life's work. As my high school years drew to a close, my parents became especially concerned that I choose a productive path in life. Both of my parents were college graduates, and my father had taken me on several occasions to visit his alma mater, Virginia State College. As Dunbar High School was known to be a college preparatory school and expectations of its alumni were high, there was no question that I was destined for higher education, even though my grades at Dunbar were never as good as they could have been. My father was worried that my obsession with music had gotten in the way of any serious thinking on my part about the necessity of earning a living. It was the era of the Great Depression, and times were hard. Even though my father managed well with his dental practice, his patients were sometimes poor people who bartered goods and other services as payment to my father for their dental care. He was generous and compassionate, and he understood the difficult situations that his patients faced. I never knew my father to turn anyone away. Nonetheless, he'd lecture me: "Do you see these people that come in and out of my office?" he'd say; "I don't ever want you to be without the means to provide for yourself. I don't ever want you to be beholden to anyone. You *must* be able to stand on your own two feet!"

My initial dream was to attend Juilliard. Juilliard was a dream destination that many African Americans had already reached by the time I was thinking of colleges. The famed composer and conductor Hall Johnson attended Juilliard. Pianist and composer Luther Henderson graduated from Juilliard, as did Ann Wiggins Brown, who played the original Bess in the 1935 premiere of *Porgy and Bess*. Hazel Scott studied classical piano at Juilliard before proceeding to a career in jazz and motion pictures. Dean Dixon was a conductor who studied at Juilliard. And then there was my own uncle Percy who'd attended Juilliard, and a friend of mine, a saxophonist named Billy White, who'd recently gone to Juilliard. These and other African Americans had already proven that if I was serious enough about music, Juilliard was definitely within my reach.

It was briefly suggested that I consider attending Howard. Although Howard had a fine music department, the emphasis there seemed to be entirely upon music in the European classical tradition, and I knew that this direction didn't interest me. Besides that, Howard was already very familiar and too close to home. Attending college there would have been like going to high school again. I wanted a chance to get away and learn to do things on my own.

After some discussions with my parents, it became clear that my dream of going to Juilliard was not plausible. My father disliked the idea of an education that was narrowly focused on conservatory training. Like others of his generation, he believed that an education should prepare you for as much of life as possible, and learning to play the piano was simply not enough. It was decided that I should relegate music to the status of an enjoyable pastime and major in sociology. In my view, sociology was no match for music, but it was a good, solid field that my parents felt would position me to earn a living, and in those days, children simply didn't question their parents. And so in 1938, I followed in my father's footsteps and headed to Petersburg, Virginia, to enroll at Virginia State College, where, beneath my sociology major, my love for music continued to simmer to the boiling point.

TWO

College Years

1938–1942

$\mathcal{T}$HE TIME HAD COME FOR ME to test my wings, a prospect that
both excited me and frightened me. I had the utmost respect and
admiration for my parents, but I believed I had the moxie to move forward, although it was that of a typical seventeen-year-old male. I was
bursting with the kind of restlessness that signaled due time for a new
level of responsibility. But there was also a great unknown before me.
Despite the fact that I had visited Virginia State College on several occasions, and despite the fact that my parents had helped me to determine
the major I would pursue and the fraternity I would pledge, I had very
little concept of life apart from the sanctuary of my upbringing and its
hallowed landmarks and artifacts—U Street, Florida Avenue Baptist
Church, Dunbar High School, the Howard Theatre, and Aunt Alcinda's
dinner rolls! Added to the uncertainty of my own life was the shifting
tide of the late 1930s. Both America and the world were changing.

As I prepared to leave the comforts of boyhood and home, America
was digging out from beneath the Great Depression while war clouds
gathered across the Atlantic. We huddled around the radios in our living rooms to listen to President Roosevelt's "Fireside Chats," during
which he tried to assure us that our country would remain neutral despite instability around the world and Adolph Hitler's troubling rise to
power. We also gathered around our radios to listen to Joe Louis knock
out James Braddock in New York's Madison Square Garden, and later
to listen to him defeat the German Max Schmeling in June of 1938, the
same summer that I graduated from Dunbar High. When the "Brown

Bomber" conquered the German, the symbolism could not have been more potent. Here was a black man whose native country confined him to "Colored Only" drinking fountains, to "Jim Crow" cars on the train, to the backs of buses, to the back doors of restaurants, and to the balconies of theatres. Yet this black man emerged the victor over the German whose native land was considered the real threat to democracy. Joe Louis seemed to speak for all of us. Throughout the South, any African American who dared to challenge a white man risked being lynched. Untold numbers of black men were castrated, hanged, or burned alive for this reason, and even if they were innocent, the law offered them no protection. Because he could stand equal to a white man without risk of being lynched, Joe Louis became our proxy.

Joe Louis was not alone, as there were other African Americans who were beginning to pierce the veil of segregation in new and exciting ways. Mary McLeod Bethune was not only an accomplished and respected educator and activist, but she was also an advisor and personal friend to President and Mrs. Roosevelt and, at the president's invitation, was a frequent visitor to the White House. The Roosevelts were open to African Americans in a way that none of us had ever seen before. It seemed ironic to me that we were finding this new place in the government's sandstone-and-marble wonderland at just the time I was leaving Washington, D.C., to go further south to the decidedly more conservative experience of Petersburg, Virginia! The soundtrack for those months before I left for college was "A Tisket, a Tasket," performed by Ella Fitzgerald and Chick Webb, a very popular tune during that summer of 1938. Even though millions of radio listeners turned their dials to the racial buffoonery of the *Amos and Andy* show, Jesse Owens, Joe Louis, and Mary McLeod Bethune were our heroes, intelligent and sophisticated individuals who challenged these old stereotypes. In this moment filled with national irony and racial pride, I headed off to Virginia State College to conquer the next phase in my young life.

I said goodbye to my neighborhood friends as I set out for what would be my new home for the next four years. The drive to Petersburg was about three hours to the south of Washington, D.C. In actuality, the school was located in Ettrick, Virginia, which was just outside of the city of Petersburg. I listened respectfully as my father extolled the virtues of the sociology major and preached to me about the importance of being financially secure during difficult economic times. The Depression had taught all of us that lesson. Despite the concern in his voice and the wisdom in his advice, I was already imagining myself at a piano somewhere on the campus, performing my best to the delight of the young ladies who, at least in my own mind, were certainly there anxiously waiting to hear me. I was thinking of how much practicing I'd do, and how amazed my buddies back home would be at my improvement when we reunited in Washington.

The transition from home to college can be a somewhat traumatic experience for a young person. Fortunately, however, my father's connections with Virginia State eased things for me. Segregation kept most other American colleges and universities off-limits to us. At a college like Virginia State, however, segregation ensured that both average students and history makers would be united in a single campus community. It was perhaps for this reason that I found campus life to be a world both entirely different and completely familiar. In that pastoral scene of manicured landscaping and hallowed academic buildings I met new friends, each of whom had a background and a hometown at least somewhat similar to mine. My college mates came from places like the Sweet Auburn district of Atlanta, the 18th-and-Vine area of Kansas City, the South Side of Chicago, and other all-black communities around the nation whose boundaries had been forged by segregation. We'd each left our respective hometowns to form another all-black community on this campus, where heritage was heavy and thick and our parents' expectations of us loomed large. The school itself was situated on a hill overlooking the city of Petersburg on a small but beautiful campus. With college life came a new collection of safe places where we could meet up between classes, swap stories, and share laughter. We knew that we were welcomed at the Green Leaf Café, at Becky's Coffee Shop, and at the College Grill, and we knew that we could venture as far as the popular student hangout near the Appomattox River, without fear of violating any custom. But we also knew the places we were forbidden to go, and we avoided those types of places just as we had each done back at our respective homes.

I found the faculty at this college to be just as nurturing and dedicated as were the teachers at Dunbar High School. Like Howard Uni-

versity, Virginia State College (now Virginia State University) was one
of the institutions of higher learning established specifically for African
Americans in the late 1800s. World-class professors were on the faculty
of Virginia State College. J. Harold Montague, a graduate of Oberlin
and Syracuse University, was the chair of the Music Department and the
choir director. Undine Smith Moore taught in the Music Department,
and I was heavily influenced by the way she played piano and taught
theory and harmony. I had no way of knowing this at the time, but she
would become one of the first African American female composers of
note. Professor Moore became especially known for her choral pieces.
She earned honorary doctorates and, much later her life, became a Pu-
litzer Prize nominee for her major choral piece *Scenes from the Life of a
Martyr*, a tribute to Martin Luther King. And attending Virginia State
along with me in the early 1940s was Camilla Williams, the first African
American singer to receive a contract with the New York City Opera; she
debuted in the title role of Puccini's *Madame Butterfly*.

In those days, we were required to attend the college chapel every
Sunday. Fortunately for us, Professor Moore was the chapel pianist. And
since we were a captive audience for her, she used those opportunities
to expose the student body to music that we might not have otherwise
encountered. Regardless of our opinion of the music, we were forced to
listen reverently. She knew this and took every advantage of it.

In accordance with my parents' wishes, I dutifully followed the cur-
riculum for the sociology major, all the while indulging myself in music
at every opportunity. At the university, there was no serious course of
instruction for jazz, which was considered strictly extracurricular, something you did in your spare time. So I took advantage of every available
moment to hone my skills at the piano. While living in Washington,
D.C., I had many opportunities to sit in at clubs and various places, but
I never got a job playing with a band until I went to college. When I was
a very young boy, Fats Waller and Art Tatum were the jazz celebrities
that interested me most, and the stride approach to piano playing was
the popular style of the day. By the time I got to college, however, the
music had evolved and *swing*, featuring the big band, was all the rage.
By the mid-1930s, the big-band celebrities were Duke Ellington, Cab
Calloway, Count Basie, Chick Webb, and Jimmy Lunceford, and theirs

were the sounds that we young people craved at the dances and parties
that enlivened our weekends and where we could two-step, slow-drag,
jitterbug, and Lindy-hop the night away, all, of course, under the moral
policing of our watchful chaperones.

There were lots of pretty girls at Virginia State, but the guys on campus always had competition from the soldiers at nearby Camp Lee. On
weekends, they would show up in their starched and pressed military
uniforms, invade our dances and parties, and scope out the girls on our
campus. This irritated us to no end.

Back in those days, personal appearance was a big deal. In Washington, D.C., there was a tailor shop, Willmuth's, where you could go and get
a suit made for 25 dollars. I was a big fan of Duke Ellington and the other
stars I grew up watching, and they were always impeccably dressed. So
in order to emulate them, I saved my money for whatever length of time
it took and I purchased tailored suits of my own from Willmuth's. By the
time I got to Virginia State, I had amassed quite a wardrobe and prided
myself on being one of the most sharply dressed students at the college.

Before I arrived to Virginia State, I had heard that there were a
couple of student-led bands on campus, one called the Virginia State
Rhythm Boys, another called the Virginia State Collegians. They each
had a faculty sponsor for a time, but neither group was sanctioned by the
college and both had disbanded by the time I arrived. I was eager to find
a group that I could play with, and my search finally led me to Richmond
and my first big-band experience. I spent my freshman year playing piano
in Benny Layton's Dance Band, a local upstart group whose piano player
had just been drafted. Benny was a few years older than me and was a
tenor-sax player. He was from a well-to-do family that supported his
try at a career as a professional musician, and it was to my benefit to
have this early big-band experience with several guys who were all more
seasoned than I was. I gained a great deal of insight from learning to
be a part of an ensemble, from having to listen and respond as part of a
larger musical team, which was a very different experience than playing
solo or playing with some of the small combo groups I'd experimented
with back in Washington, D.C. By playing with Benny Layton's band
I also learned that I could get arrangements for one dollar. We played
"Take the A Train," "Tuxedo Junction," and some charts by Mary Lou

Williams. These charts, including the solos, were transcribed right from the records, so even though the solo was right there on the page for us to read, we always added our own original touches. With such easy access to good music, I couldn't help but entertain the notion of someday leading my own group. After my freshman year, Benny was drafted and became an officer in the army.

I also took every music course that was offered, and I played in the marching band and sang in the chorus. I even took up the cello for a time while at Virginia State. My teachers gave me solid instruction in the music of Bach, Handel, Haydn, Mozart, and Beethoven, as this was the music that they had been educated to teach. But there were no college courses in jazz, no jazz experts on the faculty to challenge and guide me in the music that I loved most. Although my heart's desire was to play jazz, it was through the influence of my classical teachers that I developed a desire to write and to arrange music. They deepened my understanding and broadened my perspective in a way that sparked my interest in becoming more than just a "star."

Along with my musical activities, my membership in Kappa Alpha Psi Fraternity was an important part of my life at Virginia State. Just as my parents had the last word on my college major, it was also typical in those days for parents to have a say in the social activities of their college-age children. My father had pledged Kappa Alpha Psi during his Virginia State days, so it was simply assumed that I would do the same. In the late 1930s, black Greek organizations were still relatively new, and they were another means of uplifting the race. My father's love for discipline and achievement made him perfect for Kappa Alpha Psi, a fraternity whose members were known for earning high marks and accomplishing great things. By my freshman year at Virginia State, there was already a lengthy roster of Kappa men who were high achievers—doctors, attorneys, university presidents, and the like. It frustrated my father that I was never as serious a student in high school as he would have liked for me to be. Perhaps he hoped that by becoming a Kappa, I would reap the benefits of positive peer pressure and become more focused during my college years, maybe even to the point of shifting my heart and soul to the field of sociology and to the possibilities it offered for a respectable profession. In my father's view, pledging had ultimately failed to have the

desired effect upon me, but becoming a Kappa was something in which
I took great pride, nonetheless.

I became popular on campus because of my ability to play. There
was a steady demand for musicians to play for parties and dances, and I
jumped at every chance to show what I could do. On one particular occasion, my popularity, combined with a dash of my youthful cockiness,
actually served me well. I was hanging out with some guys in the dorm
one evening listening to a program on the radio called *Tobacco Tags*. The
show was thus named both for the musical ensemble it featured (a country string band with mandolins) and for the fact that a tobacco company
was the sponsor. (Literally, a "tobacco tag" was a little metal label that
identified the brand of tobacco in a package.) I commented to my pals
that the music was unbelievably corny, to which one of them responded:
"So, do you think you can do better?" At that time, my reputation as a
good pianist was becoming established. So when they dared me to prove
that I could do better than the *Tobacco Tags*, I accepted the challenge.

With no hesitation and very little forethought, I ventured beyond the
safe haven of the Virginia State campus and did the unthinkable. I went
to downtown Petersburg, found the radio station, and asked to speak to
the person responsible for hiring musicians to play on the air.

"What do you play?" the station manager asked, no doubt intrigued
by the bold approach of this foolishly confident young colored man. I
answered, and he then directed me to the piano to show what I could
do. And so I did. With that, he gave me a fifteen-minute weekly radio
spot, which increased my notoriety considerably! It didn't occur to me
to ask for any money, so the station manager didn't offer any. But I was a
freshman with my own radio show, a true "big man on campus," and the
popularity afforded me because of it—especially with the coeds—was
worth gold! At eighteen years of age, I certainly had no inkling that I
was taking the first step of a journey in the broadcast media that would
span the rest of my life. I was also quite oblivious to the fact that I had
unwittingly challenged segregation in downtown Petersburg! Had my
father known of this, he would have seriously questioned my judgment,
if not my sanity.

It must have been late in 1938 that some representatives of a corporation were visiting Petersburg for the purpose of demonstrating some

new technology that would soon be available to the public. They were particularly interested in trying out their contraption on people in radio, since the radio personalities were the broadcast experts of the day. They came to the radio station and explained to us that they could produce the same effect as a moving picture, and their invention would enable us to see ourselves moving and talking on a small screen affixed to a large box. To demonstrate this new technology, they wanted to showcase everyone who worked at the radio station, and that included everyone on the air, black and white. (I recall this particular instance as perhaps the one fleeting moment that there was no segregation in downtown Petersburg!) To view ourselves on the small screen was exciting, sort of like looking in a high-tech mirror; but it was no more than a fun diversion from the normal business of the workday. No one could see its relevance. So we thanked the salesmen for their demonstration, wished them well on their new-fangled experiment (they called it a *television*), and went back to listening to our radios!

It may seem strange that we were so unimpressed with this new technology. But in a segregated world, the beauty of radio was that you could become known for your talent while remaining anonymous. Had audiences been able to see at that time that I was African American, my skin color might have been a distraction to many people, especially in the South. But radio gave me access to listeners who enjoyed my music, who judged me only with their ears and hearts. And that's the way it should have been.

During the spring of my freshman year, I returned home to Washington, D.C., to be a part of a moment that has since been immortalized as one of the high points for African Americans in the twentieth century. My teacher Mr. Grant, who was one of the founding members of the National Association of Negro Musicians, was therefore one of those who had a hand in selecting its first scholarship recipient, Marian Anderson. By the late 1930s, Marian Anderson had achieved world acclaim as a singer but had yet to present a major concert in the United States. Attempts were made to secure Constitution Hall for Ms. Anderson's performance, but this facility was administered by the Daughters of the American Revolution, which opposed the use of the building by African American performers. Ms. Anderson was a queen, a graceful and strikingly beautiful woman with an inimitable voice and, through the grace and dignity with which she carried herself, had amassed friends and admirers around the world. Fortunately, one of those friends was Mrs. Eleanor Roosevelt, whose openness and sensitivity to the African American community was well known. Hearing of Constitution Hall's refusal to host Ms. Anderson, Mrs. Roosevelt angrily resigned her membership in the DAR and helped to arrange for her to perform on the steps of the Lincoln Memorial. When word got out that Ms. Anderson would be performing there on Easter Sunday, the entire African American community in Washington, D.C., erupted with excitement! It was nearly unbelievable, almost too good to be true, and definitely not to be missed.

The city was chilly and overcast that day as throngs from both Washington and surrounding cities and states began to gather hours in advance to hear Ms. Anderson's concert, which was set to begin at 5:00 PM. There were also many law-enforcement officers and news people present. While we eagerly anticipated the performance, there was a sense of caution, even a slight sense of foreboding in the air, as there had never been such a large crowd of African Americans to fill the expanse between the Lincoln Memorial and the Washington Monument. Having been confined to our section of the city, none of us quite knew what to expect from the local white citizens, who were unaccustomed to seeing us in such large numbers.

After a short speech by one of the dignitaries on the platform, Ms. Anderson was introduced and the audience held its breath. We huddled together against the cold, but as if on cue, the clouds made way for a hint of sunshine as her pianist played the introduction to her first piece. Wearing a dark fur coat, Ms. Anderson readied herself before the bouquet of microphones. A hush fell over the already spellbound crowd. Then she parted her lips to sing her first words: "My country 'tis of thee, sweet land of liberty. . . ." We forgot about the chill in the air and felt a pride that was beyond expression. In a short program that was not quite an hour long, she concluded with the beloved spiritual "Nobody Knows The Trouble I've Seen" as eyes, young and old, filled with tears. Within the safe boundaries of our segregated neighborhood, we enjoyed frequent and intimate contact with the celebrated artists of our race. But to see Ms. Anderson performing triumphantly in the world beyond those safe boundaries was a beacon for those of my generation. She had left the lake for the ocean, in effect, testing the water for us all. She showed us that where there was excellence, the waters are welcoming. I couldn't help but to think of Roland Hayes singing "Du bist die Ruh," and I wondered about the cost that he, Ms. Anderson, and others had paid to earn a place on the national stage. At the same time, I was deeply moved by the supernatural power of music to melt away the fears that keep people separate from each other. Even though my hometown remained segregated after that day, there is no question in my mind that all of us—black and white—were transformed by that pivotal event.

After the concert, I returned to Petersburg to finish the final exams of my freshman year. The end of the school year held special excitement for me because I'd made the decision that, instead of returning home to Washington, D.C., I would spend my summer vacation living with a friend of my father's in Harlem. I loved the sound of the very word *Harlem!* This was a place of legends and dreams, where the very best of jazz had become the entertainment of choice for New York's ordinary people, as well as for its sophisticated society folk. In spite of my sociology major, Harlem was a possibility flickering stubbornly like an ostinato in the back of my brain, a light beckoning me to the Apollo and to the Savoy, soon nicknamed the "Home of Happy Feet." It was beckoning me to the clubs where the older lions held court, where cutting sessions separated the weaker musicians from those who were daring enough to lay bare their skills to the tough love guaranteed to sharpen those skills even further. I knew that Harlem offered a jazz education that Virginia State could not provide for me. It was impossible for me to be in Harlem without seeing myself at the piano in one of the clubs where young musicians proved their worth. But, alas, my major was sociology.

The excitement of living in Harlem that summer was compounded by the fact that the New York World's Fair had just opened on April 30. For a ticket that cost 75 cents, you could get into the fair and view the attractions all day, from 9:00 in the morning until 10:00 at night. The fair had lots of futuristic exhibits that allowed us to sample glimpses of a world with superhighways, automatic dishwashers, free long-distance phone calling, and televisions—all of which seemed like science fiction to us at the time.

I had fun going to the World's Fair, but my real purpose for being in Harlem was to get a glimpse of my own future. I wanted to hear the pianist Teddy Wilson; my all-time favorite tenor player, Ben Webster; Count Basie; Coleman Hawkins; trumpet player Shorty Baker; Benny Goodman; Fletcher Henderson; and the other greats that I'd known from radio but who I could now find playing at Smalls Paradise, at the Savoy, and at the Golden Gate Ballroom.

My father had instructed me that once I got to Harlem I was to stop into a club called the Yeah Man and say hello to a friend of his, Bill Garrett, who was the manager there. So after I'd gone to see the musicians that really interested me, I decided I'd better make this visit to the Yeah Man just long enough to be able to say that I went, which would satisfy my father. I went to the club, which was around 7th and 135th Streets, and walked in, not paying any attention to who was playing there. I found Mr. Garrett and introduced myself to him as Bill Taylor's son.

"Oh, yes, your dad tells me that you play the piano, so when the house pianist gets his break, why don't you go on back and play a little something for me?"

The club was tiny but lively, and people were eating and drinking and having a good time as I took my place at the piano, eager to show what I could do with the tune "Lullaby in Rhythm." I finished my piece and was pleased to get a nice applause from the people in club and a compliment on my playing from the house pianist when he returned; I was especially pleased when he invited me to an apartment to visit some friends of his after his shift was done.

When we arrived at the apartment, there were three guys engaged in a game of cards. There was a piano there, and my newfound friend remarked again that I'd played pretty well, and he asked me to sit and play "Lullaby in Rhythm" once more. One of the men put down his cards and his cigarettes and sat beside me on the piano bench: "Is this what you're trying to do?" he said, proceeding to show me a version of "Lullaby in Rhythm" that far exceeded any one that I'd heard, one that certainly trumped the version I had just played. The men at the card game each took at a turn at the piano, each humbling and schooling me in this private jam session. I soon learned that the house pianist who'd invited me to the apartment was Clarence Profit—composer of "Lullaby in

Rhythm"—and the other three card-playing pianists were Marlow Morris, Stephen Henderson, and Thelonious Monk! The lesson they taught me that night was both unforgettable and exactly what I needed. I have always been grateful to Clarence Profit for taking out time to mentor me in that way. Sadly, he passed away within just a few years after I met him.

During the winter of my sophomore year, I spent the holidays with a buddy of mine from Virginia State named Noel Torres, who lived in the Bronx. This guy was an athlete, very popular, and very much a "ladies' man." I'd already taken Noel to my mother's house in Washington, D.C., and introduced him to some of the pretty girls there, so he was returning the favor by taking me home with him to New York.

Compared to Washington, where you could go anywhere on foot, Harlem seemed to me to be a huge metropolis. Noel took me from house to house introducing me to his lady friends. Finally, after introducing me to one girl after another, he decided that we should make one more stop on the way back to his place. There were some sisters who he claimed were crazy about him, and so he thought we should pay them a visit.

When we knocked, their younger sister answered the door. My friend greeted her, joked around for a bit, and then asked if her two older sisters were at home. They weren't, so he asked her to tell them that we'd stopped by and that we'd be around later to visit.

I was immediately stricken by the sight of her.

"Who was *that*?" I asked, noticing how pretty she was. He told me that her name was Teddi, short for Theodora, and that she was the baby of the family. Theodora Castion.

Later, Noel took me to a dance at the YMCA in Harlem, and I noticed her again. This time, however, she was all dressed up, and although I was certainly taken aback by how beautiful she was, I hardly recognized her as the girl I'd met just a few days before. I spoke to her and took down her address, but nothing came of it at the time. As pretty as she was, she was still only sixteen. Years would pass before our paths would cross again.

For the first two years of my college enrollment, I majored in sociology in accordance with my parents' wishes. But my love for music, for jazz, was unabated, a fact hardly lost on the classmates and teachers who noted the curious gulf between the sociology major that I professed and the music activities in which I constantly indulged. As had been the case with my teachers at Dunbar, my professors at Virginia State were deeply committed to our success, keenly observant of our activities, and generous and forthright with their advice.

The course of my life may well have changed the day that Professor Undine Moore called me into her office and asked me:

"What's your major, Taylor?"

"Sociology," I answered.

"Wrong," she replied. "You're no sociology major; you're wasting your time. Change your major to music." And so I did.

Professor Moore was very open to jazz and very supportive of my desire to go in that direction with my music. The department chair, however, J. Harold Montague, was of a very different opinion. He believed that the European tradition was the only thing worth studying and had such a disdain for jazz that he forbade students to play jazz in the practice rooms. I had many clashes with Professor Montague, and had it not been for Professor Moore's intervention, I may well have gotten thrown out of school. Even though I was forbidden to use the practice rooms for playing jazz, she came to the rescue with an alternate plan. She discreetly provided me with a key to the rehearsal room down the hall and encouraged me to not only practice there, but to rehearse any jazz groups there as much as I wanted. Perhaps emboldened by Professor Moore's unwavering support, I eventually broke the rules and started playing jazz in the practice rooms.

It was Professor Moore who helped me to end the charade and to commit to my true calling. But my doing so came with a price. There comes a point in every young man's life that marks the end of childhood and the beginning of adulthood. In my family and in our community, we valued our elders and we were taught to respect their wisdom and to submit to their guidance. There is, however, a sort of gray area, where submitting to the wishes of our elders amounts to a denial of our own destiny. I knew the day would come when I would have to face my father with the decision I'd made, and I dreaded the very thought of it. When he finally discovered that I had changed my major to music, he was furious! Incensed, he said to me: "Since you were mature enough to change your major without my knowledge, then you're mature enough to pay your own tuition. I know you won't be able to make a living in music. Half of the people that don't pay me for getting their teeth fixed are musicians, and I refuse to create another freeloader!"

So for my junior and senior years, I worked and struggled to keep up with my studies and practicing while scraping together enough money to pay my own way. I was reminded of Roland Hayes, who also worked and paid his own way.

By my junior year, I was playing with "Johnson's Happy Pals," a much more advanced and popular band than Benny Layton's group and quite a step up for me. But the particular events of my junior year at Virginia State are much more difficult to recall than the winter of 1941. On the morning of December 7, the Japanese attacked Pearl Harbor, and suddenly the United States was at war! Since television was not yet commonplace, radios and newspapers were our main sources of information. Within months, weekly newsreels were shown at movie theatres bringing news from the war front. The population at Virginia State suffered a marked decline as students enlisted for military service or left college altogether to take advantage of a new surge in wartime industry jobs, especially in northern cities. Soon, everyday goods like sugar, shoes, coffee, and eventually gasoline were rationed. The onset of the war seemed to unite all Americans—both black and white—in a common cause. Everyone, whether at home, on the front line, or in college, was expected to do his or her part.

Like all young men at that time, I had the war very much on my mind as I entered my last year of college. My senior year was an especially busy time for me, and I had the chance to test my wings in music in new ways. During that year, I got my first taste of leading my own group, a big band called the Virginia Statesmen (our school newspaper was the *Virginia Statesman*), with a vocal ensemble called the Debs and the Playboys. One of my schoolmates, a guy named Phil Medley, started the Debs and the Playboys. The group was a jazz ensemble modeled on Tommy Dorsey's Pied Pipers. Back in those days, labels like "jazz" and "pop" were often blurry, since there wasn't much difference between the two genres. Once I took over the group from Phil, I experienced all the joys and headaches of being a leader. I was responsible for securing the music, for rehearsing the group, and for making sure everyone showed up on time. Knowing that good big-band arrangements were incredibly easy to come by, I went to a music store in Richmond and bought a transcription of the original arrangement of Basie's "One O'Clock Jump." For the staggering cost of one whole dollar, I got the complete score with parts. I also purchased an arrangement of "Jumping at the Woodside," another classic Basie tune, at an equally affordable price. In addition to rehearsing the group, there were those occasions that I had to play the bad guy and lay down the law, as leaders are sometimes compelled to do. It was a healthy learning experience, however, one that prepared me for leading my own groups in later years.

Phil Medley was as serious about music as I was, and while my life would take me in the direction of jazz, he was destined for a successful career in the popular music that was later called "rhythm and blues" and "rock and roll." Once we were out of college, Phil started his own publishing company and became a very successful songwriter whose songs were recorded by a number of artists, including the Beatles.

There was another incident during my senior year that foreshadowed things to come. We were all big fans of Count Basie, so when his band passed through Petersburg to do a one-nighter, our whole band went to see the show. During the intermission, we were hanging around the bandstand trying to strike up conversation with the guys in Basie's group, when someone from my band said, "Hey, you ought to hear *our* piano player!" Now, I was popular and confident with my friends around campus, but this was an entirely different matter altogether. I was embarrassed at the suggestion that the great Count Basie would get up and surrender his piano to me, and there was no way that I'd be bold enough to ask Basie to do that. Intimidating me further was the fact that Basie's rhythm section that night included the former leader of the Blue Devils Band, Walter Paige, on bass; the legendary Freddie Green on guitar; and Jonathan "Jo" Jones on drums.

"Papa" Jo Jones grew up in Alabama and had been a carnival tap dancer and drummer when he was young. He moved to Kansas City and had been with Basie's band since 1934. Jo was a practical joker and a good-natured troublemaker. He approached Basie and told him that there was this kid who wanted to sit in. Basie, being the very gracious man that he was, invited me to the piano. Though I would never have had the nerve to do such a thing on my own, thanks to Jo Jones, I got to perform with the Basie band that night.

Jo Jones was one of those people that showed up in my life at just the right times, and I encountered him for the first of many times at that Basie concert during my senior year in college. I'm sure he got a kick out of getting me to play that night with Basie's group. It was a bit later that Jo would come into my life again as both a mentor and a true friend.

While I was in college I first encountered another great musician who was destined to turn up later in my life. By my senior year, I had fully succumbed to the lure of Harlem and had started sitting in at some of the clubs there on occasions when I could get away. I wanted to learn jazz, and since there was no professor to guide me or class I could take, I filled this gap in my education in the way that was customary at that time.

I'd gone to many late-night jam sessions in Harlem. On this one particular occasion, a guy was there challenging all of the other bass players. He outplayed them all, one after another, until there was a single bassist left standing. Slam Stewart was an entirely unique and virtuosic bass player. He had attended Boston Conservatory and was fluent in both classical and jazz. He'd started as a violinist, and despite the size of his instrument, he had incredible dexterity and was every bit as agile on the string bass as any classical violinist I'd ever heard. He was also a master showman and was known for simultaneously humming along while he played, vocally doubling his own improvisations an octave higher. In short, Slam was a lion of a musician.

So this guy decided to make his victory complete by challenging Slam, and what's worse, he decided to do so by playing one of Slam's tunes. Now, Slam was a fun-loving guy who liked to laugh and joke a lot, but when it came to playing the bass, he was dead serious. So for this guy to challenge him with one of his own tunes was just about as foolish as teasing a hungry lion with fresh meat. To challenge Slam Stewart was one thing; but to taunt him with his own tune . . . well, this fellow was in trouble.

Slam allowed the guy to revel in his arrogance for a few minutes. Then Slam came to the bandstand, took the guy's bass away from him, and proceeded to rip him to pitiful shreds. I'd never seen anyone take such a merciless beating at a jam session before, and by the time he was done, he'd earned the respect of every musician in the place. I had no idea at the time that I would be fortunate enough to encounter Slam again later in my life.

Those last two years of college were a time of learning responsibility for myself, as well as responsibility for others. After my dad's lecture, I knew that I had to depend on myself for my income, and I worked tirelessly, earning money mostly from playing gigs around Petersburg and other nearby towns. I also spent the latter part of my senior year practice teaching in a nearby school, a requirement for students majoring in music education. Although I didn't do a senior recital, I had to conduct several pieces in concert in Virginia Hall and play on someone else's recital, all requirements to fulfilling my degree. There were times that I had to choose between buying my meals and paying my tuition. I'd sometimes fall short or get behind on my tuition payments, but for some mysterious reason, the administration always let me slide. I learned much later from one of my fraternity brothers that my father had arranged it so that he'd make up the difference of my delinquent or insufficient payments. My father never intended for me to discover this, and he was much too proud to acquit me of my wrongdoing. Making me sweat through those last two years was his way of preparing me to support myself during a time when many people struggled to earn enough money for the basic necessities of life. Yet, by rescuing me when I needed it, he proved his love for me in a way that transcended our difference of opinion.

After a grueling schedule of study, practice, and work, I graduated from college in 1942 at the age of twenty-one with a bachelor of science degree in music. When I applied for a teaching job, however, I was very disappointed to find the wages less than what I had earned playing gigs around the Petersburg, Richmond, and West Virginia area. So rather than take the teaching job in Virginia, I decided to return home to Washington, D.C. Once home, I got a government job, in which my two years of sociology training came in handy. Employment prospects were always good for African Americans in D.C., since there were ample government jobs available to anyone with a mind to work. World War II was in full swing at that time, and with college life behind me, I was eligible for the draft. So I worked and fully expected that I'd be called up for military service at any time. Just about everyone I knew, including my younger brother Rudolph, was drafted. When I received my draft notice, I expected to spend the next phase of my life in service to my country. As it turns out, however, the military had no use for me. They took one look at me, standing over six feet tall but weighing only 145 pounds, and they rated my health 4F, which meant that I was physically unfit to serve. I was actually diagnosed with tuberculosis, a very serious and often fatal disease back in those days. Along with the disease, my relentless activity left me quite run down, and although I did not feel sick, the doctor assured me that I was just on the verge of a nervous breakdown. At that time, there was no penicillin for tuberculosis, so rest was the only thing that doctors could prescribe. Fortunately, my parents had many friends in the medical field, and I got the best of care. And while resting, I had plenty of time to practice and spent eight, sometimes ten hours per day at the piano.

There was about a year (from June of 1942 until the latter part of 1943) between the time I graduated college and the time I decided to really strike out on my own. I soon found that my college degree was of little use when it came to finding gigs in the D.C. area. There were plenty of good players who had laid claim to jobs while I was away at college. Consequently, opportunities to play were difficult to come by. But the silent mandate was ever with me. I'd stood in the shadow of Fats Waller, I'd heard Jelly Roll Morton in person, I'd gotten pointers from Billy Kyle and placed my own fingers on the very keys where Count Basie's had been. And my trips to Harlem left me with a nagging sense that my degree in music had only partially prepared me to become the kind of musician who could thrive in the real world of jazz.

Sometimes, you need a swift kick in the pants to propel you on to the next phase in life. Mine came when I got the idea to enter the Tommy Dorsey Amateur Contest. I'd recovered enough to resume working at my government job, and I was practicing and playing as much as I could; yet, musically, I felt as though I was just treading water. So when I heard about the contest, it seemed like a great opportunity. This was a national competition, and the winner not only got some prize money, but the opportunity to go on the radio with the Tommy Dorsey Band. Having already proven myself in amateur contests before, I thought I had a chance. But I never even made it past the audition. I was crushed.

That was it. I quit my job and announced to my family that I was going to New York.

"With what?" my father asked, still doubting my ability to stand on my own two feet. I responded that I'd saved a few dollars, which I had.

"I'm giving you one hundred dollars," he said, "and that is all that you will ever get from me. I don't want you calling asking for more. Either you'll make it or you won't. If things don't go as you'd like, son, you can always come back home."

With those words and with that challenge, my father sealed the deal for me. I was going to New York and I was going to make it, *no matter what*. If I had to beg, or starve on the streets, or work in exchange for food, I was going to New York and somehow, someday, I was going to become a *real* musician, a jazz player. The collective voices of Paul Robeson, Ms. Mary Europe, Mr. Grant, and Professor Moore were always speaking to me in a chorus of wisdom and inspiration. Mediocrity was not allowed. Music was my mission, jazz was my calling, and there was a train ticket waiting for me down at the station.

I packed my belongings and, once again, said my goodbyes to Washington, D.C., and to my family. I said goodbye to my father, whom I loved, and to whom I had so much to prove. He wished me well, and in my own mind, I said to him without speaking: "Don't worry, Dad; you'll see."

THREE

Making Waves

1943–1946

O N A CHILLY FRIDAY NIGHT late in 1943, I boarded the train for
the big city, my pockets filled with the money I'd saved, my head
filled with dreams, and my heart pounding a syncopated rhythm of nervous yet hopeful anticipation. New York was jazz heaven, and I couldn't
wait to get there and take my place. As the train moved farther and farther away from Washington, D.C., the bittersweetness of permanently
leaving home and family gave way to blurry yet bright and enticing vi-
sions of the unknown. As soon as I could, I intended to head for Minton's, the legendary Harlem club where the Who's Who of the jazz world
gathered to jam. Minton's Playhouse was the regular stomping ground
of people like Dizzy Gillespie, Charlie Parker, and Thelonious Monk.
Everybody knew that if you wanted to make it in music, Minton's was
the place to be.

When I first arrived in New York, I had arranged to stay for a short
time with my mother's older brother, my uncle Walker Bacon, and his
family. So I got off the train, and contrary to Duke Ellington's advice
to Billy Strayhorn about taking the "A train," I took the Lenox Avenue
subway to 145th Street. I got off the train, and with my luggage in tow, I
walked three very long blocks in the bone-snapping cold to the Dunbar
Apartments in Harlem. I quickly greeted my aunt and uncle and told
them I had to depart immediately to meet someone, which was part lie
and part truth. I dropped off my bags and was swiftly out the door again.
Having now relocated to this city whose lights, sounds, and possibilities
had beckoned to me, I was making a total commitment. I had no idea

what lay ahead, but I knew that I'd arrived someplace where *to dream* and *to dare* were one and the same. There was no time to waste.

On that very first night as a new resident of New York, I enrolled in the school of jazz known as Minton's Playhouse. Upon arriving at the club, I introduced myself and joined the company of eager young musicians who, like me, craved a chance to display and hone their skills. The players who had already passed muster enjoyed the hard-won privilege of going on first. All of the rest of us were waiting in line to play after them, some guys sitting nervously while clutching their instruments, others furrowing their brows in apparent fear of following the guy ahead of him (the guy he never figured to be *that* good), and still others wringing their hands and glancing down at their watches as the minutes and hours ticked by. Tapping feet kept the pulse as we waited, listened, and took it all in—new twists of harmony, melody, and rhythm, new hot-off-the-press musical ideas to incorporate into the improvisations we each rehearsed inside of our heads. Despite its legendary status, Minton's was the kind of place where the older guys considered it their role to scold, correct, and encourage the youngsters, just as seasoned masters do to their apprentices. Anyone with a desire to play could walk into Minton's, wait his turn to sit in with the band, and, if he had enough nerve and the right thickness of skin, get a jazz education *par excellence* from veteran musicians who taught by example and cared deeply about the music.

I was the new kid in town and nobody had ever heard of me, so on that night, I waited for what seemed like eons to play. Since the pecking order was well established, the best I could do was to listen and wait with sweating palms for several very slow-moving hours. When I first got to the club, there were only about five or six guys on the bandstand and four or five guys waiting to sit in. By the time people started arriving after work, there were about twelve guys on the bandstand, and everybody was eager to make music. I was tired and a little frustrated, but I didn't dare give up my spot. Finally, at around 3:00 AM, my long-awaited chance came. I didn't get to play solo very much, but I did get the chance to do some accompanying. At that time, I was very interested in the style of harmonization that you hear in the introduction to Duke Ellington's "In a Mellow Tone." I wanted to emulate that sound, so I used a four-note chord in the left hand along with an octave/fifth combination in the right

hand. And I was at the piano just long enough for my prospects to suddenly take a turn for the better.

I started my tune, and when I looked up, to my utter amazement,
there was one of my idols right in front of my eyes: Ben Webster! He was
one of the great saxophonists of that era and had played with Cab Calloway, Teddy Wilson, Fletcher Henderson, Benny Carter, and many others. He was also the first tenor sax player in Duke Ellington's orchestra
and left Ellington the same year that I came to New York. I am unsure of
Ben's specific reasons for leaving the orchestra, but by the time I arrived
in New York late in 1943, Webster was in Harlem and he and Duke were
on very good terms. In fact, Ben would be the one to formally introduce
me to Duke Ellington some time later. At that particular moment, Ben
Webster was at Minton's and he was listening to *me!*

My heart was about to explode in my chest. I kept my composure;
I kept playing. Yes, this was a big deal, but I had to stay cool. Soon, he
walked toward the piano and looked over my shoulder. After I finished,
he struck up a conversation with me and asked me where I'd been, what
I was doing, and so forth. I told him that I'd just gotten into town, fresh
off the train. I didn't realize at the time that Ben was also a very fine
pianist, and he'd immediately picked up on my unique style of accompanying. He then remarked that he thought my playing was, well, "kind
of interesting."

"Why don't you come down to the Three Deuces on 52nd Street
where I'm working on Sunday," he said. "Saturday, it'll be too crowded
and I won't be able to really listen to you. So come on Sunday and I'll
take a listen to you and we'll go from there."

Did he say "52nd Street"? He couldn't possibly be serious.

I left Minton's in the wee hours of that morning and headed back to
my uncle's apartment. I was numb, not from the cold, but from meeting
Ben Webster and getting his highly unlikely invitation to 52nd Street.

Needless to say, Saturday moved in slow motion, and Sunday morning was an eternity. Finally, on Sunday evening I headed to the Three
Deuces. The Three Deuces, the Onyx Club, Trocadero, the Downbeat
Club, Jimmy Ryan's, Kelly's Stables, and the Hickory House were among
a dozen or so famous places all concentrated in the two blocks between
5th and 7th Avenues on 52nd Street, where colorful, blinking neon signs

heralded an exciting escape from the daily grind. At one time, most of these clubs were speakeasies, and the earliest jazz they featured was played by white musicians who imitated blacks. As early as the 1920s, white musicians often traveled uptown to Harlem to sit in at black clubs. Although many blacks in Harlem welcomed them, it was in the mid-1930s that the 52nd Street clubs began to reciprocate by hiring black musicians, among the first of whom were Art Tatum and violinist Hezekiah "Stuff" Smith. Gradually, the Prohibition-era speakeasies were converted into small jazz clubs that attracted all kinds of people. By the time I got there, these clubs were serving both African American and white patrons, even while segregation persisted elsewhere. This small slice of 52nd Street showcased an entire history of jazz, and you had to walk but a few steps to find Billie Holiday and Coleman Hawkins in one place, Billy Daniels and Erroll Garner in the place just next door, and Stuff Smith, Wilbur DeParis, and Sidney Bechet in the club next to that one, and so on. On that Sunday evening, I was in a cloud of euphoria, and as I headed to the subway, a thousand thoughts, melodies, chords, riffs, and turnarounds flickered through my mind. Just three days earlier, I was packing my bags for New York, hopeful but uncertain as to how things would pan out. In what seemed like an instant, my dream of playing professionally was coming true. I'd always figured that after a period of working hard, meeting the right people, and paying my dues, I might get a chance to land a gig at a place like the Three Deuces if I was lucky. Never in my wildest dreams, however, did I imagine that I'd be headed there for an audition after just three days in the city!

In those days, the clubs on 52nd Street were typically each in the basement of a three or four-story brownstone, and they were usually small and crowded. I got off the subway and walked up to the south side of the street, and the first club I came to right on the corner was the Three Deuces, which was at 72 West 52nd Street. I entered the club and walked the few steps down from the sidewalk into a long basement room, where there were three rows of tables on each side of a center aisle. Moving swiftly past the puffs of cigarette smoke and happy chatter of patrons, I headed toward the back to where the piano was. On my way, someone grabbed me by the hand and asked, "What are you doing here in New York?" It was Norma Shepherd, the best pianist in Washington, D.C., at the time that I returned home from college. Norma had come to New York sometime earlier and was well established in the city by the time I arrived. In my opinion, Norma could outplay anyone in D.C. Nevertheless, it was hard for women to make a career out of playing back in those days. She made a decent living as a cocktail singer, however, and it seemed a strange but wonderful coincidence to run into her at the Three Deuces. Norma was always gracious to me whenever I came to hear her perform back home, and I admired her as much for her skill as for her generous spirit. Even now, I realize that I'm indebted to her for fostering the respect and admiration I've had for the female musicians that I've encountered over the course of my career.

Although seeing her was a pleasant surprise, my entire focus at that moment was on my audition. So I told her that I was there to play for Ben Webster, and I promised her that I'd come back to chat with her afterward.

But Norma was between sets, and for that reason she was in a hurry to introduce me to her friends, because she needed to return to her own gig. So she insisted: "Wait, I have to leave in a few minutes, but first I want to introduce you to some people." She then proceeded to introduce me to this person, and to that person, and to someone else until, finally, she said, "and here's Mr. Tatum."

I quickly thanked her and said, "Nice to meet you all," my sights set entirely upon the opportunity waiting at my fingertips. I rushed up the steps and was on the bandstand before I felt the significance of the prior moment dawn on me. I thought, *Did she just say "Art Tatum"?*

Art Tatum was a superhuman pianist, truly one of my idols, and I had known of his music from the time I was a boy. Meeting him in person just moments before the biggest audition of my life was ironically both a thrilling distraction and a bit of divine inspiration. Somehow, I gathered my wits, sat at the piano, and gave it my utmost, pouring every bit of my thought, my energy, and my desire into getting that job. To make a long story short, Ben Webster liked what I did and I was hired!

With the audition a success, I was able to regain my senses enough to realize that indeed, Art Tatum was the headliner for the gig I'd just gotten with Ben Webster! Had I not been so intent on making a beeline for the bandstand, I might have noticed that Art Tatum's name was all over the billboard on the front of the club! So, that evening, I stayed around, and for the first time, I heard him play in person. In an almost providential moment of synchronicity, I was witnessing with both my eyes and my ears his signature technical feats, the ones that I heard so often as a boy on Uncle Bob's records. It was the second of two life-altering experiences for me that day, and I was immensely thrilled.

Had I auditioned for Ben Webster at any other time, it's unlikely that I would have been hired so quickly. Under normal circumstances, a newcomer to the city would have had to wait months before qualifying for a card from the local Musicians Union. During those months, I would have had to find some other way of making a living while waiting to obtain my card. In my case, however, the war helped to expedite things. The clubs were hurting because they'd hire musicians one month and the next month they'd be drafted for military service. This rapid turnover was very bad for business, so the club owners negotiated with the union officials to bend the rules. This is what made it possible for me to receive my union card almost immediately after I was hired at the Three Deuces.

Over time, I got to know Art Tatum personally and found him to be a wonderful mentor and human being. By working at the Three Deuces, I got to hear him every single night, and I began to follow him around like a puppy, eager to soak up every bit of what he could teach me. Lots of people were disciples of Art Tatum, but he seemed to see that I was someone who was genuinely overwhelmed by everything he did. He'd listen to me and offer critiques of my playing with suggestions like, "Did you ever think of doing this [and he'd demonstrate] . . . ?" Of course I hadn't thought of doing it that way at all! Although he was generous with his critique of my playing, there was one thing he really disliked: He didn't respect anyone who imitated him. I remember one occasion when we went to an after-hours spot, and there was a very fine pianist who approached Tatum and said, "I'd really like to play your version of *Tiger Rag.*"

Very nonchalantly, Tatum responded, "Oh, yeah?" and sort of shrugged his shoulders. The guy began to play, and it was clear to me that he'd definitely done his homework! I thought, *Wow, Art, this guy's* really *been listening to you!* Art, on the other hand, couldn't have cared less. He ordered another beer and virtually ignored the guy.

His disdain for pianists who imitated him was initially confusing to me.

I couldn't understand why he'd show me new ideas if he didn't want me to use his suggestions. I eventually came to understand that what he intended was for me to take his ideas and then generate new, original ideas of my own from what he'd shown me.

I recall the time that the two of us went to a club uptown, and both Art and I were supposed to play. I played first, and Art was then to go on after me. Before he went on, I warned him that the piano was in terrible condition. There were several notes right in the middle of the keyboard that simply wouldn't sound. He reassured me: "Don't worry; I know." He then sat down and, before starting his piece, swept his hands up and down the piano keys, as if to take a quick tactile survey of which notes were there and which notes were missing. He then proceeded to play his piece with florid passages that went by so fast that it was impossible to detect any of the sound gaps I'd warned him about. I was bewildered that he could instantly recalibrate his improvisations around the missing notes with such perfection!

Tatum's trio at the Three Deuces consisted of Slam Stewart and Tiny Grimes. Like Slam, Art was classically trained and his first instrument was the violin. I remember once when Art was listening to some Bach, he turned toward me and said, "There's a lot going on there, isn't there?" Like Slam, Art also had absolute pitch. It was fascinating to hear the two of them volley seemingly impossible passages back and forth to each other, both with ears so sharp that neither could be unnerved by the other. Tiny Grimes once confessed to me that he was sometimes frightened to be caught between these two and was content to stay out of their way!

Well-known classical artists were fans of Art Tatum. There was one wonderful encounter that I recall between Art and the famous pianist Vladimir Horowitz. Horowitz wanted to impress Art with a set of variations on "Tea for Two" that he'd meticulously written out. So he played the variations and then asked Art if "Tea for Two" was a tune that he also had in his repertoire, which of course he did, as this was a very popular tune with jazz pianists at the time. Horowitz then invited Art to sit at the piano and play his version of the tune, which he did with all of the melodic and harmonic complexity characteristic of his signature style.

Horowitz, clearly impressed, asked Tatum: "How long did it take you to make that up?" to which Tatum responded: "I don't know; how long was it just now?"

My respect for women in jazz was reinforced by Art Tatum's example. There was a dynamic young pianist named Dorothy Donegan who, like me, used to hang around Art Tatum. She could easily rival any one of her male counterparts but was often overlooked because she was a woman. On several occasions, Art took great delight in having her at jam sessions, deliberately holding her back while allowing the other guys to play ahead of her. And just when the fellows were comfortable in their presumption that they had conquered all, Art would put her on afterward in order to show them what she could do, thereby putting them all to shame.

Art was legally blind, but in addition to perfect pitch, he had a photographic memory. He loved sports, and on several occasions, I took him to baseball and football games. There I was, watching the game, observing everything on the field with my two good eyes. Art would get back from the game and recall in fine detail every play, every player, all of the stats, every run, and every hit even better than I could! Art was truly someone from out of this world, and the friendship that started between us at the Three Deuces impacted me for the rest of my life.

Up until I started at the Three Deuces, I was known as Bill Taylor Jr., the namesake of my father, Bill Taylor Sr. My family, my friends, my teachers, and everyone from back home called me Bill. But when the owner of the Three Deuces added my name to the sign at the entrance to the club, he listed me as "Billy" Taylor instead. I suppose this error was easy enough to make, since there was an older African American bass player named Billy Taylor Sr. who was also a native of Washington, D.C. That particular Billy Taylor had played with Duke Ellington in the 1930s and was very well known on 52nd Street. He also happened to have a son, also a bass player, who was around my age but slightly younger.

I approached the owner and attempted, as subtly and respectfully as I could, to get him to correct the error. Referring to the sign, I asked him, "So, is Billy Taylor playing here tonight?"

He thought I was being facetious. "What, don't you *want* to play here tonight?!" he answered, hearing sarcasm where none was intended.

"Oh, no, of course I want to play!!" I answered and decided to let the issue rest. Whether as Bill Taylor or as Billy Taylor, I had every intention of making the most of the opportunity I'd just been given. In the larger scheme of things, answering to a new name was a small price to pay. I've been Billy Taylor ever since.

It wasn't long before I was able to leave my uncle's apartment and get a place of my own. The Dunbar apartments were very small, and although my uncle welcomed me and was very gracious, there were four of us there, including his wife and son (my aunt and cousin), which made for very cramped conditions. So I made it clear that I was only there temporarily. With the help of Buddy Bowser, a song-and-dance man whom I'd befriended in D.C., I was able to get a place at the Graham Court, which was between 116th and 117th Streets on what is now Adam Clayton Powell Boulevard. I'd worked with Buddy back in Washington, D.C., at Ike's Stockade. He was a comic and, along with his partner, Burt Howell, was playing on the theatre circuit. Buddy arranged for me to sublet an upstairs room there. The Italian-style building had a distinctive air of luxury, with its regal archway, palatial columns, ornate ceilings, and fountain courtyard. Until 1933, no African Americans were even allowed to rent apartments at the Graham Court, so when I first moved into my room there only a decade later, I felt myself to be on the road to real upward mobility.

My apartment at the Graham Court was right around the corner from Minton's and was also near the subway, close to the Apollo, across the street from a couple of theatres, and just six or seven blocks away from the center of Harlem's nightlife. Even with my new gig at the Three Deuces, Minton's was a very important part of my getting along in those days. In fact, my new job made it even more crucial that I continue my education at Minton's.

Minton's was partitioned into two sections, the front and the back. As you entered the club, in the front section you'd find a bar on the left with tables arranged as you might find in a restaurant. In the back, there was entertainment where, instead of 35 cents for a drink, you might be charged 75 cents. In addition to the jam sessions there, Minton's always had a house band and a musical director, a guy who made sure that both the scheduled entertainment and the jam sessions all occurred in an orderly fashion. The musical director made sure that the show went on and that everybody who wanted to got a fair shot at sitting in. There was a large dance floor and always dancing at Minton's, regardless of who was playing. Sometimes, the dancers were even involved in jam sessions with the drummers. There was another place in Harlem called the Rhythm Club, where tap dancers would compete with each other in jam sessions of their own. But sometimes, these tap dancers followed their musician friends to clubs like Minton's, where they would trade fours with and challenge the drummers, something especially exciting to watch. Minton's opened for business at about 9:00 at night and closed around 4:00 in the morning. I went there often, met many wonderful artists, and had extremely valuable learning experiences as a result.

I was fortunate to get a place near Minton's, but this wasn't exactly a great neighborhood. Henry Minton, who'd been with the musician's union, was the person who initially bought the place. Minton's was actually inside of a cheap hotel, and the club occupied the space where the hotel's dining room would normally be, although it was run as an entirely separate operation. Along with the hardworking, upstanding citizens who lived in the neighborhood, there were also lots of pimps, prostitutes, hustlers, and numbers runners who resided there and who hung around the club, and there was plenty of any vice you wanted to sample if you were so inclined. Even though there were many elements of the fast life in this neighborhood, it was still generally very safe. Even women could come into the club alone in the evening just to get a drink and hear the music, and they could do so without being bothered.

My job with Ben Webster at the Three Deuces was a very visible one, and I got to meet and perform with several other well-known musicians. In Ben's quartet, I played along with drummer Sid Catlett and bassist Charlie Drayton. Sid Catlett stood about six-foot-three and was such a large man that his twenty-eight-inch bass drum appeared to be too small for him whenever he sat down to play. He had a couple of nicknames—"Farm Hand" because of his size, and "the All-Season Drummer" because of his extreme versatility and his ability to play in any style. In the 1940s, he transitioned from swing to bebop playing. Before joining Webster's group, he'd recently been with Louis Armstrong and would eventually return to work with Armstrong in the late 1940s. Despite his large stature, he was an extremely smooth, tasteful, yet innovative player who brought both excitement and musicality to his performances. He influenced many bop players of the 1940s and was easily considered by many to be one of the best drummers around.

Charlie Drayton had been with Louis Jordan and Benny Carter. Although he was not yet well known on 52nd Street at that time, he was an excellent bassist. I was replacing Johnny Guarnieri, a very well-established virtuoso pianist who'd played with Benny Goodman and Artie Shaw. Guarnieri was in high demand, and he'd left Ben Webster to join with Raymond Scott. Although I'm sure that Guarnieri was paid much better than I was, I was perfectly happy with my salary of about a hundred dollars per week.

It was at this point that I got to reconnect with Jo Jones, the drummer with the Count Basie band whom I'd met when I was a student at Virginia State. When Jo came backstage to say hello to Ben's drummer, Sid Catlett, I reminded him that I had heard him play while at Virginia State. He remembered meeting me, and immediately from that point on, he took me under his wing. Between sets, Jo would take me around to meet famous players like Coleman Hawkins, trumpeter Charlie Shavers, trombonist Trummy Young, and many other guys that I knew about or heard on the radio but had never met before. In particular, I remember the way Jo introduced me to Coleman Hawkins. He said, "I'd like you to meet this young, up-and-coming musician. His name is Billy Taylor, and he can't drink."

I wondered why he'd say that, since I was over twenty-one and of legal age. Back at Virginia State, I'd get together with my frat brothers on Saturday nights and we certainly drank. Yet I was smart enough to avoid any argument with Jo. I kept my mouth shut, even when he'd buy drinks for the other guys and a Coke for me. I'm sure that these older musicians wondered whether I had some special impediment or disease that made me unable to consume alcohol, but these guys respected Jo enough that they took him at his word, and whenever I was around them, they simply wouldn't allow me to cross that line. I remember once going to a bar and offering to buy Coleman Hawkins a drink. He gladly accepted my offer, ordered a double for himself, but then turned to the bartender to let him know that "Billy here will have a Coke." With time, the way that

Jo introduced me almost became like an extension of my name: "Here's Billy Taylor, and he can't drink."

Along with Jo Jones, Sid Catlett was like a big brother to me, another watchful pair of eyes to encourage me along the straight-and-narrow path. On one occasion, Sid shortened my visit to the White Rose Bar, where 35 cents could purchase a large drink. Before I could do any damage, Sid put his arm around me, said, "See you later" to the bartender, and ushered me out the door. Even though I hadn't known Sid for very long, I didn't question him or resist his authority.

I came to realize that Jo and Sid were only protecting me. Whiskey was really the narcotic of the day, and lots of very promising individuals ruined their careers over the bottle. There have been some excellent jazz players to fall victim to drugs or alcoholism. It is both unfortunate and unfair, however, that some writers have blown the issue of substance abuse out of proportion, to the extent that many believe this behavior to be the norm in jazz. Nothing could be further from the truth. All humans have struggles, because they are human. I wish writers would spend more time talking about the many, many jazz musicians who have remained clean and sober. Many of these players were lucky enough to have someone in their lives like I did, a Jo Jones or a Sid Catlett who was there to ensure that I avoided the kinds of pitfalls that might have awaited me.

After Ben Webster left the Three Deuces, I stayed on and had the privilege of playing with lots of different musicians. There were so many who came and went that it would be impossible to recount them all. But one who stands out was a little guy who was one of the most powerful trumpet players around. Legend had it that this fellow came to the Howard Theatre to challenge "Georgetown," a rival trumpet player, and during his solo, he played with such intensity that he actually disfigured the tubing on his instrument. I'd heard this legend time and again and was thrilled when Roy Eldridge came to the Three Deuces.

Though small in stature, Roy was a bigger-than-life musician and a very exciting player who transfixed his audiences. On one particular occasion, Roy had just driven in from Chicago. He was exhausted from the trip and complained that his "chops" weren't up to par. So the job started and Roy played, but not quite with his usual bravado. Toward the end of the set, he acknowledged his friend the great trumpeter Charlie Shavers, and invited him to sit in, much to the audience's delight. *Suddenly, miraculously,* Roy's chops were revived, and the fatigue that had plagued him until that moment vanished instantly. Soon, Roy was up to the challenge that Charlie offered, and the two tigers were at each other's throats, neither one about to back down. It was one of the most exciting nights I ever had on 52nd Street!

Much later, Jo stopped in at the Three Deuces when I was playing accompaniment for someone. I'd been offered a drink, and feeling my independence, I accepted. Jo saw me take this drink of scotch. The very next night, he came into the club with Art Tatum on one arm and Teddy Wilson on the other. By that time, Teddy Wilson was a respected veteran of 52nd Street who had played and recorded with some of the biggest names around. He was also the first African American pianist to play with Benny Goodman's trio. Jo brought both of these giants to hear me play, and I'd already had one or two drinks. Well, to put it mildly, I didn't like the way I played on that occasion. Just a couple of drinks seemed innocent and harmless enough at first, but the cost of the scotch was more than the money I'd paid. I noticed that my reflexes were duller, my memory cloudier, my energy lackluster, and my fingers sluggish and uncooperative. And besides all that, I was ashamed of myself. No, the cost was too much. Yes, I was of age and the money was in my pocket, but I really couldn't afford the musical liability. That kind of embarrassment in front of Art Tatum and Teddy Wilson drove home the lesson that Jo was trying to teach me all along. From that day, I vowed that I'd never drink before playing, a promise to myself that I kept for the rest of my career.

My work at the Three Deuces placed me in close contact with people who are remembered today as the architects of jazz. They are immortalized in recordings and in jazz history books, but I remember them as colleagues, as mentors, and as friends, people I saw on an everyday basis. For example, Billie Holiday worked at the Downbeat, a club right next door to the Three Deuces. She was a fascinating woman, and I already had all of her records by the time I actually got to meet her. Included in her vast recorded output was a piece she'd done just a few years before I came to New York. Her rendition of "Strange Fruit" was a bold and courageous song that spoke plainly about lynching in the South, and only

Billie Holiday could paint such powerful pictures with the timbre of her voice. Because of its disturbing content, that particular song was banned on many radio stations. Despite that, Billie's performance has survived as the classic rendition of the piece, which is considered by many to be the very first modern protest song.

Whenever I had time, I'd go next door and chat with her or with the guys in her band. She had a reputation for being temperamental, but I never saw that side of her; she was always very kind to me. Billie was an artist in the truest sense of the word, but she lived a hard, tragically self-destructive life. In the end, drugs and alcohol got the best of her, something that always saddens me when I think of it.

When I started working on 52nd Street, the most popular sound was that of the big band. At that very moment, however, swing was giving birth to something completely fresh and new. Just across the street from the Three Deuces, Dizzy Gillespie was playing with his band, which included Don Byas, Max Roach, and Oscar Pettiford. His pianist was supposed to have been Bud Powell, but Powell was underage, and his guardian, Cootie Williams, wouldn't allow him to take the gig. So I would run across the street to the Onyx Club and sit in.

There was a lot of multitasking on 52nd Street. For example, Don Byas might be playing as the leader at the Three Deuces but at the same time have a gig as a sideman with Coleman Hawkins at another club just across the street. For a while, I was juggling both gigs, alternating sets at the Three Deuces to play with Dizzy's band at the Onyx Club. It was for this reason that I got to witness the birth of "bebop." It was also for this reason that I was eventually fired from the Three Deuces! I was so irresistibly drawn to what was happening musically with Dizzy's band that my moonlighting at the Onyx Club made me later and later for my sets at the Three Deuces. As my tardiness became chronic, Sammy Kay and Irving Alexander, owners of the Deuces, let me know that they were not pleased. The day came when I completely lost track of time and was so late at the Three Deuces that Irving Alexander fired me. But this wasn't the last time I played there. (I later played at the Three Deuces with Slam Stewart's group.)

My work with Dizzy was only temporary, and he eventually hired George Wallington as his permanent pianist. But that brief experience in his band was priceless. It was fascinating to observe Oscar Pettiford, who was really the first bebop bass player. While I was working at the Onyx Club, I heard him get really annoyed with Dizzy Gillespie. Gillespie was playing the tune "BeBop" way uptempo, very fast. Dizzy took a solo, Don Byas took a couple of choruses, Max Roach took a couple of choruses, but there was no bass solo. Oscar was fuming. He put his bass down and walked over to Dizzy, and I honestly thought he was going to hit him:

"Why didn't you give me a solo?!?" he demanded.

Dizzy answered, "Well, I thought it was too fast."

"Well, you played it! If you can play it, I can play it!" And that's the kind of musician he was. He could play anything in any tempo; he played the lines in the same way that the horns played. He was really a bass player who took the things that Jimmy Blanton did with Duke Ellington and moved them a notch up.

Bebop was innovative and exciting. Dizzy once explained that the term *bebop* came into being in this way: Many new tunes were composed on 52nd Street during this period, and it was often the case that the guys had no clue of the titles, even though each tune had its title. Instead, the musicians in the band tended to be more familiar with the notes in the melody. So some guy would call out the name of a tune, and nobody would know what he was talking about. Then someone else would chime in and say, "You know, the tune that goes be-op-a-dee-dop-de-bob-de-bop!" sort of scat-singing the melody, which, suddenly, everyone recognized. These generic syllables, used to communicate how a tune went, morphed into the description of this music as "bebop."

Bebop's most obvious departure from the familiar, more predictable big-band tunes was its complexity. However, even before its golden age in the 1940s, artists like Tatum, Ellington, Willie "The Lion" Smith, Clarence Profit, and Billy Strayhorn had already started experimenting. By the 1930s, they were using extended harmonies, innovative modulations, new melodic patterns, and more highly syncopated rhythms. Despite these new developments in the music, bebop retained both its foundational metric swing as well as its improvisational emphasis, two elements that are indispensable to any style of jazz.

No single person can take credit for creating bebop, but people like Dizzy, Charlie Parker, Kenny Clarke, and Sarah Vaughan were the ones who really helped shape and popularize the style. When it came to actually teaching the music, Dizzy took the lead. He was excited about bebop and took the time to put it all on paper and make the music understandable to those of us who needed guidance. He was the one who showed us what to do melodically, rhythmically, and harmonically.

Dizzy was a great teacher, although he never thought of himself in that way. He considered himself to be a player and a bandleader, but in all actuality, he was one of the first people to teach jazz in the true pedagogical sense of the word. With his hands-on schooling in the fundamentals of bebop, Dizzy was giving in the 1940s the sort of instruction that is typical in many high-school and college band rooms today. But mentoring and teaching came so naturally to those older musicians that it would be inaccurate to suggest that Dizzy was unique in that regard. Years earlier, I was the beneficiary of Billy Kyle's impromptu schooling after my win in the Amateur Night contest, and although he was perhaps no more inclined to label himself a teacher than was Dizzy, I learned important lessons from them both. When I think of my teachers, I must add the names of Dizzy Gillespie and Billy Kyle to those of Mrs. Streets, Mr. Grant, and Professor Moore. In different ways and to varying degrees, they all were my teachers.

Fifty-second Street offered a potpourri of different jazz styles to suit nearly any taste. Down at the other end from the Three Deuces, there was a club called Jimmy Ryan's where a lot of the New Orleans musicians played. You could go there and hear guys like Sidney Bechet, trumpeter Jimmy McPartland, and another trumpeter, "Wild" Bill Davison. Several Chicago-style jazz musicians also played there. The interesting thing is that there was free musical exchange between these artists. Even younger players who were more into bebop would go down and sit in with the older guys at Jimmy Ryan's and play with them in the context of those older styles. Not many people remember this kind of interaction, but as late as the early 1950s, players on 52nd Street would jam together in a way that transcended style. Two musicians who liked each other personally were totally comfortable jamming together even though they might each play totally different styles from each other. Performing with such a diversity of players made for a learning experience that was totally comprehensive and unique to that golden place and time.

It's ironic that I got my first big break in the professional world at a time when the music business was undergoing tremendous change. I got my job with Ben Webster soon after the start of the long-running ASCAP–BMI feud and right in the middle of a musicians' strike known as the "Petrillo Ban."

I was in college when the battle lines between ASCAP and BMI were first drawn. In 1939, ASCAP doubled the licensing fee that broadcasters were required to pay. This sudden move sent the radio industry into a tailspin, since it meant that they either had to pay the fee, or they had to discontinue airing ASCAP-protected music altogether. Back in those days, broadcasters aired mostly Broadway and Hollywood show tunes as well as a wide variety of classical music, but when it suddenly became too expensive to do so, on many stations, that music went silent.

Outraged, the broadcasters decided to fight back by forming their own alternative to ASCAP, and in 1940, Broadcast Music Incorporated (BMI) was formed. BMI thus became a competitor to ASCAP, which created important opportunities for many African American artists, many of whom would never have been afforded the protections and privileges that came with membership in ASCAP back in those days. The skirmishes between ASCAP and BMI would affect working musicians for the next several decades.

The start of the ASCAP–BMI battles was soon followed by the musicians' strike. Since the 1930s, James Petrillo had been a fierce advocate of musicians' rights, especially when he perceived a threat to musicians who belonged to the union. By 1941, radio stations had begun to experiment with using records on the air. Angry that this practice would threaten the wages of live musicians, Petrillo thought the solution was for the musicians to go on strike. So as president of the American Federation of Musicians, Petrillo launched a very vocal protest and promised a strike in 1942 if his conditions were not met. As a result, no recordings were made with AFM musicians between August of 1942 and November of 1944. Petrillo's tactic was a failure, however, since radio stations continued to use records on the air, and there were others waiting to take the place of the striking AFM musicians. The vocalists belonged to a different union, AFTRA (American Federation of Television and Radio Artists), and therefore were unaffected by the Petrillo Ban. So while the AFM members stayed out of the studios, singers stepped in to fill the gap. This dealt a devastating blow to big-band musicians, who found themselves in much less demand once the strike ended. While the musicians were on strike, the public had developed an appetite for the singers. Many union musicians were forced to find some other kind of work while vocalists were becoming increasingly popular.

Along with the Petrillo Ban, wartime politics affected the music business. Back in those days, a material called shellac was used to press records. Shellac had to be imported from Japanese-controlled Singapore, so during the war, it was impossible to get. The major labels, therefore, had to do lots of downsizing and make the best use of the resources they had. One way they did this was by recycling old records. The major labels also abandoned their production of all but the most lucrative, mainstream American music. Because the major labels were no longer meeting the huge demand for blues, jazz, gospel, and folk music, this opened the door for literally hundreds of new, independent record labels to step in and supply what the big companies would not.

Together, the ASCAP–BMI battles, the Petrillo Ban, and the shellac shortage had a huge impact on the music industry, and we were all acutely aware that things were changing. The new focus on singers, resulting largely from the strike, made for a very thin line dividing jazz from what was often called "popular" music. Louis Jordan was an example of that. He started out in Chick Webb's big band but then started doing these very catchy, singable and danceable arrangements. He was fun to listen to and watch, and the audiences responded to his antics. Even though his roots were in jazz, Jordan really helped to popularize a sound that had been around in some form since the 1930s when Rosetta Tharpe sang with Lucky Millinder's band. This sound was later called "rhythm and blues."

Back then, no matter how good you were, the life of a musician could be difficult, especially for African Americans. There were dance halls and ballrooms all over the country, and most musicians earned a living by touring from town to town. Generally speaking, the white bands got good jobs in hotels and other well-known establishments, and they traveled comfortably by train, going just short distances from one place to the next. For African Americans, however, things were quite different.

Segregation often made for long hauls between jobs, and accommodations could never be guaranteed. Racial prejudice put severe limits on the number of hotels available to African Americans, and if there were no "Colored Only" accommodations, musicians could sometimes stay as guests in the private homes of local fans. But while on the road, everything from using the restroom to getting a bite to eat was a challenge.

Because of all the challenges that African American travelers faced, there was a little book that sometimes came in handy. Back in the 1930s, a man named Victor Green got the idea to publish a travel guide for blacks trying to navigate through the complexities of segregation. He got the idea from the Jews, who had their own publication which informed Jewish travelers about places that were friendly and those that were restricted. Especially when traveling to unfamiliar places, African Americans sometimes had no way of knowing which places were "white only" and which were "colored only" except through trial and error, which could be embarrassing at best, and dangerous at worst. So Victor Green published an annual travel guide called *The Negro Motorist Green Book*. In the *Green Book,* you could turn to the section on California, go to the page for San Francisco, and see, for example, that African Americans visiting that city could find lodging in one of three hotels (the Buford Hotel, the Skaggs Hotel, or the Powell Hotel), could go to one tavern (Jack's on Sutter Street), and could get a meal at one restaurant (the California Theatre on Post Street).

This is one reason that I was so fortunate to have landed solid work in New York. Since most of what I did to make waves in those early days was right there in the city, I was spared much of what traveling African American musicians usually endured.

Several times in my life, I've had the privilege to work with very special, God-gifted musicians who somehow fell through the cracks of history. Some were born too soon, some met with a premature demise, but too many just didn't get the recognition they deserved. In Washington, D.C., there were musicians like Harold Francis, Norma Shepherd, Jimmy Mundy, and drummer Eugene Burrell (nicknamed "Streamline") and a marvelous trumpeter known by the nickname "Georgetown," whose real name was Daniel Brashears. These people were celebrities in our community back then. Today, however, their names are rarely spoken, their achievements have all but slipped into obscurity, and their music is heard nowhere but in the memories of those of us who knew them. Billy Kyle was one of those, and so was Claude Hopkins. History was unfair, but I mention them here because I'm indebted to them. They were first-rate artists, and their music helped to shape mine.

Thanks to 52nd Street, I had the good fortune to connect with two men, both violinists, neither of whom is as well known today as he deserves to be. After working at the Three Deuces, I got a short-term job at the Famous Door. The featured act was Pearl Bailey, who was known at that time as a singer and dancer who'd worked with Cootie Williams, Cab Calloway, Duke Ellington, and Count Basie. (Later, of course, she would become a legendary star of Broadway and film.) I was hired to play piano along with her big band. The Pearl Bailey show only lasted a week or so, but the leader of the big band liked my work, so he hired me to play with a trio that he was starting. His name was Eddie South.

Eddie was the consummate musician. He'd have me up to his home in Harlem and we'd play through classical pieces as easily as if we'd both been in recital at Carnegie Hall. But Eddie wanted to have a jazz trio consisting of himself on violin, me on piano, and a bass player. My first time going on the road after working on 52nd Street was with Eddie's trio, and my job with him took me away from New York for several months. The tour took us first to Chicago, and from there, we spent four bitter-cold weeks in Grand Forks, North Dakota. After that, we headed straight for the warmth and sunshine of Los Angeles.

Eddie had studied in Budapest and was very familiar with the music and culture of the Gypsies there. During one performance in Chicago, a large group came into the small club where we were playing, and from the way that one man was greeted and acknowledged, it was clear that he was of some importance. We soon learned that this man was the king of the Gypsies, and he'd come to hear Eddie. Soon after Eddie started to play, there was the king with tears streaming down his face because he was so moved by the music. Eddie had a real gift for getting his audiences emotionally involved in his music, and this helped to inspire me not only to get people to hear what I was doing, but more importantly, to *feel* it.

The entire time that I played with Eddie, he took great delight in throwing me one difficult piece after another, and there was plenty of time to practice and rehearse. So while we were on tour in Grand Forks, I decided one day that I'd be a wise guy and try to throw Eddie a curve. I did my own arrangement of *Rhapsody in Blue,* one that I thought would make Eddie sweat at least a little. But he picked it up and played it just as perfectly as if he had written it himself!

For several months, we were on the West Coast. It was during this period that we had a standing gig at a club called the Streets of Paris. By that time, Art Tatum was living on the West Coast, and he'd come every night to hear me play. This tour afforded me another very special opportunity to really hang out and spend quality time with him. One night while we were in Los Angeles, Art and I sat together to hear this guy play two tunes for which Art was known, "Elegie" and "Tea for Two." In fact, like the man who had played Art's "Tiger Rag" for him, this pianist was actually playing extremely accurate, note-for-note transcriptions of Tatum's recordings of those two pieces. While he impressed the audience with his display of polished technique, Tatum leaned toward me and said, "He knows what I did on the record, but he has no idea why I did what I did." This well-meaning pianist had captured the notes but had missed the spirit altogether. Had he truly understood the artistry of Tatum, he would have done more than simply play a reproduction; he would have used Tatum's work to create something original of his own.

My time on the West Coast afforded me a period of valuable learning from both Art and Eddie South. Eddie is one of the great jazz artists who isn't known today simply because he was born at the wrong time. A versatile, world-class musician who had studied overseas and who spoke fluent French, Eddie was an ill fit for the prejudiced and segregated world of the mid-1940s. There was a time when Paul Whiteman needed a special violinist, and Joe Venuti, who was himself a jazz violinist and member of Paul Whiteman's orchestra, recommended Eddie. Eddie came to the studio to audition, and he got the job. Because he was African American, however, a curtain was placed in front of him so that he'd be invisible to the studio audience. He was already invisible to the radio audience for which he was performing, so being hidden from the studio audience in this way because of his race was both ridiculous and humiliating. Joe was thoroughly embarrassed and upset at this sort of treatment but was powerless to do anything about it. This was the kind of racial discrimination that was a major factor in Eddie's decision to stay in Europe as long as he could until the war started. He was not only respected there, but was also accepted and celebrated there as both a jazz and a classical musician.

One of the unique things about playing with Eddie South was that he featured a lot more musical variety than was typical of the other groups I played with. We'd often play a combination of jazz, pop, and Latin tunes during our shows. On one particular night, however, we happened to be working at the same club where the king of the Gypsies had come, and all of the songs Eddie announced were jazz tunes. Afterward, Eddie introduced me around to a few people and then he said, "Billy, I'd like you to meet Stuff Smith." Also a violinist, Stuff Smith was one of the swingingest musicians I'd ever heard, and by the time I met him that night, I already had all of his records. Stuff was a very funny guy, and when I was a kid, I'd hear him on the radio. He had a reputation for being a comedian, and he always tore the audience to shreds! It turns out that Eddie South and Stuff Smith were good buddies and friendly rivals. After several months of working with Eddie South, I returned to New York and got the chance to play with the Stuff Smith Trio at The Onyx Club on 52nd Street. We were also later featured in a historic concert at Town Hall. That was my first time playing at Town Hall, and it was one of the most memorable experiences I've ever had. Stuff epitomized jazz playing, and that night stands out in my mind as one of the hottest performances of my career.

The violin would normally have difficulty competing with the more powerful timbres of a jazz ensemble. Yet Eddie South and Stuff Smith somehow developed a way to be heard with microphones and amplifiers even before this technology was in common use. These two great musicians were giants, and their names deserve mention not only here, but in every discussion of jazz in the 1940s.

I hadn't seen my family in months, so after we returned from touring, I arranged to go to Washington, D.C., to visit my mother and my brother Rudy. (By this time, my parents were no longer together.) I also wanted to impress everyone with my connection to this world-famous violinist, so I got Eddie to agree to come to Washington and had a list of places where I thought he should be booked. This was a very big deal for me, because Eddie was a huge star and it was his first time performing in my hometown. Although Eddie had agreed to play there, he made the mistake of turning everything over to his manager, who failed to get him the billing he deserved. Instead, he booked Eddie as though he was an ordinary guy, and as a result, we were severely undersold. From this disappointment, I learned a crucial lesson. I saw that even with the best management, it would always be important for me to take responsibility for my own career.

Upon returning to New York after touring with Eddie South, I took up residence again at the Graham Court, where I'd had an apartment before, and I found work again freelancing on 52nd Street. My apartment was so large that I was able to rent a Steinway grand, and I practiced for six or seven hours a day, determined to continually sharpen my skills and retain my ability to compete, since eventually there would be plenty of musicians returning from the war.

During the mid-1940s, I made my first recordings. Today, landing a record deal with a major label can be a pretty complex affair, nearly impossible unless you work hard and connect to the right people at exactly the right time. But back during the World War II years, the whole recording industry was still very much in its infancy. There were a few major labels, but the ones that really popularized African American music were the independent labels that started recording music that the major labels ignored. The independent record companies of the 1940s were far from glamorous. Instead, these companies usually had very little overhead, and many were started in basements, in attics, and in garages by entrepreneurs who had a knack for finding good music.

One of those independent companies was Savoy Records. Herman Lubinsky founded Savoy just the year before I arrived in New York, and he was one of the first to recognize that there was a wealth of music on 52nd Street, and that in most cases, the musicians who performed there weren't signed to anyone. So in the early 1940s, he'd canvass all of the clubs on 52nd Street in search of artists to record. It was with Herman Lubinsky that I made my first record on 52nd Street. I played with a trio consisting of Al Hall on bass and Jimmy Crawford on drums. On the day of the recording, Herman Lubinsky came out after the first take or two and asked me if I could play a little more like Erroll Garner. This sort of threw me for a loop! But I settled down and finished the date. The four tracks completed were "Mad Monk," "Solace," "Night and Day," and "Alexander's Ragtime Band."

"Mad Monk" was actually the first bebop tune I tried to compose, and I wrote it as a tribute to my friend Thelonious Monk. For a time, he was the house pianist at Minton's, and he was a real support to me when I first arrived in New York. He was often misunderstood. People dismissed him as crazy because his style was so rhythmically complex and what sounded like "clunkers" were actually Monk's way of reconciling his stride technique with more contemporary elements.

Today, digital technology accelerates the whole process of recording. Furthermore, digital editing makes it possible to create recordings that are virtually flawless from a technical point of view. In the early 1940s, however, there were no shortcuts, no magic buttons that enabled you to delete a wrong note or to erase a missed cue or an early entrance. Instead, making a record back in those days meant doing a tune for as many takes as necessary in order to get it just right. If someone sneezed, missed a cue, or dropped a drumstick in the middle of a session, we'd have to stop, go back to the beginning, and do the whole thing again. This could create a dilemma for jazz artists. On one hand, I was determined to make the best recording possible, even if it meant doing a hundred takes of the same tune. On the other hand, I wanted to keep the freshness and spontaneity in every performance. This can be tricky after the tenth or twelfth take!

There were no industry rules or oversight committees to govern the way independent labels did business back in those early days. They had no big corporate structure, no voluminous contracts, no legal departments. Business instead was done more or less on a handshake. Consequently, many artists felt that they were cheated or unfairly exploited. Despite their ethics or lack thereof, the independent labels deserve credit for capturing our music at some of its most important evolutionary moments. And for a young fellow like me who still pinched himself to make sure my life on 52nd Street wasn't just a dream, being recorded was an honor. My first exposure to many of my own idols came through records, and there was something truly magical about hearing Fats Waller and Art Tatum on those old 78s, and then seeing them perform those magnificent feats in person. And to some degree, to record was to follow in their footsteps. Were it not for those early pioneers in the recording industry going door-to-door on 52nd Street, the early days of bebop may never have been immortalized on vinyl and preserved for posterity. That music might have been lost to us forever.

During the period when I had worked for Eddie South and, soon after, was working for Stuff Smith, I approached Teddy Wilson for advice about some damage I'd sustained from playing too forcefully on a poorly maintained piano. Teddy lived in Harlem a few blocks from me, and he was already playing with Benny Goodman and doing lots of professional work. He'd also just started teaching at Juilliard, so although he liked me well enough, he literally didn't have the time to teach me. So he suggested that I take lessons with his teacher, Richard McClanahan. Richard taught at the Riverdale Country School, but his real studio was in Steinway Hall, and his students included Teddy and Hazel Scott. Richard taught the Tobias Matthay method of piano playing. Matthay was a scientist and musician who had spent many years observing great pianists in order to conduct a very scientific and detailed investigation into the ways that the muscles of the arms and the fingers worked when playing easily and effortlessly. His research resulted in several books, including *The Act of Touch* and *The Visible and Invisible in Pianoforte Technique*. Richard based his own teaching on Matthay's discoveries. In order to help me develop a healthy and effective sense of touch, he used various techniques during my lessons, like having me ball my fingers into a fist to make me aware of the various ways that weight was being distributed from my shoulders, from my elbows, and from my wrists. Ultimately, Richard was a tremendous help in correcting the damage, and I credit him for helping me to develop the touch and the sound that I was able to achieve.

Perhaps the most elaborate and spectacular production in New York in late 1944 was a show called *The Seven Lively Arts*. The revue, produced by Billy Rose, opened on December 7, 1944, and included a smorgasbord of just about every aspect of show business that you could imagine. Billy Rose had recently purchased and remodeled the Ziegfield Theatre, and the show opened there at a reported cost of $350,000, a huge sum of money at that time. The tickets to the show's opening night were $24 for orchestra seats, again, not much by today's standards, but very expensive back then. *The Seven Lively Arts* featured some of the biggest names in show business, including comedienne Beatrice Lillie, comedian and actor Bert Lahr (best known for his role as the Cowardly Lion in the *Wizard of Oz*), ballerina Alicia Markova, dancer Anton Dolin, Benny Goodman, and Cole Porter. He even hired the composer Igor Stravinsky to write the score for the ballet that was included in the revue. The chorus for the show was under the direction of Robert Shaw, and the orchestra director was Maurice Abravanel. The audience on opening night was equally filled with big names, including Alfred Hitchcock, Oscar Hammerstein, gossip columnist Elsa Maxwell, George Kaufman, and many others. During intermission, the audience was treated to champagne, as Billy Rose spared no expense in attempting to please his patrons.

Partway through the show's run, Benny Goodman had to leave to fulfill other obligations. So there was need for another band to close the first half of the show just before intermission. Billy Rose knew Cozy Cole, the celebrated drummer who just the year prior had done a drum solo in the all-black Broadway production *Carmen Jones*. Cozy Cole assembled the band, and he hired me, Don Byas, Tiny Grimes, and bass player Billy Taylor. (It was the only time I ever worked with the other Billy Taylor.) During rehearsals and performances, we were surrounded by the statuesque chorus girls that Billy Rose called "glamazons." The last act just before the intermission, we were wheeled out on a platform in the middle of the stage to play, and once we finished, they'd bring the curtain down to close the first half of the show. The second half then opened with the ballet. That experience was entirely unique in that it was my first time performing onstage as a part of the production rather than as an invisible pit musician, as would be the case, for example, when I played in the pit band of the 1945 production of *Blue Holiday* starring Ethel Waters.

Ultimately, the critics felt that *The Seven Lively Arts* was a bit too ambitious of a production, and it received poor reviews for that reason. It lasted for 183 performances. Over time, however, I would reap the benefits of the exposure I received as a result of being in that most unique and highly publicized of shows.

After the show, I returned to my regular work in the clubs on 52nd Street. As bebop developed, jazz artists were recognizing the vast creative resources available in Caribbean and Latin music. My love affair with the Latin sound began because of an opportunity I had to play a gig with tenor saxophonist Walter "Foots" Thomas, who was the partner of Cozy Cole. Foots was also an arranger, and he and Cozy Cole shared an office on 48th Street. Foots and I were playing intermissions regularly on Monday nights at the club on Broadway where the legendary Machito was performing. Machito was a charismatic bandleader who was famous for bringing Afro-Cuban rhythm to American jazz. It was during the war, and as luck would have it, Machito's regular pianist was drafted. It would take several weeks to bring the replacement "star" pianist from Cuba, so Machito's manager and brother-in-law, Mario Bauza, recruited me to play with the band in the meantime because I knew the show. That was the start of several career-changing weeks that I spent playing closely with Latin musicians and learning, for example, the *montuno*. That experience schooled me in the fundamentals and nuances of performing Latin music, a sound that had me hooked from that point on.

There were new learning experiences awaiting me at nearly every turn, and I remained open to these lessons. For example, spending time with Erroll Garner opened my eyes to the many ways that jazz musicians can develop their craft. Erroll was a guy who didn't read music, but he studied music in a different way than those of us who were formally trained. He'd listen to the artists that he admired, and emulated what he heard. Moreover, he wouldn't just emulate the musicians he admired, but he'd run their stylistic gestures through his own creative computer and come up with things that were totally original. Although he had no use for sheet music, Erroll knew what the notes were on the keyboard, but this didn't concern him at all. To him, it made no difference whether something was in the key of G or in the key of F$\sharp$. He understood the relationships between notes and therefore had mastered the ability to navigate easily from one key to another as though the two different keys were exactly the same in terms of the mechanical process. The fact that he really made no distinction between being in one key or another was frustrating to those with whom he worked. He was known for rehearsing a tune in the key of A, but then doing the tune a third up in C$\sharp$, because they were all the same as far as he was concerned. Of course, the two keys were certainly *not* the same to the other guys, who had to think quickly on their feet when he would spontaneously transpose in this way! Erroll's unique way of internalizing and performing made him completely unique from any other pianist around. Erroll was also very special because of his sensitivity to the audience. Regardless of what he did with his playing, he always made sure the audience got the melody. The melody was his way of remaining connected to them despite any improvisation he brought to a piece.

In those days, New York's music scene was my universe. Yet there was a war raging, and many of our friends and loved ones were detained overseas engaged in a conflict that we all hoped would end soon. Finally, in early May of 1945, Hitler's regime fell. Back then, televisions were still a rarity, so international news was broadcast in movie theatres in the form of short informational films called newsreels. The newsreels would typically be shown before the featured movie. The newsreels reported the celebrations that erupted around the country when Americans received news of the war's end in Europe. In New York City, two million people poured into the streets to celebrate the Allied victory and the forthcoming happy reunions with our enlisted family members and friends.

Soon after the news reported Germany's surrender, the newsreels began broadcasting scenes that shocked and horrified us. We knew that Hitler was a racist, but until we were sitting in the theatres watching the actual footage of the prisoners that were liberated from the concentration camps, we had no idea of the extent of his evil. Hitler's racism had reduced millions of innocent human lives to piles of rotting corpses. The pictures on the movie screen were more grisly and macabre than any of us could have ever imagined. Prisoners that were little more than skeletal remains with bulging eyes mustered barely enough strength to smile at the long-awaited arrival of their American liberators. Black people were all too familiar with racial discrimination, and ironically, many who viewed these newsreels did so while seated in the "Colored Only" sections of America's many segregated theatres. Hitler's unthinkable oppression of the Jewish people began with small acts of segregation and discrimination; these acts then escalated into a full-fledged holocaust in which countless beings were senselessly put to death. For anyone who would discriminate on the basis of race or gender, the tragedy of the Holocaust teaches an important lesson.

The evil that humans can inflict upon each other magnifies, at least for me, the importance of the unifying power of music. Jazz has never discriminated. Jazz is a creative democracy that gives everybody a voice. Although rooted in the African American experience, the music itself has always been inclusive. On 52nd Street, there were many interracial musical partnerships, many genuine and meaningful friendships between black and white musicians. Al Haig, a white pianist, played with Dizzy and Charlie Parker. John Robinson, a white drummer, played with Erroll Garner and Slam Stewart. White bebop trombonist Frank Rosolino played with Charlie Parker and Oscar Pettiford. Shelly Manne, wearing his military uniform, once came into a club on 52nd Street and sat in with a racially mixed group of musicians. Nobody thought a thing of it, because he was just looked upon as a great drummer. Of course, there were different pay scales, with white musicians earning more than comparable black musicians. But that kind of disparity in wages was the norm back in those days. The point is that there were many musicians, both white and black, who transcended the color line in order to come together for the purpose of playing the music.

Being in New York placed me in contact with important people in the industry, people who loved the music and championed its cause even though they themselves were not musicians. One of those was a good friend of mine, Timme Rosenkrantz. Originally from Denmark, he was a jazz enthusiast and an interesting man who should have gotten more recognition for his contributions. Rosenkrantz was also a very fine writer, and at the time that I met him, he was preparing an article on Erroll Garner for *Esquire* magazine. Rosenkrantz was the one who discovered him, and Erroll and I spent lots of late hours at his home. Those of us who played in clubs typically got off work at 3:00 or 4:00 in the morning, but none of us wanted to go to sleep afterward. Instead, Erroll and I often went to Timme's apartment on 46th Street and 5th Avenue to hang out and jam, and by the time we finished, we'd go somewhere for breakfast in the wee hours of the morning, and then go home.

Back in those days, there were not many tape recorders. Instead, wire recorders were more the rage, and Timme had both a tape recorder and a wire recorder that he used to collect all kinds of music. Wire recorders preceded the invention of magnetic tape by just a few years, and they were used by the U.S. Army during World War II. After the war, companies started making wire recorders, and they were first available for sale in the United States around 1946. The music was played into a microphone and recorded onto a steel wire held in place by a spool. It took over seven thousand feet of wire to store one hour of music, but the wire itself was no thicker than a strand of hair. The sound quality of wire recordings wasn't that different than the quality of 78s, but to us, it was brand-new technology, and it allowed us to enjoy Timme's vast collection.

Although Timme became very well known in New York, it was rumored that his family disapproved of his attraction to Harlem. Timme was living with an African American woman, Inez Cavanaugh, something that was not entirely acceptable at a time when racial segregation and conservative values prevailed. He was a good friend to me, however, and a good friend to jazz, although his influence has gone unheralded.

I came to know Timme at a time when many new doors were opening for me in Harlem. Playing at the Three Deuces afforded me lots of exposure, and this, in turn, made it possible for me to access other opportunities. For example, between sets at the Three Deuces, I got to go across the street and play with Dizzy Gillespie when Bud Powell was released from the gig. I also played with my mentor Jo Jones, along with Eddie South, Coleman Hawkins, Roy Eldridge, and Machito's Afro-Cuban band. Timme would later be the catalyst behind another opportunity to come my way in the late 1940s, one of the most significant opportunities of my life.

Another important champion for jazz was John Hammond, one of the investors in Café Society. The original Café Society opened in Greenwich Village in 1938 and was unique at the time for its integration and equal treatment of both African American and white customers. John was the classic rich liberal when a second branch of the Café Society opened in 1940. It was John who came up with the idea that both clubs should feature folk, blues, and gospel singers alongside jazz greats. John also worked for Columbia Records and several other labels, so he was in a position to get people jobs. He got Teddy Wilson and Lionel Hampton the opportunity to perform with Benny Goodman. He was very clear about what he liked and disliked, however, and even though I was very fond of him, we argued a lot. He preferred Billie Holiday over

Ella Fitzgerald, and Basie over Ellington, and this was reflected in what and where he enabled them to record and perform. So he was a powerful figure, but a very nice man and a true lover of African American music. In the late 1930s and early 1940s, he sponsored some concerts at Carnegie Hall called "Spirituals to Swing," which were very popular. I was in school at that time, and although I didn't attend those concerts, everybody who loved jazz knew about them because we heard them on the radio.

In those days when I was freelancing on 52nd Street, I started dating a girl in Harlem whose brother was a friend of mine. One day, he called me up and said, "Hey, man, you gotta help me out. I know you're dating my sister, but there are a couple of girls who are crazy about me and I can't make up my mind. Why don't you take one of them off of my hands for a minute, and we'll double date and have some fun." I agreed.

So, I went to meet these two girls and found out that one of them was Teddi, the beautiful young lady whom I'd met a few years before when I was visiting Harlem during the Christmas holiday with my friend Noel from my college days. I'd last seen her at the YMCA dance, and now she was more mature and even prettier than I remembered. So, I put the guy's sister down and started dating Teddi.

During our courtship, I took her to various places on 52nd Street to show her the clubs where I'd worked, and I enjoyed name-dropping as much as I enjoyed showing her off. She loved to dance, and one of her favorite musicians was Charlie Barnet, a saxophonist and bandleader who had assembled an integrated band as early as the 1930s.

During the period that we were dating, I got a call to play a show with Ethel Waters, whose regular accompanist had fallen ill. Both Ms. Waters and Bill "Bo Jangles" Robinson were working on shows at the same time, and Ms. Waters was in a hurry to open hers first. Although she was wonderful to me, she had a terrible reputation for losing her temper. As it turned out, she won the race with Bo Jangles Robinson, but we opened so quickly that there was barely any time to rehearse. The show featured Mary Lou Williams, the Katherine Dunham Dancers, comedy, and drama. Although tempers flared and nerves frayed, we got through the show, which lasted about three weeks. Through it all, I'd managed to remain on Ethel's good side, and she even recommended me to a couple of other singers. Most importantly, however, I got to impress Teddi with my association with such big stars.

It was also while I was dating Teddi that I got a call to play with Slam Stewart, the incredible bassist I'd first seen perform back during my college years. I never forgot the way that Slam had blown everyone away, so when I got the call to work with him, I jumped at the chance. Despite his conservatory training, there were no classical venues where he could work, as African Americans were rarely seen in major symphony orchestras back in those days. But Slam was a star on 52nd Street. As half of the duo "Slim and Slam," he'd been featured frequently on the radio and had already had quite a few big hits. When I got the call to play in both his trio and his quartet, I was actually taking Erroll Garner's place. It was while working with Slam for several months that I had my first opportunities to play in major theatres. We played the RKO in Boston as well as a couple of the white theatres in Philadelphia, places I'd heard and read about but had never been to before. We also played at the Apollo, at the Howard Theatre, and at a black club in San Antonio Texas, back in the days when traveling by air was no luxury.

The performance in San Antonio was full of unwelcome surprises. Slam was such a celebrity that it came as a shock to us that the people in the club there didn't seem to know who he was. Even as Slam performed some of his biggest hits, the crowd was unmoved and the reception was, at best, lukewarm. This was a blues crowd, not at all into our jazz, and the club owner decided to replace us with an R & B pianist for whom, much to our embarrassment, the crowd went crazy! We were more than ready to leave the lazy little Texas town and head back to our next engagement at the Apollo, but we found ourselves stranded, bumped off of our scheduled flight by military personnel. So Slam and I waited around for the next plane to arrive. Meanwhile, as if things couldn't get any worse, someone noticed the two of us sitting and waiting, and as was the custom of the day, went to get a "Colored" sign to place above our heads in order to properly label the spot where we were. Segregation.

Teddi and I got married in 1946. She was a stunning bride; I, on the other hand, decided for some reason to wear a striped suit and a really bright tie! My dad and I were not on the best of terms at that time. Although he refused to attend the ceremony, I was thankful that he came in after the service to wish us both well. We'd had our ups and downs over the years, but he was still my father.

After the wedding, we took the train up to Connecticut to honeymoon for a few days, and once we returned home, I learned that I'd lost my job! Not good. All of my father's oft-repeated admonitions about financial independence, self-sufficiency, and adult responsibility came rushing back into my head like one big, giant "I told you so!" The only thing worse than being unemployed was being an unemployed newlywed, so I determined that my jobless state needed to be as temporary as possible.

In retrospect, I can say that my loss was someone else's gain, someone who needed that job and the opportunity to play more than I did. While I was away, a gig came up for Slam and he needed a pianist right away. I was on my honeymoon, so he hired Beryl Booker to replace me. Beryl Booker was yet another woman whose contributions to jazz have gone unheralded. Beryl was a fabulous, self-taught pianist and singer who didn't read music. Though relatively short-lived, her career was impressive, nonetheless. I took no joy in losing my job at that most inopportune time; the fact is, however, that her work with Slam Stewart was the gig that launched her career. Beryl would go on to play and record with other greats like Count Basie, Dinah Washington, Billie Holiday, and Miles Davis, and even had her own all-female trio for a time. Like most female jazz musicians of that era, Beryl had to go against the tide of a male-dominated field. Looking back, I can only be grateful that circumstances created a space for this talented and deserving lady to shine. Hindsight is twenty-twenty.

I knew that in the music business, the show had to go on without me. Yet I never forgot the feeling of being both a newlywed and newly unemployed! Thankfully, Teddi had a job that sustained us until my next opportunity came along. And my experience with Slam, though short-lived, was one of the shaping forces of my career.

Teddi loved to go dancing, so one night I took her to the uptown Café Society for an evening out. The star of the show that particular evening was the lead dancer with Katherine Dunham, whom I'd met earlier when I played the show for Ethel Waters. As I danced with Teddi, I noticed that the pianist on the bandstand was Ellis Larkin, a classically trained and wonderfully versatile musician who had accompanied Ella Fitzgerald. So before the evening was over, I went over to chat with him.

"What are you doing these days?" he asked.

I told him that I was freelancing.

"That's cool," he said. "Would you like to have this gig?"

He informed me that he was leaving soon and that the management would be looking for another pianist. So the very next night, I came back, got the job at the Café Society, and worked for a time with New Orleans–style clarinetist Edmond Hall.

Teddi and I were still newlyweds when my career headed for the next important milestone. In the 1930s and 1940s, Paul Whiteman, Jimmy Dorsey, Bing Crosby, Fletcher Henderson, and Count Basie were all household names, and their lives and accomplishments are well documented in today's histories of jazz and popular entertainment. But these and other artists owe a degree of their fame to someone whose name is far less familiar to the current generation. All but forgotten, this man was the one who set the standard for jazz composing and arranging. It was he who gave swing its characteristic instrumentation, featuring parts for both choirs of instruments as well as for improvised solos. He was never the kind of charismatic showman who would bring the house down, like a Cab Calloway or a Duke Ellington. But his charm and appeal were of a different sort, and historically, he is just as important. His big-band arrangements helped to make people like Dorsey, Crosby, and Whiteman famous, and without him, the sound of swing might have never come to be. He changed history. His name was Don Redman.

By the 1930s, Don Redman had already recorded, worked in film, and done numerous performances on radio. And by the time my generation came along, he was known around the world. A child prodigy, Redman was conservatory trained and performed in several bands as a reed player before leading several bands of his own. His first recordings and some of his earliest arrangements were with Fletcher Henderson back in the early 1920s, so guys my age viewed him both as a celebrity and as a very seasoned veteran.

Playing with Ben Webster was one unfathomable dream come true, and having the chance to play with Don Redman was another! Soon after Teddi and I were married, Timme Rosenkrantz started to talk to me about the possibility of going to Europe on tour with Don Redman. The idea was for Redman to assemble a band to tour Europe for a few weeks, and this tour would be distinguished as the first to bring an American band to Europe since the end of the war. It was a thoroughly exciting and tempting proposition, the kind of opportunity not to be missed. But I was a new husband, and I loved my wife. I told Rosenkrantz that I didn't want to leave Teddi so soon after getting married.

"Then bring her," Timme said. And with that, arrangements were made for both of us to go to Europe. What was originally planned as a six- or eight-week tour turned out to last for several months. I was the only guy in the group who was allowed to bring his wife, and for Teddi and me, it was an extended honeymoon and a rare chance to see places like France, Belgium, Holland, and Switzerland.

There's no way to describe how unique that experience was for us as African Americans. In the 1940s, much of the country—the South, in particular—was still segregated. By the World War II years, however, the economy was prosperous and things were starting to look up for African Americans. During the war years, thousands left the South to take advantage of the plentiful jobs and better wages in the steel and automobile plants of the northern cities. Consequently, by the late 1940s, this country saw the first generation of African Americans with significant disposable income. For the first time in our history, large numbers of African Americans could afford to spend money on recreation.

Despite this, however, our mobility was limited. Even those who could afford to live in wealthy neighborhoods were not allowed to because of segregation. Even though many African Americans could now afford cars that went farther and faster, there were severe restrictions on where they could travel. Even if you had the money to take your family on an excursion to the beach or on a nice vacation, back in those days, most beaches and resorts were closed to African Americans, regardless of income. And regardless of your prestige within the black community, you couldn't even ride the train from one state to the next unless there was a seat available somewhere back in the "Colored Only" section.

African Americans in those days had a difficult enough time getting around their own country. So the opportunity that Teddi and I had to visit *eight* foreign countries was absolutely unheard of among the people of our community, especially since we were not going for military service. We were going overseas to play our music, and this made our situation entirely unique. When Teddi and I arrived in Europe, we experienced culture shock. For the first time in our lives, we were in a place where there was no segregation, and we were treated like royalty. Whenever we'd get off of a plane, there'd be a band to greet us, and these European musicians were often quite good. They had heard American jazz on records, and they were already quite familiar with Don Redman through records and radio by the time we arrived. The Europeans also fell in love with my young, beautiful wife. Luckily for me, there were two older women who traveled with us, and they helped to fend off the guys who were among my wife's many admirers. This, in turn, kept me out of trouble!

There were also sobering moments during our time there. The war had ended just three years before, and its residue and devastation were still evident. We were able to see with our own eyes the kind of suffering that people endured. I recall vividly being in Germany and watching people walk barefoot down the streets in the dead of winter, and seeing mothers and children sift through trash heaps in search of some token of normalcy. Ghostly facades of once grand structures stood as barren, empty reminders of where bombs had fallen. What were once homes and businesses were unattended piles of rubble. Thankfully, I didn't see too many of these kinds of scenes. But the few times I encountered such misery was sufficient to remind me of how blessed we were that the brunt of war had never come to American soil in my lifetime. It also reminded me that people have the capacity to suffer cruelty at the hands of others regardless of their race, their status, or their nationality.

I was fortunate to tour Europe with a great group of musicians, both African American and white, some of whom were already major figures in their own rights. On the tour, Don Redman wore several hats, including bandleader, arranger, and alto and soprano sax player. He wanted to do more than just entertain the Europeans; he wanted to educate them, to give them a sense of the new direction that jazz was taking at that time. So he very strategically included both older, more conservative players and younger, up-and-coming players in the group. With this combination, he was able to do both swing tunes and some of the newer bebop material. Don Byas was the featured tenor player and the musician in our group best known to the Europeans. Don had played with everybody, from Lionel Hampton, to Lucky Millinder, to Count Basie. After the tour, he decided to settle in Europe and lived there the rest of his life. Other sax players on the tour were Ray Abrams, Peter Clark, and Chauncey Houghton. On trombone, we had a white player named Jackie Carmen, Quentin Jackson (also known as "Butter"), and Tyree Glenn, the latter two of whom had already played with Cab Calloway and several big bands. Tyree Glenn actually played both trombone and vibraphone. On trumpet, there was Herbert Lee "Peanuts" Holland (who also served as vocalist), Bob Williams, and Allan Jeffries, a young white guy who was into bebop. The bass player was Ted Sturgis, and the drummer, Buford Oliver, fell and broke his ankle during our first week in Europe. Inez Cavanaugh, Timme's girlfriend, was the female vocalist on the tour. She went on to become quite famous in Europe, but when she returned to the United States, nothing was ever made of her success overseas. She faded into obscurity, and I was saddened to learn many years later that she was among the followers of Jim Jones who died in the mass suicide in Guyana in 1978.

While in Europe, we basically lived in hotels and rode a bus when touring with the band. Although we attended lots of parties and played with many of the local musicians, we mostly did concerts, sometimes two concerts in different locations in a single day. There was one occasion when the State Department asked us to go to Germany to play for American soldiers stationed there, but otherwise, we were doing concerts.

Timme Rosenkrantz was from Denmark, so we stopped there first. Consequently, our initial impression of the Europeans came from the Danes, who were delightful and incredibly welcoming, warm, and hospitable. In general, people were friendly toward us wherever we went, but we couldn't help but perceive the people of the other countries there to be somewhat reserved in comparison to the Danes. We were playing some pretty well-known halls, and the very first place we played was KB Hall in Denmark, which was larger than Madison Square Garden, one of the most gigantic halls I'd ever seen! At that time, many of the musicians we met in Denmark and Sweden were a lot more modern than the

French, which may seem strange since France was the first European country to show great enthusiasm for jazz.

There's no way to recount all of the music we played during our visits to each of those eight countries. There were some favorite numbers, however. Don Byas had recorded "Laura," and that was a popular tune with European audiences. My solos were "Tea for Two" and "Alexander's Ragtime Band." We played, among other things, "How High the Moon," "Stomping at the Savoy," "My Melancholy Baby," "Stormy Weather," and several tunes by Don Redman.

We always faced a language barrier to one degree or another while traveling around Europe, but the necessities of day-to-day living motivated us to pick up key phrases here and there. Fortunately, however, most of the Europeans spoke at least some English, and they were hungry to learn as much as they could about who we were and what we were doing musically. I was the first bebop pianist that many of them had ever heard, and while there was lots of curiosity about bebop, there were just as many who wanted me to show them how to play stride, since this is what they were familiar with. Where our spoken language failed, our music communicated in ways that transcended anything we could have expressed with words alone.

As the bandleader and arranger, Don was wonderful, sensitive, easygoing, and a great musician. His biggest challenge may have been regulating the band's consumption of liquor. Because we were treated like celebrities, there was never a shortage of alcohol, and on a few occasions, this didn't bode well for us. And then, of course, there were the hangovers, which were a major problem whenever we had two concerts scheduled in a single day. Thanks to the mentorship of Jo Jones and my embarrassment back at the Three Deuces, I had learned well the importance of sobriety. But for some of the guys in the band, this lesson was still a long way off.

Fortunately, there were no major catastrophes during the tour. But there was a close call. Gas was being rationed at the time, so we did lots of walking while there. Our trombone player, Tyree Glenn, was a superb musician and very popular with the Europeans. A rather portly fellow, however, he tired easily from all of the walking, and he found someone to lend him a bicycle. Given his rotund size and shape, Tyree balanced atop that bicycle seemed like a miracle of gravity! And as if that weren't comical enough, he went riding in the wrong direction down a one-way street! Concerned pedestrians waved and yelled urging him to turn around, but he was oblivious to the danger of oncoming traffic. He knew that he was a celebrity, and he thought that their gestures and screams were enthusiastic greetings from his adoring fans. Thankfully, someone stopped him and pulled him over, and saved both Tyree and the brass section of our band!

Aside from the typical conflicts that arise when people spend long periods in close contact, we all got along reasonably well. Music was changing, however, and this was evident in our individual styles and preferences. The majority of the guys in the band were older and there-fore much more comfortable playing swing. But there were some young-er guys who wanted to play bebop, the new, emerging sound. I was in the process of honing my own bebop chops at that time and I got lots of attention because, to the Europeans, what I was playing was entirely new. Some time passed before bebop came into vogue in Europe.

The European tour was both memorable and fun, and I recall fondly those with whom I shared those eight months. My wife and I enjoyed sightseeing, strolls around Paris, and a relatively carefree existence since my contract with Don provided for all of our needs. After the formal tour was over, I was part of a smaller band that worked in Paris over the Christmas holiday. Following that, we spent a couple of weeks in Holland.

After nearly a year of royal treatment, it was time to return home to the United States. I was in for a major period of readjustment, since there were no adoring crowds, welcoming bands, red carpets, or steady jobs waiting to greet me. For Teddi and me, Europe was like a beautiful, harmonious dream, far removed from the mundane, far removed from reality. But I was about to quickly learn that the honeymoon had come to an end.

FIGURE 1.

With my Uncle Nathaniel Bacon and my mother,
Antoinette Bacon Taylor.

FIGURE 2. With Art Tatum and friends at a club in New York. *(above)*

FIGURE 3. Performing with Artie Shaw. *(below)*

FIGURE 4.

Performing with Candido, 1952.

FIGURE 5.

At a rehearsal for *The Subject Is Jazz.*

FIGURE 6.

A portrait from the late 1950s.

FIGURE 7.

With Duane and Kim, early 1960s.

FIGURE 8.

On the air at WLIB.

FIGURE 9.

One of many performances at the Newport Jazz Festival, mid-1960s.

FIGURE 10.

Taking a break in the offices of WNEW.

FIGURE 11.

On the set of *Captain Kangaroo.*

FIGURE 12.

Vacationing with Teddi. (*facing*)

FIGURE 13. An early Jazzmobile street performance. *(above)*

FIGURE 14. Relaxing with Teddi. *(left)*

FIGURE 15. Laughing with David Frost. (*above*)

FIGURE 16. With Teddi, Duane, and Kim. (*below*)

FIGURE 17.

Promoting Jazz Month in New York City, mid-1970s.

FIGURE 18.

Performing and promoting jazz education in Chicago, 1973.

FIGURE 19.

Celebrating one of the annual mayoral proclamations in support of jazz in New York City.
From left to right: Leonard Goines, Sylvester "Sonny Red" Kiner, Larry Ridley,
Joe Lee Wilson, mayoral representative (unidentified); unidentified man, Billy Taylor,
Jimmy Owens (large afro, standing rear and to the right of Billy), Jimmy Heath,
unidentified man in rear, Reggie Workman (in dashiki), Lenny McBrowne, Jim Harrison.

FIGURE 20. "A round of applause for Dexter Gordon and Frank Wess!" *(above)*

FIGURE 21. At New York's jazz station, WRVR-FM, before its demise. *(below)*

FIGURE 22. Another proclamation from the New York City
mayor's office in support of jazz. *(above)*

FIGURE 23. Duke Ellington with two of his many admirers. *(below)*

FIGURE 24.

Applauding Lionel Hampton.

FIGURE 25.

Doing what I love best of all.

FOUR

The Subject Is Jazz

1946–1958

O NCE BACK FROM EUROPE, it didn't take long for reality to set in. My early years in New York gave me lots of exposure, but when you're absent for months at a time, people tend to forget about you. While I was overseas with Don Redman, the music scene in New York went on without me, so I needed to reestablish myself. And with a new wife to support, I was desperate for work and willing to take just about any job I could get. One day, I was at the Musicians Union Hall to attend to some business when a guy approached me and said, "Hey, man, someone's looking for a piano player. Do you want the gig?" Of course, at that time, I was in no position to refuse.

The job was on Eighth Avenue at a lousy bar, the sort of raucous, seedy joint where you'd find ladies of the evening and every other imaginable vice. The piano was on top of the bar, behind the bartender. The manager's instructions were succinct: "Play as loud and as long as you can, and when you get tired, stop and I'll come and turn on the jukebox."

Of course, I didn't take this literally. I began to play, and after a few upbeat numbers, I started in on a ballad. Immediately, the manager came rushing out from the back in an angry fit.

"What are you doing!?!" he yelled. "I told you to play as loud as you can for as long as you can!"

With that, he put on the jukebox and motioned for me to come down from the piano.

"I know what I'm doing," he said. "This is a *loud* bar, and I want you to do *exactly* as I said. As loud as you can, and as long as you can!"

Needless to say, there were no more ballads that night. I soon realized that these people came to this bar for the noise, not for the music.

At around the same period, I got another job from the Musicians Union, this time at a car dealership. On the night of the gig, there was a torrential downpour, and when we finally arrived at the location and unloaded the bass and the drums, the manager came out of the dealership and asked, "Where's your piano?" I wondered what he could possibly mean. Puzzled by such a question, I went inside, and to my surprise, there was no piano anywhere in sight. Now, this was long before the days when people carted around their electric pianos, so I'm not sure why this fellow thought we'd bring our own. But I needed the money, and *there was no way I was walking away from that job!*

As it turns out, we were in an Italian neighborhood, so it occurred to me to ask around for an accordion. My accordion skills were the result of my friendship with Peter Rabbird (nicknamed "Peter Rabbit"), a fellow who worked opposite me at a club back in Washington, D.C. From him, I learned just enough accordion to get myself into trouble. My wife heard me play accordion when we were in Europe, and her only comment to me was "Don't ever do that again." Nevertheless, our trio that night consisted of accordion, bass, and drums. As I struggled through the gig, I looked over to see someone setting up microphones! No one told us we'd be on the air, but to my horror, my unrehearsed and profoundly mediocre accordion performance was about to be broadcast all over New York!

Shortly thereafter, I was at the Musicians Union when a friend of mine stopped me: "Hey Billy, there was some guy on the radio playing accordion and using your name, and he was just *awful*!" Happily, that performance was never to be repeated.

These were the kinds of lackluster jobs that I took during a dry spell that lasted longer than I care to remember. But I used my time wisely. I was still taking lessons with Richard McClanahan, whom I'd met a few years earlier while working on 52nd Street. So whenever I wasn't pounding the pavement or searching for work at the union, I was at the piano practicing.

Finally, things began to look up when I got a job at Wells Supper Club on Seventh Avenue in Harlem. Famous for its chicken and waffles, it was an after-hours place open all night to serve customers who came there after leaving dances and various clubs. You could leave the Savoy at 2:00 in the morning and stop into Wells for a bite. If you were too confused to decide between a late dinner and an early breakfast, at Wells, you could get both. It was while I was working there that I came to know Bob Wyatt.

A classically trained organist, Bob was a bright, articulate, and mature man, and at Wells, we played opposite each other. Our show started at 9:00 PM and we typically opened with me on piano, followed by Bob doing an organ solo. Twice each night, we'd get together and play for our vocalist, Sylvia Syms, yet another wonderful artist who never got the credit she deserved. Bob and I later became partners, and we were billed as "Wyatt & Taylor."

At that time, many people believed that presenting jazz on equal terms with classical music was tantamount to committing some kind of sacrilege. This belief came from the notion that one type of music was inferior to the other, a myth to which I never subscribed, one that I felt the need to challenge intellectually. And I soon found opportunities to do so, one of the earliest of which came as a result of my connection to Bob Wyatt.

While working at Wells, there was a publisher named Charles Hansen who came in to see Bob about writing some organ music for Ethel Smith, a well-known organist who played for the movies. Hansen was an independent publisher who was doing lots of imaginative things back in those days. Before big jazz anthologies like the *Real Book,* Hansen had published something very similar called *1001 Jazz Songs.* At the time he came into Wells, Hansen also happened to be looking for someone to write a book on bebop—nothing huge, just a short instructional booklet to explain the history of the music, discuss some devices typical of the style, and give a few music examples. When he first approached me to do this, my initial reaction was to suggest that he get someone else, Dizzy Gillespie or Charlie Parker, perhaps. But Hansen had been unable to persuade anyone else to write it, so I agreed. I actually completed much of the work on the book later while Bob and I were engaged at the Royal Roost, one of the major hot spots on 52nd Street in the 1940s. The book was published in 1949. Hansen liked what I did, and *Billy Taylor's Basic Bebop Instruction for Piano* became the first instructional book I wrote on jazz piano playing. I followed *Basic Bebop Instruction* with several similar instructional books on earlier styles like ragtime.

Hansen had difficulty getting other artists to write the book, even those who were on the cutting edge of the style. This was very likely due to the fact that artists didn't want to get taken advantage of, which was too often the case. It was a well-known fact, for example, that Irving Mills put his name on many pieces that were actually written by Duke Ellington. In addition to the fear of exploitation, there was also a prevailing attitude at that time among jazz artists that the music couldn't really be taught; you either had the natural ability to play jazz, or you didn't. Louis Armstrong was once famously quoted as saying, "If you have to ask what jazz is, you'll never know." I begged to differ, however. I believed back then, as I do now, that it is most certainly possible to teach jazz. Writing *Basic Bebop Instruction* was an opportunity for me to act on this belief, and to make history in the process: It was the first book ever published on bebop.

Despite those prevailing attitudes, there was a genuine hunger for knowledge about jazz, and I soon found myself with invitations to lecture and to write for *Esquire* magazine, for the *Saturday Review,* and for other well-known publications. For a time, it seemed as though mine was the lone voice crying in a wilderness ripe with the desire to know more about this music that many believed should never be discussed, only heard. But there were lots of people who wanted to sit down and talk about jazz, and I soon found that this was something I enjoyed doing.

My mother was a teacher, and my grandfather a preacher, so perhaps I inherited from them a desire to discuss, to exhort, and to impart the music to people in ways that transcended performance alone. And it wasn't just jazz that I wanted to share, but jazz as a part of my heritage, music forged in the flames of the African American experience. I'd grown up with some of the best musicians and singers in the world, African Americans who could have graced any stage but whose gifts were confined by segregation. Even as I branched out into the world as a professional musician, the indelible imprints of Fats Waller, Art Tatum, James Reese Europe, Mary Europe, and Henry Grant were ever with me. My childhood teachers not only taught me the music, but they taught me a history of the music that was nowhere to be found in books, a history that already had me thinking about the word *classical* and how that applied to American music. Back in the 1910s and 1920s, you could pick up a copy of a magazine like *The Literary Digest* or *Current Opinion,* the equivalent of modern-day *Newsweek* and *People* magazines, and in them you could find all kinds of articles about the virtues of classical music and the dangers of inferior styles like blues and jazz. But the music they praised was imported from elsewhere, borrowed from an earlier time and from an overseas culture. Thanks to my teachers, I formed the opinion early on that European music, though "classical," did not truly belong to America. Jazz, by contrast, was born and raised on American soil and gave voice to a uniquely American experience. Jazz was really America's Classical Music.

Although this seemed obvious to me, a common prejudice prevented many from seeing the value of music beyond the European classical tradition. I felt the call to dispel this blindness and to challenge the myth of European musical superiority. Mozart and Beethoven hadn't cornered the market on great music. Beauty, substance, and craft were every bit as present in African American music, every bit as present in jazz.

Basic Bebop Instruction was a small but significant beginning. Another important beginning came through Undine Moore, my former professor at Virginia State. When she was a graduate student at Columbia College, with her teacher's blessing, she invited me to come and speak in her class about jazz. University jazz courses were nonexistent in those days, but there were serious musicians with curious minds. I gained a special satisfaction from talking about the music, perhaps because I knew that there was a growing demand for people who could both perform jazz and discuss it intelligently. Those early opportunities to speak and to write about jazz foreshadowed things to come.

Bob and I shared lots of interesting experiences, some great, some not so great. Although we met at Wells, Wyatt & Taylor performed in other venues both in and outside of New York. Our first out-of-town engagement was in St. Louis, one of a number of road trips during which we loaded Bob's very expensive organ into the trailer attached to the bumper of the car. To ensure the safety of the organ, we drove more slowly than normal, a necessary precaution that added considerably to our travel time. After the painstaking odyssey from New York to St. Louis, Bob and I finally arrived at the Chase Hotel, where we were on the same bill with Guy Lombardo. We were exhausted from the trip and anxious to get cleaned up and settled in, but we soon found that there was a problem.

Our manager at that time was Mike Levin, a young white man who was one of the editors for *Down Beat* magazine, and he simply didn't know any better. Innocently, he'd booked the two of us for rooms at the hotel, not realizing that blacks weren't allowed. Unlike our manager, Bob and I were well acquainted with segregation. But we thought of St. Louis as one of the more progressive cities and assumed it to be more "northern" than "southern" in its mindset. So we were also surprised to find ourselves performing at a "Whites Only" establishment, one where we weren't permitted to sleep. I was disappointed, but Bob was furious, and understandably so. He was older than I and thus more battle-scarred, and this latest insult just added to many other unsavory experiences. The manager was kind to us but refused to relax the hotel's policy for fear of jeopardizing his own position. So we found lodging at a hotel on the African American side of town, and traveled back and forth to the Chase to perform for our whites-only audience.

To be denied lodging because of our race was one thing; but to be denied the chance to play for African Americans was quite another, an even more egregious insult. At a time when we had to swallow our pride and "make do" as best we could, nothing would be more affirming and uplifting than applause from our own people. There were many African Americans in the St. Louis area who were disappointed that they couldn't see our performance at the Chase. This was unacceptable to us, so we approached the owner and offered to do an extra show on Sunday, our off day. This way, we could perform for our African American fans and the hotel could uphold its segregationist policy. The owner agreed to the Sunday show, and this was the only time that African Americans were allowed to enter the hotel while we were there. Oddly enough, however, whites also wanted to attend the Sunday show even though that performance was designated for blacks who were banned from seeing us during the rest of the week. Therefore, albeit briefly, the Chase Hotel had a taste of integration in 1948, after all!

We finished in St. Louis, and immediately, we were loading up the organ and hitting the road again for home and our next engagement in

New York. In order to make it to Carnegie Hall for the show, we drove the entire night and arrived just in time to set up and rehearse. Having just finished our sobering engagement at the Chase Hotel, we were primed and excited to come back home to be a part of something that was no less than a celebration.

The show was *Billie on Broadway,* and it was one of the high points of Billie Holiday's career. She had just finished serving eight months in prison for heroin possession, and she was sober, optimistic, and seemed to have a new lease on life. But her conviction made it impossible for her to resume working in clubs as she'd always done. So the show gave Billie an opportunity to sing again for her adoring and supportive fans. She was absolutely at her prime and sounded better than ever. *Billie on Broadway,* opened in March of 1948 and was held over in response to popular demand. Bob and I rushed back to play in the extended performance. Unfortunately, Billie's troubles didn't end in 1948, but during that show, the public rallied around her with such support and appreciation that she knew she was loved.

After we finished working with Billie Holiday, Bob and I were invited to do an extended engagement at the Royal Roost. Though comparatively short-lived, the Royal Roost was a jazz landmark, and Wyatt & Taylor was engaged there at the same time that the club hosted Miles Davis's first performance with what was later called the "Birth of the Cool" band. In those days, big bands were giving way to smaller combos, and there was enormous excitement when the Miles Davis group came to play.

Davis's more subtle, lyrical style was in contrast to the kind of complexity and percussiveness that were in bebop. Anyone who has tried to emulate him knows that it is more difficult to play with simplicity than it may appear. Miles was known for allowing the musicians in his band great expressive freedom, and he was not one to limit or dictate to them in any way. There is a famous story, however, about Miles Davis and John Coltrane. Coltrane would seem to go on and on and would sometimes play thirty or thirty-five choruses on a piece of music. Once, Miles asked him: "Why do you play so long?"

Coltrane answered, "Well, sometimes, I just can't think of how to stop."

Miles replied: "Did you ever think of taking your horn out of your mouth?"

Even though Miles had attended Juilliard for a time, he was a completely free spirit and had an entirely personalized approach to playing that was a big contrast to the complex styles of bebop. Someone once asked him how much playing he did on a daily basis. He answered that he never touched his horn unless he had a gig. He claimed that this was the way he kept his musical ideas fresh.

Wyatt & Taylor had the night off on the evening they performed, but we learned when we came in the next day that they were a smash hit. Miles Davis and the *Cool* album were to attain legendary status, but Bob Wyatt wasn't impressed. Instead, he was upset that in his absence, the guys had tampered with his organ!

Along with our vocalist, Sylvia Syms, Bob and I were broadcast nationally from the Royal Roost every night, which enabled each of us to establish a reputation. By that time, I'd had an opportunity to introduce Bob to the Latin sound which first captivated me during those early days in New York when I played with Machito's band. I took Bob to a club to hear the music performed, and he found that he could replicate the sound of the conga drums and other Latin percussion on the organ. Today, such a thing is taken for granted, but back then, the electric organ was a novelty, and the ability to reproduce percussion sounds on an organ was new and fascinating to our fans. In fact, it was so new that people would write to ask about the other players in our ensemble. Of course, there weren't any other players, just Bob doing his magic on what was then a new-fangled instrument.

For a time, the Royal Roost seemed to be emerging as the new, important club in town, and the same people who ran it later opened other establishments, including Bop City and Birdland. The Royal Roost eventually folded, however, and it was the last place that Bob and I played together. Wyatt & Taylor had a successful run, but Bob and I had different goals. Although he loved jazz, it wasn't his greatest passion. He was classically trained in the repertoire of the European masters, and he really wanted to go that direction. I tried to convince him that we could create a special niche for ourselves by combining jazz and classical, but he didn't share my conviction that this could work.

After the split of Wyatt & Taylor, I went to Bop City, a much larger club that catered to a younger clientele. Bop City served no alcohol but instead had a soda fountain in the back where the bar used to be. A unique establishment, it featured a variety of acts, including comedy and rhythm and blues, alongside jazz, and for 50 cents you could enjoy entertainment all night long. On one particular night at Bop City, I played for a show which included Dizzy Gillespie's big band, Dinah Washington, and a couple of other acts. I then had to come on and play solo for an entire hour, undoubtedly the longest solo of my career! It might have gone even longer if not for the union rule which stipulated that a musician get an hour break after each hour of playing.

I had another interesting experience at Bop City, involving the great clarinetist Artie Shaw. By this time, Shaw was retired, but he was interested in experimenting with new sounds, so he hired a quartet of us—me on piano, John Collins on guitar, Charlie Smith on drums, and Joe Benjamin on bass—to play with him at Bop City. During the performance, as Artie was in the middle of playing a ballad, this guy from out of nowhere emerged from the audience, walked right up, put his arm around Shaw, and started going on and on about how big a fan he was, how much he loved his playing, and so on. The audience wondered whether this was some sort of comedy routine and wasn't quite sure whether to be shocked or entertained. Artie was incredulous and looked ready to punch the guy. When it became clear that Artie was furious, waiters and busboys came from everywhere to hustle the guy off stage. Bop City could be a fascinating place!

Around the same time, I had another opportunity to tour outside of the United States, and this time, our purpose was to educate as well as to entertain. Bud Johnson was an excellent arranger and sax player who had performed with Earl Hines. (Earl Hines was the pivotal pianist largely responsible for changing stride into the freer, more melodic right-hand style of playing.) Bud was somewhat older, but unique in that he managed to make the transition from swing to bebop, and it was because of him that I got the opportunity to go to Haiti. He'd been to Haiti on several occasions and was the friend and one-time instructor of Issa El Saieh.

A dynamic advocate of Haitian art and culture, Issa El Saieh had studied in the United States, was himself a clarinet and sax player, and had organized his own uniquely Haitian big band in the 1940s. More than anything, perhaps, he was an organizer, and he was very interested in exposing the people of Haiti to the latest in American jazz. In 1949, he invited Bud Johnson, his friend and former teacher, to bring his band to participate in a music festival that combined both performance and education. So we were playing in clubs and doing bebop clinics, and the people were very receptive and excited about it.

While there, we came to know a wonderful local drummer named Tiroro, yet another unsung hero who should have become much more widely known. Tiroro was the inspiration for a piece that I wrote, and through an accidental misspelling, that piece is known and performed today as "Titoro."

Because of the strong European influence, the use of rhythm in African American music tends to be very westernized despite the fact that syncopation is often present. Caribbean music, by contrast, features percussion performance which is much more highly developed. Because the music of the Caribbean islands is much more closely tied to its African roots, in a place like Haiti, drumming is quite an advanced art form. So it was especially interesting to watch our African American drummer, Charlie Smith, go head-to-head with Tiroro. It was the kind of percussive dialogue that you had to actually see to believe! The Haitian ignited the air with impossible rhythmic feats, and Charlie fired back with riveting explosives of his own. To be caught in the musical crossfire of these two geniuses was an excitement that I still have difficulty putting into words.

I went to Haiti at a time when race relations in the United States were beginning to change. The civil-rights issue was brewing in the White House, and to African Americans, it appeared that President Truman was on the side of progress. It was Truman who desegregated the armed forces and ended racial discrimination in federal jobs. Although he fought an uphill battle, Truman, like FDR, went further than many of his predecessors in acting on behalf of civil rights, and for African Americans, this was a reason for real optimism. Having grown up in Washington, D.C., I had long been aware of the civil-rights struggle of a small group of vocal and progressive African Americans who were well known in my community. But by 1949, that struggle was gaining national attention to a degree not seen before. Going to Haiti at that particular moment broadened my perspective in another way. Back in the United States, whites were the majority and African Americans were careful to observe the boundaries that kept the races separate. In Haiti, however, the people of color were the majority, and this was a completely new experience for me. Yet, the average Haitian had no participation in the control of his homeland's natural resources. Tourists poured into Haiti, but the profits from tourism never quite seemed to reach the pockets of the Haitians themselves. I found the Haitians to be very proud people, but too many of them lived in abject poverty. It seemed to me that there should have been some way for them to help each other, especially since they were the majority. But no one seemed to even know where to begin. I found this both puzzling and disturbing. This political disparity was impossible to ignore, but there was some consolation in knowing that we'd come to enrich the people of this small and vibrant country with our music and, in turn, to be enriched by theirs.

I went to Haiti and observed these problems at about the same time that my hero Paul Robeson was heavily involved in global activism. Interestingly, Robeson became involved in the struggle for global civil rights in the late 1940s, and by 1949, his outspokenness made him the target of government suspicion. Just a year later, Robeson was banned from international travel because he refused to sign an affidavit stating that he was not a communist. When I went to Haiti in 1949, I saw with my own eyes the kind of injustice that people of color suffer the world over, the kind of injustice to which Paul Robeson was passionately opposed.

The period following my return from Europe was both a rude awakening and a test of patience. In what seemed like an endless valley, there were certainly a few high points, like playing with Bob Wyatt and working at the Royal Roost and later at Bop City. But those engagements were generally fleeting ones, lasting a few months at best before the future became uncertain again and I was forced to fill my days with job hunting, practicing, and waiting for the phone to ring. During these periods of financial instability, my father's voice echoed in my head loudly and clearly. In fact, it may have been his dismal prognosis of my future that kept me on such a driven path. Days without work could have easily become periods of idleness, but I had no choice but to press ahead and fill those jobless phases with as much productivity, as much practicing and job seeking as possible. Not only did I have a burning need to prove my father wrong, but I also needed to prove to Teddi that she was right to believe in me.

And then it happened. I was at home practicing one day when the phone rang. It was Al Haig, Charlie Parker's pianist. I'd known Al for some time.

"Man, I'm sure glad you're home because I've called a number of guys and I just haven't been able to reach anybody today. I'm scheduled to open tonight at Birdland with Charlie Parker, but I have a conflict and I just can't be there. I really need somebody to cover for me."

I'd heard of this new club called Birdland, and at that time, it had only been open a few months. The owner was Morris Levy, one of the most important nightclub impresarios in the music business and a real champion of bebop. Late in 1949, he opened the club, which he dubbed for his favorite musician, Charlie Parker, whose nickname was "Yardbird." Birdland opened just at the time when the jazz scene on 52nd Street was starting to wane.

Charlie Parker started playing the saxophone when he was eleven or twelve years old. Inspired by Coleman Hawkins, Lester Young, and Ben Webster, he left his native Kansas City for New York just in time for the emergence of bebop. Parker became friends with the likes of Dizzy Gillespie, Thelonious Monk, Billy Eckstine, and Earl Hines, and developed a distinctive style that was highly complex and individualized. Despite his innovations, however, he was really unappreciated in the United States for much of the early part of his career. It wasn't until his European tour in the late 1940s that he achieved the kind of spotlight he deserved. In December of 1949, Birdland opened on Broadway, about a block or so west of the now declining 52nd Street.

Needless to say, Al's call that morning couldn't have come at a more opportune time, so I hurried and dressed and got down to the club in time to make the remainder of the afternoon rehearsals. When I arrived, the place was abuzz with activity. It was filled with the kind of excitement and anticipation you feel when something big is about to happen. I knew many of the musicians there, but the place was also jammed with onlookers who came to observe the rehearsal as though it was the actual concert. I soon learned that I'd be playing along with Roy Haynes on drums and Curly Russell on bass, both of whom I knew and with whom I'd played before.

The opening that night was a smash! Charlie featured strings in the concert, something different from the norm, and people absolutely loved it. There was no question about the significance of that opening night with Charlie Parker at Birdland, and I was thrilled to have the chance to be a part of it. But as far as I knew at the time, I was just substituting for Al on that single occasion. So after that show, I went back home with no prospects other than the modest gig I had on 49th Street.

On the afternoon of the very next day, I was at home practicing when, again, the phone rang. It was Monte Kay, the man who did the booking for Birdland: "Man, drop whatever you're doing and get down here right now! We can't find Al Haig, and the first set has just started, so we'll use you until he gets here."

Again, I dressed, hopped in a cab, and rushed down to the club. Sure enough, just as everyone feared, Al never came. That was the beginning of my tenure as house pianist at Birdland.

The show with Charlie Parker at Birdland was such a success that Monte Kay arranged for us to take a bigger show to the Apollo for a week's engagement. The band he assembled featured Stan Getz on tenor and several of the younger bop players. We did so many back-to-back shows at the Apollo that we barely had time between the end of one and the start of another to grab a quick bite.

It was rumored that Al left the music business altogether and took up gardening. Actually, he returned to the business after doing a variety of different jobs. Whatever the case, I am glad that I was at home that day to take one of the most pivotal phone calls of my life.

If playing at the Three Deuces was like going to high school, then playing at Birdland was like earning a graduate degree at an Ivy League college! As house pianist, I had to be ready for anything that came my way. Every night, I was onstage with incredible people, in many cases people whom I'd never have the chance to play with again. Often, the rehearsals at Birdland were like master classes, since many of the artists would bring their music and explain to us in detail the sound they were trying to achieve. The list of artists that I played with during those two years is too long to reproduce in detail, but it includes everybody from

Miles Davis to Lester Young, to Stan Getz, to Sarah Vaughan, Art Blakey, and Jo Jones.

Charlie Parker was an interesting person, very intellectual, but always in touch with the audience. And he knew much more about music than just jazz. On one occasion, I'd been to a piano lesson and, rather than going home, I decided to head straight to the club to work on a piece that my teacher had just gone over with me. I started playing, and Charlie walked over to me to listen.

"Hey, that's nice, B. I like that," he remarked.

I said to him, "You like this? How do you know? You don't even know what it is."

He answered, "Sure I know. That's Debussy."

I told him it was a lucky guess.

He said, "That's Debussy's *Arabesque*." At that point, I conceded that he knew what he was talking about, but by then, it was too late. Bird was insulted, so to show me a thing or two, he took out his horn and played the next section of the work, the part that I hadn't gotten to yet. This gave me an even deeper respect for Charlie Parker.

One night, Dizzy Gillespie was scheduled to play at Birdland when he'd just come in from off of the road. The show that night was to be broadcast. He and his vibraphonist, Milt Jackson, were going over this tune they were going to do, and I asked what the name of the tune was. They answered that the tune didn't have a name, but they needed to call it something since it was going to be on radio. Now, everyone knew that Dizzy was always a ladies' man, and there were lots of beautiful women who came to Birdland. Dizzy had a habit of hitting on the young ladies, and having just noticed him flirting with one of the pretty women moments earlier, I said, "Why don't you call it 'Birks Works'?" (Dizzy's real name was John Birks Gillespie.) "Birks Works" has been a standard in the jazz repertoire ever since.

I had the opportunity to work with John Coltrane at Birdland, and he was absolutely one of the nicest human beings I ever met in my life. He was very kind and thoughtful, and it was really during that period that I had the only chance to really talk with him. Between sets, we talked about all kinds of things. In fact, I never felt as comfortable with many of the musicians I met during that period as I felt with him. John had a very interesting grab-bag approach to his playing. He heard and assimilated lots of different musical styles and devices and found ways to incorporate them into his saxophone performance whenever and however it pleased him. He was really interested in some of the Tatum-esque harmonic devices and glissandos that I used on the piano. So we talked about it and I slowed one of the glissandos down enough for him to hear the specific patterns of notes that were actually being played. He decided, "Yeah, I'm going to try to do that on saxophone." I didn't see how he would pull it off, so imagine my surprise when sometime later he did just that on his instrument.

At Birdland I developed the versatility of a musical jack-of-all-trades, and that made some experiences less glamorous than others. I had to be spontaneous and versatile enough to play with all kinds of musicians and under all kinds of circumstances. But there were moments when I had to draw the line and speak up for myself. There was a Steinway at Birdland, but the instrument had been very badly abused. One of my coworkers at the club was another pianist named Slim Gaylord, whose habit was to prop a giant glass of Coca-Cola right on the piano. I was paranoid that it was just a matter of time before this large glass of Coke would topple over, so I kept moving it out of the way; and no sooner than I'd move it, Slim would move it back to where it was. Gaylord was a large man with long arms and big, sweeping motions, and sure enough, the day came when that glass of Coke went crashing right down into the piano—liquid, ice, broken glass, and all. The moisture and sugar ruined the soundboard, and at that point, I had to let Morris know that it was time to exchange the beat-up old model for a new piano.

When Morris asked me what kind of piano we should get, I insisted on a Steinway.

"But that's awfully expensive, isn't it?" he asked.

After a long conversation and a lot of back-and-forth, I finally said to him: "You drive a Cadillac, don't you?" To which he replied that he did.

"And you drive the best because you know that it will keep its value no matter what, right?" He couldn't argue with that.

So, I convinced Morris to come with me to Steinway Hall so that he could see what I was talking about. Beforehand, however, I called a friend of mine there to let him know that I needed his help to make this sale. I arranged for him to bring out a couple of the lesser-quality trade-ins so that I could play those first in order for my boss to understand the difference in the quality of the Steinway. So we got to Steinway Hall, and I played an old upright first, and then an old off-brand grand next. Finally, we go over to this fabulous new Steinway that was just impeccable, stunning in every way. Even before I played a note, Morris could see the difference. Finally, I played the Steinway, and Morris was sold immediately. And that's how Birdland got a brand-new Steinway piano.

Some of my least glamorous moments at Birdland were the times that I had to come on and play the intermission of a show featuring a major headliner. During the intermission, the audience tends to turn its attention away from the stage until the featured star returns to the spotlight. However, I took this as a part of my job and came to accept that during the intermission, I stood a good chance of being ignored. This was often the case, except on one especially memorable occasion when the headliner was Duke Ellington.

On this particular night, people crammed the space until not an inch was left to sit or to stand. Movie stars and maids, politicians and porters, everybody was there. If you sat at the tables or at the bar at Birdland, you were expected to purchase something to eat or drink. But if you didn't want to buy food or drinks, there was a so-called bleacher section where you could sit all night and enjoy the entertainment just for the price of admission to the club. Every part of the club, including the bleacher section, was completely full. Flickering flashbulbs decorated the atmosphere already electric with anticipation and excited chatter, everyone waiting for that first exquisite downbeat, those opening bars of "Take the A Train" or "In a Mellow Tone" or "Mood Indigo." When William "Pee Wee" Marquette took the microphone, the entire room held its breath. "Ladies and gentlemen," he started, and before he could finish pronouncing Duke's name, the house exploded with thunderous applause. It was unmitigated bedlam.

Duke was pure magic, a showman par excellence. With every tune, with every bow, the crowd only grew to love him even more. And then came intermission, and perhaps the only time in my life that I felt unlucky to be the house pianist. No one in his right mind would choose to follow Duke Ellington.

But instead of making the hurried departure to which celebrities are entitled at intermission, he did something incredible. He stayed onstage: "Ladies and gentlemen, Johnny Hodges loves you madly. And Cootie Williams loves you madly." And he continued in his trademark manner, calling the individual members of the band by name, declaring that each one "loves you madly." He spoke in a caressing tone that settled and silenced the audience, now attentive and eager to hear what he had to say.

"And now, ladies and gentlemen, I'd like you to listen to a young friend of mine from Washington, D.C. I want to hear him, so I'd like to have you listen, too." And then, as though to force each person in the audience to the edge of his seat, he said my name slightly louder than a whisper: "Mr. Billy Taylor." At that golden moment, I never felt luckier to be the house pianist.

"Luck" is a very funny word when it comes to music. I've been described as lucky because of the seemingly accidental way in which certain strokes of good fortune came into my life. But someone once described luck as the place where preparation meets opportunity. In music, it's crucial to stay prepared, even if you're not sure just what you're preparing for. I had no idea that I'd get the call to play at Birdland. Had I not been prepared, however, that luck would have passed me up and gone to someone else.

I was working at Birdland in 1951, the year that my son Duane was born. I was literally on the stage when I got the call from someone at home that Teddi had gone to the hospital, so I left the club and raced uptown to be with her. By the time I reached the hospital, Duane had already arrived, and aside from the fact that he was the most beautiful baby I'd ever seen, the feeling I had at that moment is one that I've never quite been able to put into words. I could say that I was profoundly and deeply happy, but even those words fall short. Now I was responsible for the lives of the two people that I loved most in the world, and this intensified my passion and drive to be the best musician that I could be in order to support them.

Teddi was an excellent mother, and she created a warm and stable life for our family at a time when work often kept me away from home or on the road. She provided the day-to-day care and discipline, and though I would like to have expressed it better and more often back then, I realized that hers was no easy job. I am greatly indebted to her even today for all she's done for each of us, individually and collectively as a family.

Like his mother, Duane had light green eyes, and this was one of the first things I noticed about him. When he was still quite young, it became clear that Duane was a very bright little boy, artistically inclined, and very good with his hands. As a piano player, I had a great deal of dexterity, but when it came to assembling toy trains for my son, I was all thumbs! After watching his frustrated dad tinker unsuccessfully for some time with sets of toy trains, Duane mercifully came to my rescue: "It's okay, Dad," he consoled. "I'll put the trains together."

Teddi and I had certainly moved a long way from our carefree strolls in Paris back when we were newlyweds. We'd taken up residence in a housing development in Harlem called the Riverton, a family-friendly place where there was a playground and a community of young parents like us, many of whom worked in some aspect of show business, some of whom were quite famous. Another kind of reality was setting in, and along with it, a new and daunting, yet very welcome, sense of responsibility.

While I was at Birdland, Jo Jones informed me that he had arranged for me to do a job at a club in Boston, a brief engagement of no more than a couple of weeks. The gig was for the opening of George Wein's new jazz club, Storyville, which was located on the ground floor of the Hotel Buckminster in Kenmore Square, and the performances were to be broadcast live on the radio. Jo arranged for my temporary release to go to Boston, after which I would resume my work as house pianist at Birdland. He even went as far as to assemble the trio, which would consist of myself, Marquis Foster on drums, and Charles Mingus on bass. I'd heard and seen Charles Mingus play, but it wasn't until the four-hour train ride to Boston that I came to know him personally. As the train moved along the tracks, he and I had very sincere, and even slightly heated, conversations about jazz and how it was being played at the time, conversations during which Mingus made clear his desire to see the music evolve beyond bebop to its next level. Although we differed on many things, we had a very good-natured and jovial relationship, and getting to know and play with him was a fascinating experience.

I was in my early thirties at the time, and my professional life to that point consisted of the many wonderful opportunities I had to play a supportive role for other musicians. Every one of those experiences—from working with Ben Webster to working at Birdland—was indispensable. My two years at Birdland enabled me to build the reputation and the foundation I would need for the next phase of my life, at the center of which was supporting my family. Times were changing and my life was changing, and the moment had come for me to test out a new kind of independence, one involving a trio of my own.

For over fifteen years, from its beginning late in 1949 until it eventually closed in 1965, Birdland was the most important answer to a dying 52nd Street. Admission was $1.50, and shows started at 9:00 PM and often ran until the morning. Marilyn Monroe, Frank Sinatra, Sammy Davis Jr., and many other celebrities were seen there regularly. Without question, it was the place to be.

But there was a dark side. Backstage, some of the band members were taking collections for heroin. I had no interest in participating, and this caused me to lose some popularity with a few of the musicians who were involved in this. Charlie Parker himself was arrested for heroin possession in 1951, barely two years after the opening of the club named in his honor. As a result of his trouble with the law, he lost his cabaret card, which meant that he lost the right to legally work in clubs in the state of New York, including Birdland. By the time his cabaret card was restored, he was already on a downward spiral.

Bird was such a sensitive guy, such a genius of a musician, that I could never understand how he could stay on drugs, knowing that the dope was killing him musically and in every other way. But that is the power of addiction. Some years after I left Birdland, there was an occasion one year at the Newport Jazz Festival to discuss the problem of drug addiction among jazz musicians, a conversation facilitated by Nat Hentoff. We organized a committee, and with a grant of $5,000 (which went much further back in those days than it goes today) from the festival, our objective was to assist in the rehabilitation of some of those who had become addicted. But although our intentions were good, we soon discovered that we were naive. You see, if an addict were to approach us for the help we were trying to offer, we would then be obligated to report that person to the police. From that point, the person would be under constant surveillance by the police, who would be on the lookout for leads to pushers and other offenders they were hoping to arrest. Not only this, this musician seeking help would likely lose his cabaret card, which meant the inability to play in any clubs, and therefore the inability to earn an income. With no way to earn his living, this would create other problems. It was due to all of these complications that our committee had little success in actually getting help to the people that we knew needed it. A musician with a drug problem who knew he could risk losing his cabaret card simply for turning himself in was more likely to try and battle the addiction on his own. For too many, like Parker, this battle was too big to win.

Monte Kay decided to give up his job booking acts for Birdland and to turn his attention instead to a new place called Le Club Downbeat on 54th Street (not to be confused with the older Downbeat on 52nd Street where Billie Holiday performed). With a trio consisting of Charles Mingus on bass and Charlie Smith on drums, I started a residency at Le Downbeat. As it turned out, however, Mingus was beginning this work with me at about the same time that he was making up his mind to go out as a leader himself. I was also doing lots of Latin jazz at the time, which was not his preference, since the bass part in this style of music was more about articulating rhythms than doing chord changes. He was really coming into his own during that period, and he wanted the freedom to explore and experiment and do more of his own compositions. So Charles Mingus went out on his own, and he was replaced by Earl May.

I'd come a long way since my first experiences with leadership back in college with the Virginia Statesmen and the vocal group that sang with the band, the Debs and the Playboys. During our yearlong residency at Le Club Downbeat which started in 1951, my trio, consisting of Earl May on bass and Charlie Smith on drums, became known for playing lots of ballads, and our soft, mellow sound was nicknamed the "the Billy Taylor style." For the first time, people were coming night after night specifically to hear us. Le Downbeat was a small club, and in the back there were stairs that led to a balcony where about a dozen people could sit and look down on the bandstand. Back in those days, ladies would leave their husbands and children at home and come into the club just to relax and listen to the music. Listening to live music was a favorite and very respectable pastime of women who needed a break from the daily grind. The club owners were aware of this, so they were very protective of their female patrons. And the musicians understood and respected the fact that so many women found relaxation and solitude in good jazz.

Earl and Charlie were both very special musicians. Earl was one of the nicest people you'd ever want to meet—honest, genuine, and a fine musician. He was a self-taught bassist who tuned his bass G–D–A–E as right-handed players did but then played from the left-hand side of the bass, literally playing the instrument backward. Charlie Smith, who was also left-handed, was a very exciting and creative drummer, and he popularized playing with brushes, since sticks were too loud for most of the places where we performed. Charlie's inventiveness came in handy with regard to a particular piece I wrote titled "Cu-Blue." Although the record didn't sell a lot, it was a local turntable hit and everybody knew the tune. There were lots of requests for us to play it, but I didn't think it would sound right because the piece really called for a conga drummer. Once, Charlie overheard me turn down someone's request to hear the piece, and he stepped in and said, "Hey, wait, I can do that." And he did. He figured out a way to get the sound of the conga from his snare drum and tom-toms.

Charlie had worked with just about everybody in jazz, and his talent and creativity ensured that he was in constant demand. Eventually, other opportunities took him away from the trio. So I needed another drummer, someone who I not only respected as a musician, but someone who was sincere and dependable. In Charlie's place, I hired Percy Brice.

I played with many trios and quartets over the years, but the trio that consisted of myself, Percy Brice, and Earl May stayed together for several years. In that time, one of the more memorable experiences we had was with a Latin percussionist from Havana, Cuba. We were working at Le Club Downbeat, which was literally around the corner from the Palladium, the main Latin jazz dance hall on Broadway. Dizzy Gillespie had been one of the first to incorporate the conga drum into his music and had featured the great Cuban conga player Chano Pozo on his tune "Manteca." Unfortunately, the hot-tempered Chano was killed in a Harlem bar brawl. When Dizzy heard of another great Cuban percussionist, named Candido Camero, he was interested in auditioning him. Dizzy brought Candido to the club where we were working and asked if the drummer could sit in with us. At first, I said, "We already have a drummer," but the guy insisted. So Candido unloaded conga drums and bongos and amazed us all when his pair of hands transformed into dozens of hands and fingers going in multiple directions, playing several instruments at once! The owner of Le Club Downbeat hired Candido on the spot, before Dizzy ever had a chance to audition him. An honorary "fourth" member of our trio, Candido added a distinctive and powerful Latin flavoring to our music. Today, he is hailed as one of the greatest Cuban percussionists to ever live.

We played at Le Club Downbeat until about 1952, after which we were engaged at the Copacabana. Following that engagement, I took the trio on the road.

Touring took us away from our homes and families for weeks at a time. We lived together while we were on the road, so it was important that we were able to depend on each other. Aside from cold weather, touring in the North was usually uneventful. Touring in the South, however, was a different story. On one occasion, we drove all the way from Toronto to Atlanta. We stopped in Washington, D.C., but once we continued southward from there, we knew there would be no stopping until we reached Atlanta. Between those two points, restrooms and hotels were practically nonexistent for us. Times were changing, but they weren't changing fast enough in the southern cities where we encountered the worst of segregation. Once in Atlanta, we headed straight for the Sweet Auburn district, where, as in Washington, D.C., the black community had developed its own vibrant business enclave. There, we could get food and lodging in establishments owned and operated by our own people.

But none of our labor was in vain. As we lived day to day in the throes of making the music that we loved, people in the industry were taking notice in ways that we were not aware of. I don't think that any of us were necessarily in the business to win awards. Jazz was our life, and its addictive beauty compelled us to do what we did. Nonetheless, in 1953, I won my first major honor, *Down Beat*'s New Star International Critics Award.

By the mid-1950s, the trio was beginning to record prolifically, particularly with Prestige Records. It was during this time that we released tunes like "Theodora," "Cool and Caressing," "À Bientôt," and many other classic recordings, both of my own compositions and of many, many other works. On December 17, 1954, Percy, Earl, and I were booked to do a concert at Town Hall. The organizers wanted to know ahead of time what we would play, and so I sent in a program. One of the pieces I listed on the program was "Theodora," a ballad dedicated to my lovely wife. The problem, however, was that we were coming in from a gig in Pittsburgh on the same day as the Town Hall concert, and I had yet to actually compose "Theodora." I had a notion of how it should go, but I hadn't found the time to put the tune on paper. So I had just a short window of time in which to clean up from the Pittsburgh trip, write the piece, and get to Town Hall for the performance. So as soon as Teddi welcomed me home from the road, I convinced her to take Duane out to the park for a while so that I could finish some important work. While she was away from the house, I wrote "Theodora," and we premiered the piece that night. There was no time to rehearse the hot-off-the-press composition, so thank God for Earl May, who knew my style well enough to follow along by ear and pick up perfectly on the harmonic changes, some of which were off the beaten path. We were arranged on the stage so that both Percy and Earl were at the far end of the nine-foot grand piano I was playing, so there's no way Earl could see any of the written chart. The recording actually captures Earl using only his ears to supply the bass part of a piece he'd never heard before.

By the mid-1950s, I was a married man with two children. Beautiful like her mother, my daughter Kim was born in 1955, four years after Duane. She had the same strikingly gorgeous light green eyes as her mother and older brother, and when I looked at her, I was in awe and felt especially protective of her. I was also thankful that my children appeared to have inherited more of their mother's traits than mine. Kim was born the year after the landmark *Brown v. Board of Education* decision, which declared school segregation unconstitutional. The changing times signaled that my children would come of age in a world very different than the one I knew as a youngster. I had grown up with segregation, and I knew its dictates like the back of my hand—where to eat, where not to eat; where to sit, where not to sit; where to buy, where not to buy. But those barriers were crumbling, thank God, and my children would never have that experience. *Brown v. Board of Education* was the most sweeping victory of our lifetime, one that my mother could have hardly imagined back during her days of teaching in Greenville. And the demise of segregation was also evident in the music.

During the 1950s, African American teenagers and white teenagers began to dance in the same halls to exactly the same music, although some felt more comfortable referring to rhythm and blues as "rock and roll." The emerging stars of that music were people like Ruth Brown, Little Richard, and Ray Charles, all of whom had both black and white fans. Many cities, especially in the South, were so resistant to the mixing of the races, however, that it was common to see a rope stretched down the middle of the dance halls that teenagers frequented as a way to divide the races, literally keeping black kids on one side of the hall and white kids on the other. In the minds of many, the end of school segregation was a big threat to the familiar social order, and many were afraid, terrified of the thought that black and white children might actually get to know one another and become friends.

For all of its pain and humiliation, segregation had given us certain blessings, like closely knit communities, and it gave those from my era a strong and proud identification with the African American race. Segregation was the reason that someone the caliber of Marian Anderson might well lodge at my home, or at my cousin's home, or at my neighbor's home if she visited Washington, D.C. Segregation enhanced the odds that an eleven-year-old boy could walk a few paces from his front porch and stand in the shadow of Fats Waller. All of that was beginning to change.

It is with a certain longing that I recall the warmth and closeness of our communities back in those days. Yet, by the mid-1950s, we were tiring of second-class citizenship. Between 1954 and 1958, I was touring with the trio, and life on the road was always a gamble. Clubs were smaller, and our engagements were typically a week or two at a time. We'd sometimes get to an engagement only to find that the club was segregated, or we'd drive for hours and finally reach a hotel only to discover that it served whites only. At the same time, however, there was great optimism, and in the mid-1950s, we permitted ourselves to wonder out loud what life would be like if we could go anywhere, stay at any hotel, and eat at any lunch counter. We were touring the country when we got news of Rosa Parks and the Montgomery Bus Boycott. The success of the boycott added fuel to a fire that was growing hotter by the week. A full-fledged, nationwide Civil Rights Movement was stirring awake, and African Americans were ready to push the dream of freedom closer than ever before to reality.

This period of prolific recording coincided with the season during which I was finally coming into my own as an artist with a distinctive flavor and style. During the late 1950s, I had an opportunity to do a different kind of recording project with my friend Quincy Jones. In the mid-1940s, a teenaged Quincy Jones arrived in New York and got his first taste of 52nd Street. With an enormous talent and a musical sensibility well beyond his years, it quickly became obvious that this was a very special young man, and he was soon in demand as a writer and arranger for many well-known artists. Although he was a musical genius, his youth and innocence left him exposed to the brutal side of the music business. Unscrupulous people had no problem taking advantage of a newcomer who was talented, eager, and trusting. Although I wasn't that much older than he was, I tried to look out for him and offer him advice whenever he asked, in the same way that Jo Jones and others had looked out for me. It was normal for the older musicians to feel this sense of responsibility for their younger peers. In that context, we became friends. By the mid-1950s, Quincy was fully initiated, very well established, and highly regarded.

We had the opportunity to work on an exciting project. I'd done lots of playing and recording with my various trios, but we planned a recording for a much larger ensemble, for which Quincy would do the arranging. *My Fair Lady* had been a very successful musical on Broadway, so the idea was to do jazz versions of some of the signature tunes from the musical. Along with Earl May on bass and Ed Thigpen on drums, we had saxes, trumpets, mallet percussion, and guitar. The result was the album *My Fair Lady Loves Jazz*, which was released in 1957. The arrangements that Quincy did were just magnificent. Don Elliot was featured on the album doing quadruple duty on vibraphone, mellophone, bongos, and trumpet. Two sax players, Charlie Fowlkes and Gerry Mulligan, played on the album, but Gerry was not contracted to do the recording. It just happened that Gerry stopped into the studio while we were recording, and Charlie, who was playing baritone, had to leave for an engagement with the Count Basie band. So, since Gerry was there, he did the baritone sax parts in Charlie's absence, and that's how he ended up on the record. Today, that sort of spontaneous substitution might create some legal hassle, but back then, there was a different kind of easygoing camaraderie among musicians who knew and worked with each other. I miss that. After the release of the album, we had the opportunity to play the music for the cast of the musical, which was a thrilling experience.

By about 1957, I'd begun working regularly at a popular club called the Hickory House, a place known for its casual jam sessions and free and comfortable interaction between black and white musicians. The Hickory House also featured the great pianist Marian McPartland, a woman whom I'd actually met earlier while I was working at Birdland. Marian started working at the Hickory House in the early 1950s and is another woman whose work has gone largely unheralded. Born in England, she was a great admirer of Duke Ellington, Thelonious Monk, Count Basie, Bud Powell, and others, and drew a great deal of inspiration from Mary Lou Williams. Marian is someone who was destined to become very productive in jazz education and on radio, and over the years, the two of us have regarded each other as colleagues and good friends.

Although I was very fortunate to have amassed a following of fans that came regularly to the Hickory House to hear my trio, I was beginning to be faced with the challenge of keeping my playing fresh and creative. By that time, I'd recorded over 130 tunes, either on my own records or albums or with various groups. Audiences came to identify me with certain records that they liked, so they'd come expecting me to play their requests, something they certainly had a right to expect, and something that I tried my best to accommodate. In the process of fulfilling as many audience requests as I could of my most popular recordings, I found myself playing the same tunes again and again. This can be suicide for a jazz musician. I had to work hard to avoid getting into a rut, and I had to be very deliberate about finding ways to present new material, even when it meant that I had to decline to play some of the familiar pieces that fans wanted to hear. Although my busy schedule afforded me very little room for seeking out and experimenting with new material, I knew that my own musical vitality and that of the trio very much depended on keeping things fresh.

In addition to this challenge, the desire to teach about the music was still with me, and this desire may have been intensified by the new self-awareness that African Americans were embracing at that time. There were also some very progressive whites who were becoming open to dialoguing about music beyond the European classical repertoire.

One of the liberal, free-thinking whites who expressed genuine interest in jazz was Marshall Stearns, a college professor and jazz enthusiast. Stearns was connected to a larger community of artists, musicians, and scholars who gathered in the Berkshire Hills of Massachusetts at a new place called "Music Inn." A close neighbor to Tanglewood, Music Inn was established in 1950 when Phil and Stephanie Barber, a married couple involved in the arts, bought a piece of property that they wanted to dedicate to music and arts education. Managed by Jim Tite, Music Inn was a resort, a retreat, a think tank, an artist colony, a classroom, and an ongoing music festival and jam session all in one. It was open to visitors of all races and nationalities who wanted to perform with and for each other, to engage in stimulating conversation, and to learn from each other. Visitors to Music Inn ranged from dancers like Geoffrey Holder, to actresses like Butterfly McQueen, to writers like Langston Hughes, and to a whole host of musicians of nearly every persuasion, including European classical, blues, gospel, and jazz.

By the mid-1950s, I had developed a reputation in music circles as one willing to converse about jazz. So I was among the guests that Stearns invited to Music Inn. The atmosphere was charged with curiosity, and the creative and inquisitive people with whom I interacted had each come expecting to learn about the music beyond their own comfort zones. At the particular time that I attended, most of the guests there were classically trained. Consequently, much of the conversation about jazz fell to me, something that I embraced with great enthusiasm. These classically trained musicians treated me not as the "token jazz guy," but as one of their colleagues, and their interest in my perspective was both genuine and affirming. I would cross paths with Marshall Stearns again in 1958, a year during which two more opportunities brought my educational calling more clearly into focus.

The first of those two opportunities came to me along with my friend and colleague, pianist, composer, arranger, and bandleader, Stan Kenton. The two of us were invited to present at the 1958 annual meeting of the Music Educators National Conference. Founded in 1907, MENC was the largest organization in the country for music teachers at every level. I was thrilled because, in my mind, it seemed a real coup to be able to take my knowledge of jazz straight to the jugular vein of the country's most important think tank for music education. I was certain that the leadership of MENC would find my presentation informative and useful, and that they'd eagerly consider ways to develop and incorporate serious jazz-studies efforts into the music education curricula. And perhaps, in appreciation for my ideas and expertise, they'd invite me back the next year for a follow-up session.

And I couldn't have been more wrong! Both Stan and I left that meeting wondering why we'd even bothered to come in the first place. It turned out that we'd been invited to Los Angeles to merely decorate an agenda that had no intention of doing things any differently than they'd always been done. The reception that we got at that conference was very condescending and gave new meaning to the words, "Don't call us; we'll call you."

One reason for the cold reception had to do with the way that MENC evaluated credentials back in those days. I had a bachelor's degree in music, and I'd made my living playing professionally for fifteen years. I'd performed with people like Ben Webster, Dizzy Gillespie, and Count Basie, and had shared the stage with Duke Ellington. I was on records, on radio, and was the leader of a successful trio. I'd seen Jelly Roll Morton play stride piano and had watched while swing gave birth to bebop. I wrote the first book ever published on bebop. Those were my credentials.

MENC, however, couldn't have cared less. From their perspective, my lack of an advanced degree in music outweighed all of my other qualifications. This snobbery underscored a serious disconnect between music in the academic world and music in the *real* world.

But our presence at MENC wasn't a total loss. There were a few inquisitive teachers at the conference that had genuine respect for jazz and a real interest in sharing it with their students. Though disappointing in many respects, that encounter with MENC was the catalyst for some important endeavors. Out of the frustration of that experience came much of Stan Kenton's important contribution to jazz education. More acutely than ever, he felt the need to get the music into the schools, and he started using his ensemble as a laboratory band.

The very next year, he organized the country's first jazz band camp, at Indiana University, and he was instrumental in helping to found the National Association of Jazz Educators, later renamed the International Association of Jazz Educators.

A second opportunity in 1958 came by way of Marshall Stearns. By that time, his deep interest in jazz had turned to television, and in collaboration with Leonard Feather, he came up with the idea to do a series of thirteen shows as part of a program called *The Subject Is Jazz*. Although jazz had been on radio for decades, *The Subject Is Jazz* would be the very first program of its type to come to television. Stearns and Feather were both writers, however, and neither knew a thing about the practical aspects of musical direction or doing a television show. So it was for this purpose that they hired me. Having experienced rejection from MENC, it was crucial to me that *The Subject Is Jazz* develop into a high-quality, educational show.

The Subject Is Jazz was distributed through NBC network facilities to educational TV stations. Although a variety of different musicians performed on the show, my basic combo included Osie Johnson on drums, Eddie Safranski on bass, Mundell Lowe on guitar, Tony Scott on clarinet, Jimmy Cleveland on trombone, and Carl (later known as Doc) Severinsen on trumpet. The show featured some great music and stimulating conversations with people like Duke Ellington, Aaron Copland, and Leonard Bernstein, all of whom were serious connoisseurs of jazz. But a major flaw was the show's dry, stoic, and overly academic presentation. There were lots of people who knew and loved the music, people who would have made excellent commentators for the show. Even without advanced degrees, they would have been able to engage the audience and introduce the artists with heartfelt enthusiasm. Rather than get some known radio personality, the producer hired Gilbert Seldes, a Harvard-trained cultural critic who read to the television audience from his stack of handheld notes. I knew that the audience for *The Subject Is Jazz* was vastly different from the audience I typically encountered while I was performing in clubs. Gilbert Seldes was a conservative, grandfatherly type in his mid-sixties who sported a professorial bowtie and spoke in a sort of scholarly monotone, using carefully measured language as one does while delivering a lecture. He was an intellectual speaking to a Saturday-afternoon television audience of intellectuals who wanted to understand the music with their minds as much as they enjoyed it with their ears and hearts. Working in this context, it was my job to combine clear, articulate answers to Seldes's questions with musical demonstrations of whatever I was explaining.

For example, one episode was devoted to the question of improvisation. Seldes started by asking how improvisation worked in jazz. Before playing a note, I responded by discussing the importance of rapport between musicians, about the necessity of the instruments carrying the harmony—like the piano and the guitar—to acknowledge and cooperate with one another. After a short discussion, I then led the band in a performance of "Groovin'" to demonstrate what we'd just talked about.

By today's more sophisticated, high-tech standards, *The Subject Is Jazz* may seem like a very primitive and "square" attempt at using mass media to educate the public about the music. Yet, in some ways, the show was quite ahead of its time. One of the episodes, titled "The International Impact of Jazz," showcased several musicians from other countries, including Toshiko Akiyoshi, a rising star from Japan. Toshiko taught herself to play jazz piano by transcribing and studying Teddy Wilson's recorded performances. After gaining notoriety in Japan, she was discovered by Oscar Peterson and, soon after, was recruited to the United States to study at Berklee School of Music in Boston, one of the extremely rare institutions that offered any kind of collegiate jazz study at that time. Toshiko appeared on that episode wearing a kimono, and her playing erased any doubts as to whether an Oriental woman could swing! Of course, in the years since, Toshiko has enjoyed a stellar career.

During the thirteen-week run of *The Subject Is Jazz,* I also had an opportunity to perform some of my own compositions. Ed Thigpen came on the show and was the featured percussionist on "Titoro." He gave a fascinating discussion and demonstration of using the trap set to create a variety of sound effects. The last episode featured a composition that was my tribute to Charlie Parker, titled "Early Bird."

Thankfully, over those thirteen weeks, Seldes was converted. He gained an increased personal appreciation for jazz, and this enabled him to loosen up by the time *The Subject Is Jazz* had completed its run. He softened his scholarly persona, and his lectures took on a more relaxed, conversational tone. He closed the series by declaring that jazz was a legitimate form of musical expression. This is something that is taken for granted today but was a radical statement to make at the time, as few colleges and universities shared this view in the 1950s. To support his conviction about the legitimacy of jazz, Seldes's two invited guests for the final episode were composer and theorist George Russell and Columbia University Professor Dr. Robert Pace. Near the end of the final episode, viewers were given an address where they could send a postcard to request a discography and reading list to learn more about jazz. It seems ironic that this very conservative, academic, and somewhat rigid television series could serve as a vehicle for presenting music characterized by freedom, creativity, and risk taking. But *The Subject Is Jazz* was an important effort proving that if someone as straitlaced as Gilbert Seldes could become a fan of the music, anyone could!

Meanwhile, the trio was as active as ever, and in between my educational activities and appearances, Percy, Earl, and I continued to record, travel, and perform. We enjoyed some classic moments with many great artists, and one of my favorite memories is of a particular engagement we did in the late 1950s with Dinah Washington, one of the queens of song during that period. She sang with a distinctive clarity and tonal precision, and an approach so versatile that it was difficult to label her according to any one genre. Earlier in her life (when her name was Ruth Lee Jones), she was a gospel singer in a Pentecostal church. As she matured, she could be at one moment a blues singer, the next moment a jazz singer, and the next moment an R & B singer. Dinah had her share of personal struggles, but through it all, she kept a great sense of humor. She was especially fond of Percy and Earl, and whenever we played in Chicago, she made it a point to come and see us. One day, we were playing in a club and someone recognized her in the audience. He urged me to get her to come up and sing, but I refused because I didn't want to prevail upon her.

If she sang, it had to be her choice, but I didn't want to ask her. So the guy said, "Fine, I'll ask her." He asked if she'd come up and do something for us, and she responded, "Sure, I'll do something for you." So I went up to the bandstand to announce her: "Ladies and gentlemen, please welcome our very special guest, Miss Dinah Washington!"

I then took my seat at the piano, fully expecting, along with everyone else, to hear the sound of her golden voice. But to everyone's delighted surprise, she took *my* place at the piano and started to play! The Queen of Song never crooned a single syllable that night, but we were all in stitches and I laughed until I was on the floor! She'd pulled a fast one on all of us, and she loved every minute. This was very typical of Dinah Washington.

I managed to accomplish a lot during the 1950s. I'd become an established artist, and I had also accepted my calling to champion the cause of jazz, to speak and to write about the music whenever opportunities arose. The tide was also slowly turning in music education, where there was a small crack in the wall that prevented the study of jazz while it ensured that the same European repertoire and composers would be taught in perpetuity. But these hopeful signs were only a beginning.

FIVE

From "Tobacco Tags" to the Urban Airwaves

1959–1968

*I*N THE LATE 1950S, we were living in the Riverton, a very secure upper-middle-class Harlem housing development between 135th and 138th Streets. The group of ten or so buildings that made up the Riverton community served as an oasis, a peaceful and comfortable world apart from the normal frenzy of urban life. Many of our neighbors there were celebrities whose children played with ours. Although Kim and Duane were happy youngsters living in a safe and affirming environment, they'd gotten old enough to understand the disturbing images they saw on television. And they knew that people who resembled them—African Americans—were the subject of those unsettling scenes. Thanks to Teddi, we sat at dinner each evening in our tastefully appointed home where life was tranquil, fairly predictable, and good. And although we ourselves were far removed from the protests, bombings, and senseless murders of the South, Duane and Kim demanded to know why.

The air itself was charged and schizophrenic, at times invigorating us with excitement and hope, and at other times thickening with anger and frustration. Change was on the horizon, and there were signs all around. We wanted it and anticipated it. Many white Americans, however, feared and resented it. And by way of television, the fearful entered the living room of my Harlem home, spewing heated words within earshot of my innocent and curious children.

When I was a child, our people believed that achievement was the most powerful form of resistance. Our heroes were the likes of James Reese Europe, Roland Hayes, Paul Robeson, and Marian Anderson, and their lives showed us that hard work and *excellence* were the keys to gaining the world's respect. Neither hard work nor excellence could erase the color line, but they could take you around the world and earn you the high regard of presidents, kings, and other crowned heads of state. *Excellence* was the loophole, the enticing crack in an otherwise impenetrable racist wall. So we turned inward and worked hard to create ourselves in the image and likeness of what our elders believed we could become; and in the sequestered space of our warm, tightly knit communities, those elders hovered around us like eagles fiercely guarding their young. Civil Rights leaders? We had plenty of them! They were in every one of our Washington, D.C., classrooms, behind our pulpits, in our drugstores, on our street corners. But things were different now, and the community that was once a few blocks in a section of a single town was now expanded to encompass all of the black communities in all of the black sections in all of the American towns. Thanks first to radio, and now to television, we were becoming aware of one another to a degree never before possible. Television created contact between African Americans in Harlem and those in Mississippi, between the Sweet Auburn district in Atlanta and the South Side of Chicago. Television made it clear that whether in Sweet Auburn, or on U Street, or on Chicago's South Side, or in the Vine Street district of Kansas City, African Americans were engaged in a common struggle.

For much of the 1950s, I was on the road with various trios and quartets, playing and making a living. As we traveled, we encountered the usual inconveniences of segregation, as, for example, during a trip from Toronto to Atlanta. On the way, we stopped in Virginia and encountered trouble there in our attempt to use the restroom. Even so, the old order was beginning to shift in ways that signaled sweeping changes. It started with the announcement of the *Brown v. Board of Education* decision in 1954. In the summer of the next year, the murder trial of young Emmett Till was telecast. A Chicago teenager visiting his family in Mississippi, Till was brutally tortured and murdered for allegedly whistling at a white woman. Two white men were arrested for the crime but swiftly acquitted by an all-white jury. On their televisions, people across the nation viewed the perfunctory proceedings of the Tallahatchie Courthouse in Sumner, Mississippi, and, in horrified disbelief, became eyewitnesses to justice gone terribly awry. In December of that same year, Rosa Parks defied Alabama law by refusing to move to the back of the bus, and her courage ballooned into a bus boycott that went on for months. For the first time that any of us could recall, blacks in the South could celebrate a measure of success against the racial oppression that extended for generations back to the time of slavery. It was just one victory of many, but the success of the boycott energized not just those who lived in the South, but African Americans around the nation.

Early in 1960, the state of my birth began to stir awake with a new fire in its belly. I recall the North Carolina of my childhood memory as a place of quiet complacency, so quiet, in fact, that my mother was eager to move us to a more northern locale. Starting in February of 1960, however, the nation began to see another side of its black North Carolinians. African American college students in that state launched a series of sit-ins to protest segregation at stores and various businesses, first in Greensboro, and later in other cities. In Raleigh that same year, over forty African Americans were arrested for refusing to leave the sidewalk in front of the Woolworth's which refused them service because of their race. Although these protests were started by courageous young students at nearby black colleges, they soon found the support of the NAACP and the Congress of Racial Equality and gained national attention. The protestors were rock solid in their resolve and believed that it was only a matter of time before white businesses realized that they'd either have to offer equal service to black customers, or, without black support, they would have to shut down their businesses altogether. That year, students engaged in similar protests against segregation in Fayetteville, North Carolina; in Richmond, Virginia; in Chattanooga and in Nashville, Tennessee; in Madison, Wisconsin; and in many other places around the nation. Before very long, the young inspired the older African Americans, who, now in greater numbers than ever before, were willing to face being arrested, hosed down, chased by dogs, kicked and stomped, and whatever else the process required. And they were willing to face these consequences with calm, with dignity, and without flinching. Perhaps we were now on that road that would bring us freedom and first-class citizenship one step, one fight, one victory at a time.

These were our most pervasive thoughts in the 1960s, a time when the world seemed to redefine itself at every turn. And just as African Americans wrestled with a new definition of blackness, those of us who considered jazz our heritage viewed the music with a renewed sense of pride. More intensely than ever, I felt the need to impart knowledge of the music to those distracted and disheartened by the deafening turbulence of those days. And coupled with that need was a desire to attend to other matters of the heart.

For some time, I'd already been thinking seriously about my professional life in light of my role as husband and father. The road afforded us a respectable living, but it was no place for a man with two growing children. My wife Teddi made it clear that my children had reached the age where my presence was needed. Once again, it was my good fortune to be in the right place at the right time.

Jazz on radio was extremely common in the 1950s. At nearly all of the major clubs, there was a wire that put the musical performances on the air. At Birdland, for example, there were broadcasts every night, and my own recordings with John Coltrane and Miles Davis are from one of those broadcasts. The amount of jazz on radio at that time naturally led to a place for many jazz entertainers to get on television. During the 1950s, talk-show hosts like Steve Allen and Dave Garroway, and shows like *The Eddie Condon Floor Show, The Ed Sullivan Show,* and the *Colgate Comedy Hour* frequently featured jazz artists. You could turn on your television set and see people like Ella Fitzgerald, Sarah Vaughan, Louis Armstrong, and Teddy Wilson almost every night. In addition, many artists had their own local or regional programs.

I, too, was lucky enough to play several television gigs, one of the most memorable of which was a portrayal I did of Jelly Roll Morton in late 1954 on a show called *You Are There.* This television series ran from 1953 to 1957 and featured various episodes intended to transport the viewer back in time to a certain point in history. For example, one of the episodes was "Paul Revere's Ride" and the highlighted date in history was April 18, 1775. The particular episode in which I was cast was called "The

Emergence of Jazz," and the viewer was supposed to be able to imagine being in the Storyville section of New Orleans on November 20, 1917. This, of course, was the place where Jelly Roll came of age musically. Having actually met him in Washington, D.C., when I was a boy, I was very interested in bringing dignity to this role, as I felt that he never received the credit that was due him. As Jelly Roll Morton, I sat at the piano and demonstrated how the "Tiger Rag" evolved from an old quadrille, and in the process, I described the journey of jazz from Africa, to America, and finally to Storyville. Although I didn't seek any Academy Awards for my acting, I was certainly honored to present this great musician and to play his music for a television audience.

My start in radio had come back in college when several buddies of mine dared me to gain a spot on the *Tobacco Tags* radio show back in Petersburg. I never realized that this early work in broadcasting foreshadowed things to come. By the late 1950s, I'd already written more than fifteen or so show themes for radio disc jockeys around the country, including "Eddie's Theme," which was composed for a jazz disc jockey in Philadelphia; "Mood for Mendes," for disc jockey Jim Mendes in Hartford, Connecticut; and "Daddy-O," for Chicago's Daddy O'Daley. So beyond my performances, which were often broadcast over the air, I was known in the radio industry. There was a disc jockey named Phil Gordon, known to the public as Dr. Jive, who worked at WLIB. At that time, WLIB was one of the most important black-oriented radio stations in New York. Dr. Jive wanted to take some time off, so he invited me to substitute for him on the air. As it turns out, Dr. Jive never returned to that station, and what started as a temporary stand-in job became for me a permanent position.

WLIB was owned by two Jewish brothers, Morris and Harry Novik, and Harry, the general manager, changed the station's conservative, all-classical format. When I came aboard, I was the only one playing jazz on the station. Harry was committed to the kind of programming that the African American community wanted to hear, and for that reason, the station became a major sounding board and source of entertainment and information for listeners of color during that era. The radio station played gospel, rhythm and blues, and jazz, and even had a classical show featuring African American concert artists. I was still performing with my trio regularly at the Hickory House and at other venues in New York at that time, and having a daily radio program increased both my popularity and my marketability. Through this radio show, I was able to access an entirely new audience, and this became useful leverage when I approached my boss at the Hickory House for a raise. With a growing family to support, it was more important than ever that my earnings match my actual worth as closely as possible! This was all during my first period of employment with WLIB.

When I started with WLIB, the station was broadcasting from the Hotel Theresa. The year was 1959, and during my first few months at the radio station, it just so happened that the Hotel Theresa was the scene of international news. I remember being in the lobby waiting to get on the elevator, and just a short distance from me there was a bearded fellow in olive-colored fatigues with his entourage. This fellow and his bodyguards soon disappeared into the elevator as I stood intrigued at the history unfolding right before my eyes. Suspicious of whites, Fidel Castro had elected to stay at the Hotel Theresa during his first visit to the United States in April of 1959. Just months before, he'd seized power in Cuba, and already President Eisenhower was nervously watching as the revolutionary leader became close friends with the Soviets. Castro had hired a PR firm and had come to the United States that April to get the media attention that he hoped would sway American public opinion in his favor. I don't know how successful he was, but I was impressed to have chanced a glimpse of someone so much bigger than life right in the lobby of the building where I went to work every day.

At that point in my life, my focus was primarily on radio. I had amassed quite a record collection of my own, so I had the opportunity to feature recordings by many people with whom I'd already played, people that I knew personally. So in addition to playing and talking about the music, I enjoyed sharing interesting anecdotes both about the artists themselves and about my personal experiences as a performer. Although I played lots of the better-known jazz artists, I distinguished myself by also playing some of the more avant-garde, lesser-known artists. I programmed artists like George Russell and Ornette Coleman in large part because of my personal interest in what they were doing with the music. But programming the music wasn't my only job. Because WLIB was a small station, I also had to sell commercials and do assignments that were very community-oriented.

WLIB was a daylight station, and according to our license, we had to be off the air by dark. Consequently, we could broadcast for longer in the spring and summer, when daylight lasted later into the evening. Since the onset of nightfall would cause our signal to interfere with other signals, our airtime was shortened during the fall and winter months when the days were shorter. This worked out well for me, since my show rarely went later than around 9:00 PM, at which time I could leave the radio station to join the trio for our nightly performances.

During the time that I was working at WLIB, my daughter, Kim, came home one day singing a song she'd learned in school. When I tuned into what she was singing that particular day, I realized that it was a spiritual. But she didn't seem to understand the kind of feeling required for that type of song. So I immediately summoned her for a fatherly lecture on the correct and authentic way to sing our music. Kim loved to sing and did pretty well with all of the popular tunes she heard on radio and television. Motown was all the rage with youngsters at that time, and she and her brother liked the latest songs and dances. But she was the daughter of Billy Taylor, and it seemed unthinkable that there should be this gap in her knowledge of our musical heritage. So I was determined to educate her about the way a spiritual should be sung. As I sat at the piano, I invited her to come and observe: "See, I'll even make up a little tune to show you how it should *really* go," and I did. But to no avail. She had unwavering faith in the Sister at her Catholic elementary school and could not be persuaded that the song should sound any differently than she was initially taught.

For the moment, I gave up on teaching Kim the correct way to sing spirituals. But the song I created to demonstrate my point stuck with me, and its lyrics were about freedom, which, for African Americans, was the clarion cry of that era. It took me fifteen minutes to write the music and first verse of "I Wish I Knew How It Would Feel to Be Free." It took a co-writer, Dick Dallas, and almost another year, however, before I was satisfied with the final version of the song. That was how my most popular composition was born. "I Wish I Knew," for me, captured the essence of the Civil Rights Movement and was first recorded by Nina

Simone, whose classic rendition of the song has been widely emulated. Reverend Martin Luther King was a fan of the song. He was a lover of jazz and would come to the Hickory House on occasions when he was in New York. Because he could never remember the title of "I Wish I Knew," his way of requesting that I play it was to simply ask for "that Baptist-sounding song." Of course, I knew exactly what he meant and was happy to oblige. Since those days, it has been recorded by numerous artists, both African American and white, from Leontyne Price to Peter, Paul, and Mary, from Solomon Burke to Ahmad Jamal.

WLIB was at 1190 on the dial, and just next to it was WNEW, a major independent station in New York catering to a much more mainstream audience. Because WLIB and WNEW were literally next-door neighbors on the radio dial, the management of the larger station became aware of my popularity with the New York listening audience. This was the reason that, after my first two years with WLIB, I received an offer from WNEW to host a daily jazz show, an opportunity too attractive to ignore.

As I prepared to depart WLIB, I arranged for my very good friend, Mercer Ellington, to replace me at the station. Educated at Juilliard, Mercer was a fabulous jazz trumpeter, composer, and bandleader in his own right. As the son of Duke Ellington, however, he had his own unique cross to bear. Not only were there the inevitable comparisons between Mercer and his father, but there was the lingering sense of the need for his father's approval, understandable considering his father's fame around the world. But Mercer had something special of his own to offer, and those of us who were close to him realized that. Mercer was successful during his time at WLIB, and his work there was one of the times that the public had an opportunity to know and appreciate him apart from his famous father's legacy.

I was hired at WNEW in 1962 and became the station's first African American to host a daily program. Part of a large corporation, WNEW was located on 5th Avenue, three blocks from Radio City Music Hall. Situated in a more spacious studio, they could afford me extra conveniences like a piano, a turntable, and interview capability at my disposal. For example, while at WNEW, I had the opportunity to do a live taping with Count Basie, and on another occasion, I invited a young up-and-coming singer—Nancy Wilson—to come for an interview.

The comfort and safety of my job at WNEW seemed in striking contrast to the tensions ever brewing in the world around us. In 1962, along with my trio, I recorded a piece titled "Don't Go Down South." Although the piece was entirely instrumental, the title alone aptly summarized what many of us were feeling. The inspiration for the tune came from those courageous people, many of them students, who went down south repeatedly to push for freedom by bravely facing the many hardships that awaited them. They were willing to suffer indignities but were buoyed by their faith and commitment to the cause of justice and freedom. Although the title of the piece seems to be cynical and foreboding, the music itself is anything but. The music conveys the brightness and buoyancy that I associate with the undaunted spirits of those dedicated soldiers.

The year 1963 was one of rage and uncertainty, one during which televisions nationwide carried live footage of southern law enforcement turning high-powered water hoses and vicious police dogs on peaceful demonstrators. That year saw national guardsmen escort Vivian Malone and James Hood past a defiant Governor Wallace, who had attempted earlier in the day to block the two African Americans from registering at the University of Alabama. It was in 1963 that an angry segregationist ambushed Medgar Evers in the driveway of his Jackson, Mississippi, home. I was working at WNEW when I came in on a Saturday and heard the news that President Kennedy had been assassinated.

During these volatile and irrational times, a special friend of mine at WNEW was William B. Williams. A radio personality who traveled in the same circles with Frank Sinatra, William B. Williams was one of the most popular deejays in the country in the 1960s. His show, *Make Believe Ballroom*, ran from 5:00 until 7:00 in the evening, and my show, which came on at 7:00, started just after his. So it was always the case that his audience for the evening was also likely to hear me.

A kind and forward-thinking person, "William B" was very supportive of my presence at WNEW, and he took a personal interest in the simmering civil-rights struggle. He was also a high-ranking member of the Friars Club, and it was likely through his influence that the club sponsored a group of entertainers to go south to participate in fundraising activities leading up to the March on Washington, where Dr. King was scheduled to give his now famous "I Have a Dream" speech. Through his outspokenness, he made sure that WNEW could broadcast on location, and he insisted that I accompany him to Alabama early in August 1963 to broadcast and help cover the news.

The contingent of artists who arrived in Bull Connor's segregated territory that August included very well-known celebrities, both black and white. The sight of such racial mixture—dozens of blacks and whites getting off of planes and loading onto buses *together*—must have sent shock waves throughout Alabama. We were headed for the black community of Birmingham in a tired old bus that struggled to go thirty-five miles per hour on its best day. Yet, within no time, we looked behind us to see flashing lights and pealing sirens! The law pulled us over for speeding. It was their way of telling us just how unwelcome we were.

Upon arrival into Birmingham, we were informed that the City Auditorium we'd reserved for our concert was suddenly and mysteriously "closed for repairs." With high-profile personalities like Johnny Mathis, the Shirelles, Dick Gregory, Nina Simone, Joe Louis, Ray Charles, the Supremes, and many others, the concert had been widely advertised, and we suddenly found ourselves with a need for some venue large enough to accommodate thousands of fans. So we went to the football field of the nearby all-black Miles College, where the local African American community lavished us with plenty of food and warm hospitality. Eager young men quickly set about building a makeshift stage for what now became an outdoor performance.

Although this was one of the events intended to raise funds for the civil-rights struggle, I learned that there were many people in Alabama who cared much more for the music than for the politics. Even in "Bull Connor country," there were everyday white people who came with nothing in mind except to enjoy the music. I found this to be true as William B and I moved through the crowd with our microphones looking for people to interview. I approached a white gentleman who appeared to me in every way to be a native Alabaman: "Excuse me, sir, why did you happen to come to this particular concert?" I asked him, perhaps expecting to hear his opinion on the political purpose of the event. Instead, he looked at me with an incredulous expression on his face as though I'd just asked the stupidest of questions.

"I'm going to hear Ray Charles!" he said as though the answer should have been obvious, and then he walked on by. It was impossible to know whether this fellow was a fan of Bull Connor or of Dr. King, but he made it perfectly clear that he was a fan of Ray Charles! He was there to hear the music.

It was nearly nightfall by the time the bandstand was built and all of the equipment arranged, and some thirteen thousand people had gathered in the open air to see the show, many carrying their own chairs, and many others perfectly happy to sit or to stand on the grass. Every time a new act took the stage, the enthusiastic crowd jumped upon and lunged against the newly constructed bandstand, which wobbled beneath the pressure. Finally, it was my turn to introduce the headliner for the evening, Johnny Mathis. Smooth as velvet and dressed to "the nines," Johnny was the heartthrob of the decade, and I'd just introduced him when a swarm of star-struck pretty girls rushed to the front. With that, the stage and everything on it went crashing to the ground!

Understandably, there was panic. After all, this was Birmingham, and in the instant that the stage went down, no one was sure what had happened. In a city infamous for its racially motivated bombings, the collapsing stage generated a tidal wave of fear. Dr. King was sitting right in front and came to the stage. We had no high-powered spotlight, so a few people gathered around to shine flashlights on him as he raised both hands to quiet the terrified crowd.

He spoke with a father's authority: "Everybody be calm," he said. "It's nothing serious. We've had an accident because we've had too many people pulling on the stage." He took charge in a way that I don't think anyone else could. He turned to me and asked me to play something on the piano, but it was impossible for anyone to hear me, so Dr. King continued speaking, and the crowd started singing freedom songs as the stage was repaired. I don't remember to this day whether or not Johnny Mathis ever actually finished his performance.

Despite the loss of our venue, the collapse of the makeshift stage, and the sweltering August heat, the concert lasted until nearly 3:00 the next morning and was a big success.

My work at WNEW lasted two years. Afterward, I returned to WLIB, which had moved from the Hotel Theresa and was now broadcasting from the United Mutual Life Insurance Building on Lenox Avenue at 125th Street. Just a short distance from the entrance to that building was the street corner where Adam Clayton Powell preached to people about their civil rights long before there was any Civil Rights Movement. In the two years that I was away, there had been improvements, and now as an FM station, there were more programming possibilities. Although there were other black radio stations in New York, WLIB was dominant and became known for giving voice to African American concerns in a community with a long tradition of mobilizing its citizens at the grassroots level, and it was in this atmosphere abuzz with revolution that I aired my daily jazz program. On one particular occasion, I was on the air and this gentleman peeped in to ask about the recording I'd just played. After a few minutes of chatting, it became clear that he was a lover of jazz and knew more about the music than the average person. He talked about Lester Young and a few other artists, but our conversation was hurried because I was in the middle of my broadcast and had to get back to my show and he had to leave.

"When you get a minute, I'd like to talk to you again," he said to me and, with that, left me to continue my program. I later learned that the gentleman with whom I conversed that day was Malcolm X. Although I certainly knew who he was, I had never seen him before in person. It just so happened, however, that the mosque for the Nation of Islam was but a brief stroll away on 116th Street, and Malcolm X was a frequent visitor to WLIB, as the station would air programs featuring his commentary on current issues. I saw him several times after that and had the chance to chat with him about the music. His love for and knowledge about jazz left a very positive impression on me.

The year was 1964. What had begun as a movement of non-violence was now changing into something far more urgent. On one hand, the news was encouraging. In the summer of that year, President Johnson signed the Civil Rights Act, and at least on paper, it appeared that the federal government was committed to ending racial discrimination. I couldn't help but imagine what such an event thirty or forty years earlier might have meant to my parents, to Ms. Europe, to Mr. Grant, to Dr. Moore, and to the other great influences in my life. Despite segregation, they flourished intellectually, creatively, and artistically. What might they have become had they been able to soar in their early years without barriers? Within weeks, however, the passage of the 1964 Civil Rights Act was overshadowed by grim news carried over every wire in the nation: Three young men—James Cheney, Andrew Goodwin, and Michael Schwerner—were working to register black voters in Mississippi when they were reported missing. After weeks of searching, their bodies were discovered in a shallow grave. We craved freedom, but we cringed at its cost.

Even during those volatile times, people across racial lines welcomed and enjoyed our music. Throughout the 1930s and 1940s, jazz was musical fare for the common American, and back in those earlier days, the jazz of Duke Ellington, Count Basie, and Ella Fitzgerald provided the soundtrack for everyday life. Everyone appreciated jazz back then, since it was the popular music of that era, heard on radio, played on jukeboxes, and performed in clubs in cities around the nation. In those early days, radio stations featured actual musicians in their shows, which were always broadcast live. But when stations started programming recorded music, many of those musicians had to find some other way to earn a living. The AFM strike of the early 1940s also sent a good number of musicians in search of other occupations. The increasing popularity of television also changed the dynamic in the entertainment industry. Audiences who once frequented clubs to hear live musicians play were, by the 1960s, both much older and increasingly inclined to relax at home in front of their televisions and record players. And the generation that came of age in the 1950s ushered in a new sound—a blend of gospel, blues, big-band jazz, and country. African Americans called it rhythm and blues; white Americans called it rock and roll. And the record industry called it one big payday.

By the mid-1960s, rhythm and blues had become soul music, reflecting the serious and introspective mood of those anxious years. As courageous African Americans in cities around the South huddled together in mass meetings, singing freedom songs and risking life and limb to strategize and plan for the next act of resistance, lighthearted music for fun and dancing seemed increasingly irrelevant. So the freedom songs of the mass meetings and street protests became the model that transformed rhythm and blues into soul music, and many consider "I Wish I

Knew How It Would Feel to Be Free" representative of that style. I didn't set out to compose in any particular idiom; there was just something in the air, something that all of us wanted to express as best we could using the means at our disposal. For me, the means was music.

In spite of all that we stood to gain as a people, something precious was being lost. In every aspect of life, African Americans were anxious to part with any reminder of the oppressive past. But in our past were certain precious jewels, treasures not to be discarded. The spirit of the Civil Rights Movement gave rise to a generation of forward-looking people, and rightly so; yet in our drive toward the future, I felt the urgency, now more than ever, to make sure that the ties with our musical heritage were not permanently frayed. With its afros, "Black Power" rhetoric, and "Motown" moves, this generation needed to know its roots. They needed to know the heroes who provided the foundation for their hopes, people like Billie Holiday, who protested injustice in her classic rendition of "Strange Fruit," decades before the choruses that accompanied the marches and sit-ins. They needed to know that the energetic defiance they felt in the 1960s was already in the altered chords and shuffle rhythms of the jazz giants who'd gone on well before. And if they were to know this history, then someone would have to tell them.

The movement sparked questions about long-standing political practices in the arts. When it came to funding, the largest slices of the pie always went to institutions like the New York Philharmonic, to Broadway shows, and to museums. But the cultural institutions most relevant to people of color were always at the bottom of every list, if they made the list at all. It was the sort of benign neglect that sent a powerful message about what was valued and what was not.

For this and other reasons, jazz was at a delicate crossroads in the 1960s. Taking their cues from the European classical tradition, younger jazz artists began to embrace new notions of progress. Like Schoenberg's music, which was so cutting-edge that only the cerebral few could understand it, this new direction in jazz was so complex that the artists were leaving their audiences behind. Many artists of the 1960s and early 1970s were claiming a certain generational right to create their own kind of jazz without regard for audience response, an aesthetic too abstract for the average listener to follow. When I was becoming an adult, people of all ages enjoyed the *American Song Book* and *Jazz Classics*. Sure, the younger people had their own distinct preferences, but whatever our specific musical tastes, we understood our heritage and generally ate from the same table. By the 1960s, however, there was a generational split, one that was complete by the 1970s. In asserting their right to make their own kind of jazz, they broke with the artistic tradition that was the very definition of jazz itself. At its core, jazz was always meant to communicate with the listener on a personal level. Whenever music is more for the artist than for the audience, one must question both its purpose and its value.

At the same time, many of us were continuing in that traditional direction and we were trying to use music education to inform youngsters about the origin and history of jazz. It was also to our advantage that by the 1960s, there were many excellent books and radio and television programs that could help us trace the curve of the music.

It was in 1964 that I joined a new organization, the Harlem Cultural Council. This talented and energetic group was formed to promote the arts in our community. An interracial organization, the council included dancers, writers, musicians, and artists, all of whom felt the urge to bring much needed artistic enrichment to Harlem's youth. At that time, there were educational programs developed for minority children, but since they failed to include the arts, these programs essentially amounted to job-skills preparation. They included nothing to inform these youngsters about their cultural heritage, nothing to expand their sense of self-worth beyond the hope to someday be employed. The unspoken message here seemed to be that success for African American children went only as far as the ability to get a job. We considered this a serious omission, so the Harlem Cultural Council (HCC) aimed to fill this gap by providing our young people with exposure to the art, music, theatre, poetry, and dance that were so much a part of black identity and of American culture.

As with any group of energetic and passionate people, there were lively discussions and occasional differences of opinion. The council was a collection of gifted artists and arts advocates, each representing his or her own creative territory, with poets and dancers every bit as committed to their particular art forms as were the sculptors and actors. To complicate matters, there were also heated debates about race, debates that were sparked by the Black Arts Movement so prevalent at that time. There were challenging conversations and arguments about whether the European forms should or shouldn't be prioritized over African-derived forms. In the end, however, we were able to settle the question of music. It was imperative that these African American youngsters know that the only indigenous musical art form to be born from the African American experience was that which their forefathers created. Especially in Harlem, where so many jazz greats were bred and nurtured, it seemed unthinkable to me that the council would even consider overlooking this heritage. As for music, the only logical place to start with educating Harlem's youth was jazz.

But how was this to be done? Jazz education courses were not being offered at the public schools. Although a few lifeless monuments like the Apollo still stood, there were certainly no nearby theatres or places where these young people could go on any given day and chance a glimpse of someone like a Fats Waller. The once glorious 52nd Street had lost its former luster. The late-night jam sessions at Minton's that welcomed a newcomer to the city some twenty years earlier had all but hushed to a silence. A few nightclubs remained here and there in Harlem and in the Village, but even Birdland, the diehard symbol of that magical era, was singing her swan song. What had been the center, the mecca, the holy land of jazz, now lay in near ruins. Besides all of this, many of Harlem's young people were focused on survival, and going beyond the familiar in search of some new musical experience was low on the list of priorities.

One of the founding members of the HCC was New York arts patron Daphne Arnstein. Born in England, Daphne came to the United States in the early 1940s, settled in New York, and became heavily involved in all sorts of charitable and community projects. She was as committed as anyone to addressing the cultural deficiency of Harlem's youth, and one day, she proposed a radical idea, something outlandish, far-fetched, and never before attempted in New York's inner city. The idea was born when Daphne shared an experience she'd had recently at the World's Fair: "I was waiting to see an exhibit when I looked over and noticed a group of people following some musicians who were performing live around the fairgrounds. The musicians were on what appeared to be a flatbed truck that transported them from place to place, and everywhere they went, they attracted young people who walked alongside and seemed to really enjoy the music. *I wonder if something like this could be done in Harlem?"* Daphne asked.

What she suggested immediately triggered something in me, and the image she painted of musicians moving through the streets struck me as a way to reclaim the tradition of black presence and ownership in a community whose heritage included both the New York sophistication of classically trained artists like Francis Johnson, Will Marion Cook, and James Reese Europe, and the jazz innovation of the Dizzy Gillespies and Charlie Parkers of 52nd Street.

I jumped in and exclaimed, "That's it! We could do something like that, a sort of updated version of the New Orleans jazz parade! We could get the musicians to come and play right where the people live!"

Of course, when you open your mouth, you get the dubious privilege of being in charge of your own suggestion. And so there I was, faced with the task of bringing this wonderful possibility to fruition. I needed to not just secure musicians, but pay for those musicians. I'd done enough benefits during the course of my career to know that it would be unfair to impose on anyone to play for free, even for a good cause. A committee of us from the Harlem Cultural Council went to meet with representatives of the Ballantine Beer Company, and they very generously donated the money to do several concerts. We borrowed a float to transport the band and, with everything in place, were able to offer the community the inaugural season of what was to become a Harlem mainstay: Jazzmobile!

And the people loved it! We were able to bring world-class jazz artists directly to the neighborhoods and hearts of those in most desperate need of knowing their artistic heritage. I promoted Jazzmobile on the radio, and although I offered to do as many of the concerts as possible, we also invited well-known people from the community—like Dizzy and Lionel Hampton—to participate. For the first Jazzmobile performance, I put together a bebop group. We started on West 137th Street in Harlem and drove the float through about ten blocks of the neighborhood, inciting the curiosity of people peering out of their windows and from the rooftops. The music collected a crowd of curious adults and children along the way. Having amassed our audience, we circled back to 137th Street for an outdoor concert that lasted a couple of hours. The next performance was by Dizzy, and then afterward there was one by Lionel Hampton.

The summer of 1964 was perhaps both the worst time and the best time to initiate Jazzmobile. Harlem had been the scene of rioting since that July, and frustration and anger reached fever pitch when a fifteen-year-old boy in the community was shot and killed by police. Everyone seemed to be on edge that summer, and either in spite of this or because of this, the music was a welcome distraction, something beautiful and uplifting in the midst of troubled times.

In the early days of Jazzmobile, we'd start with a parade and then we'd stop and perform at a particular spot, such as a church or near a housing development. The first time we played near a housing project around 127th Street, the cops came around and warned us that our music would surely incite a riot. But instead, we were drawing people not just from that housing development, but from white, black, and Hispanic neighborhoods all around, and no riot ever occurred. The people just wanted to enjoy the music. It wasn't long before we were receiving invitations from different block associations in Brooklyn, the Bronx, and several of the other boroughs.

The reach of Daphne's idea extends to today, and on many occasions some fine young musician will tap me on the shoulder and say, "I became interested in jazz because Jazzmobile came to my neighborhood!"

As with anything new and different, Jazzmobile had its share of critics. There were those, for example, who opposed our sponsorship by a beer company. These critics, however, were unable to match their disapproval with the funds we needed. They were also uninformed. Few people stopped to consider, for example, that one of the most popular national weekly radio shows back in the 1930s, Benny Goodman's *Camel Caravan,* was sponsored by Camel Cigarettes. Many artists, including Don Redman, the Mills Brothers, and Duke Ellington, to name a few, all had sponsorship from a variety of companies that sold a variety of products. The point is that commercial sponsorship has always been partially to thank for getting jazz to audiences that might not otherwise have opportunities to hear and enjoy the music.

Still other critics of Jazzmobile resented Daphne because she was white. Here was a woman whose track record showed that she genuinely cared about the community, someone whose idea made a profound and lasting contribution. Yet some had the sense that she was condescending. This was an unfortunate perception, one that I could never really understand. This irrational and unfair assessment of Daphne was a part of a certain angry mindset shared by many young blacks in the 1960s, a mindset that automatically regarded white people with suspicion and contempt simply because they were white. Daphne was a kind and creative woman who deserved kindness in return.

In the end, however, the important thing is that Jazzmobile was a rousing success. We were not only able to entertain the people, but to inform and to uplift them in the process. The success of Jazzmobile even inspired the Harlem Cultural Council to support a similar project, Dancemobile. Jazzmobile proved back then, and continues to prove today, that age-old truth: New results require new risks.

And despite its sometimes tumultuous formative phase, the Harlem Cultural Council also grew to establish and achieve many important objectives for the community. Over the years, luminaries like Jean Blackwell Hutson, Romare Bearden, Nikki Giovanni, Geanie Faulkner, Frederick O'Neal, Katherine Dunham, Bruce Nugent, and many others came to be associated with this very important group.

If ever a community needed a Jazzmobile, that community was Harlem. The very next year, she would suffer one of her most painful losses. On Sunday afternoon, February 21, 1965, Malcolm X went to the Audubon Ballroom on 166th Street and Broadway to a rally where about four hundred people had come to hear him speak. Malcolm had recently taken a pilgrimage to Mecca and, deeply moved by the diversity he saw there, underwent a major conversion experience. This man, who once called whites "blue-eyed devils," decided that his separatist views were wrong. He parted with the Nation of Islam and, inspired by his new belief in the possibility of world brotherhood, Malcolm started the Organization of Afro-American Unity. The people gathered in the Audu-

bon that afternoon were interested in learning more about his change
of heart. He had barely begun to address the audience when a shower of
gunfire knocked him backward. The badly wounded leader was rushed
to Columbia-Presbyterian Hospital, where, about fifteen minutes after
the shooting, this champion of the people and lover of jazz—Malcolm X
—was pronounced dead.

My work at WLIB during this period was very important because I
felt that the music was necessary for the emotional healing of our community. I played lots of both new and familiar artists, and I especially
enjoyed playing John Coltrane's recordings on the air, in particular his
ballads. In 1967, John asked me to emcee a concert that he was planning
that April at the Olatunji Center for African Culture in Harlem. The
center was on 125th Street, which was just about a block away from the
station where we did the broadcasts for WLIB. Since I couldn't take
the day off from my work at the station, we decided to broadcast the
performance live. John had been away for a while and was doubtful that
very many people would turn out for the concert. But he was pleasantly
surprised that so many were there to hear him. The recording from that
concert, released much later, featured only two tunes, as his specialty
was extended improvisation. That was the last live recording he ever
did, and one of the last concerts of his life. I don't think that John ever
really realized the impact that he had on jazz, nor did he ever come to
know how much people loved and appreciated him and his music. He
would find it hard to believe that people are still fascinated with his
music today.

April 4, 1968, started out as a typical day. I'd performed with the
trio the night before and passed the day with the usual activities before
heading to WLIB for the evening's broadcast. By the time I arrived at
the radio station, however, we'd gotten the terrible news that Reverend
King had been shot in Memphis. Details were sketchy at first. The initial
report was that he'd gone there to support that city's sanitation workers
and had just given a powerful speech the night before, an eerily prophetic
sermon in which he proclaimed that he'd been to the mountaintop, had
seen the Promised Land. He'd said in his speech, "I may not get there
with you," almost as if he had a premonition about his fate and had resigned himself to it. But the rest of us could not wrap our minds around

what had just occurred. He was standing on the balcony of the Lorraine Motel, preparing to go to dinner with his close confidants. Suddenly, a shot rang out, and the great leader who had come to personify the fight for equal rights fell victim to the violence he so despised. By the time I signed onto the air, our worst fears were confirmed. He was dead. Time seemed to stand still while shock and grief settled over the entire station. Quiet tears streamed down faces in utter disbelief. The rage I felt inside was like the wakening of a long-dormant volcano, and I wanted to do something, take some action, maybe even strike out at something or someone. But my rage was encased in a sense of helplessness. Nothing seemed to matter anymore.

For many people, Dr. Martin Luther King's death marked the end of the belief in nonviolence. Soon after the news of his death was confirmed, there were reports of riots in city after city, more than a hundred according to some accounts. My heart ached at the news from back home in Washington, D.C. Rioting erupted in the black neighborhoods, causing numerous fires, injuries, and arrests. An area that was the scene of so many of my most cherished memories, the U Street corridor, went up in flames, permanently crippling once-vibrant local businesses. Shattered windows and burned-out buildings of inner-city Washington, D.C., would stand testament for the next several decades to the sad period of rage and self-destruction following Reverend King's assassination.

Unless something was done soon, Harlem would be next. Harry Novik, our general manager at WLIB, called the FCC to inform them that we must stay on the air past our nightfall curfew. Nerves frayed, tempers flared, and Harlem needed radio to escape her impending inferno. We broke the law and remained on the air. For the next several hours, we broadcast a soothing salve of words and music to people who needed us to take the edge off of the pain. Harry called every celebrity, city official, and community leader he could get and invited them to come to the station and speak on the air to the citizens of Harlem. Listeners were allowed to call in with remarks, and as they did, the broadcast took an interesting turn. Although there was an outpouring of anguish over Dr. King, the callers took the opportunity to air other grievances. For instance, someone would say to one of the city officials, right in the middle of the live broadcast, "As long as I have you on the phone, tell me how we can get someone down here to fix this streetlight!" So what started out as an effort to avert a riot evolved into a community forum as the citizens of Harlem aired various complaints. Our civil disobedience lasted the entire night, and when the morning came, Harlem, though weary and grief-stricken, was intact.

SIX

How It Feels to Be Free

1969–1990

SOMEHOW, IN THE MIDST of all of my activity, I had become middle-aged. When I was a boy back in Raleigh and later in Washington, D.C., I remember wondering why no one would speak up. Although I did as I was told, it bothered me that my place was at the back of the bus, or in the balconies of certain theatres, or at the water fountain marked "Colored." It disturbed me that the people I admired most—Marian Anderson, Roland Hayes, Paul Robeson, Fats Waller, Henry Grant, Mary Europe, and my own parents—were all confined to second-class citizenship despite their great accomplishments. And now, in the 1960s, African Americans were speaking up and paying dearly for it. The news broadcasts seemed to report one victim of violence after another, one fallen hero after another. First there was Medgar Evers, gunned down in front of his home in 1963; then there was President Kennedy, our advocate and our champion, killed later that same year in Dallas, Texas. Next was my friend Malcolm X, killed by African American separatists just two years after that. And three years later, we lost Dr. Martin Luther King. Within a few months of Dr. King's murder, our hopes that Bobby Kennedy might pick up where his brother left off were dashed when he, too, was killed by an assassin's bullet. The forward momentum of that whole decade seemed to be veiled in a cloud of mourning, confusion, and unrest. We barely had time to finish grieving over one tragedy before we were already hearing about the next one. Those of my generation understood that the birth pangs of the change we craved were a long time coming, and we knew that it would not come easy or cheap. We also knew that a cloud this thick and heavy was bound to give way to a brighter day.

Jazz was also at a crossroads. In the late 1960s, soul music and the Beatles were all the rage. In August of 1969, Woodstock attracted a half million rock-music devotees. The legendary clubs of 52nd Street, however, were either closed or virtually empty. Gone were many of the sacred places where the older lions once baptized the up-and-coming generation in jam sessions that imparted the sway, the saunter, the *swing,* and the spirit of the music. The corrective and affirming voices of those earlier jazz masters were hushed to an eerie silence that haunted barren walls of now desolate places to whose former glory I owed so great a debt. Despite the demise of the clubs, however, jazz awareness was already expanding in other ways. Through the books and articles that I had written going back to the 1940s, through the efforts of other music educators who were now taking a serious interest in understanding and promoting the music, through various radio features and television programs, we were seeing some success in attracting new audiences to the music. By the beginning of the 1970s, jazz education was beginning to emerge in a very promising way on college campuses all over the country. *Down Beat* magazine also turned its attention to jazz education and began providing instructional resources to its readers, who were curious about everything from voicing ninth chords to arranging for a combo. Many of us who'd cut our teeth on 52nd Street might not have been able to imagine the music apart from the clubs where we played in those early days, yet we were fortunate to have identified new venues for the music, as by the end of the 1960s, jazz could not depend primarily on clubs for its survival. Just as Neil Armstrong's 1969 walk on the moon signaled the dawn of a new era, jazz, too, would need to look to its own new frontiers.

I found great joy in seeing my children come into full bloom. In what seemed like the blink of an eye, Duane had gone from childhood to college, where he was majoring in art; and Kim, now an outspoken, articulate, and attractive teenager, already showed signs of a future in the field of law. As my own career evolved, Teddi had shouldered most of the responsibility for rearing our children. I was enormously grateful to my wife for the steadfast nurturing and guidance she gave to Kim and Duane during the years that my career took its many twists and turns.

We could only be proud of the healthy, intelligent, and well-balanced young adults they were becoming.

Neither of our children were musicians, but they inherited the drive and passion that were passed to me, the kind of persistence that would bode well for them, whatever their chosen fields. It was from my mother that I learned some of my earliest lessons in persistence. When I was a boy, I sat many times struggling at the piano, trying desperately to play some difficult passage or to master some technical feat. My mother had her own unique way of encouraging me to stay the course: "It doesn't sound like music yet," she'd remark as she passed me in the hallway where the piano was. It was her personal challenge to me, her tough-love way of urging me forward until the job was done. Thankfully, my children, each in their chosen fields of interest, inherited this persistence.

And yet, as I encountered my fifties, the job seemed somehow un-done. Even with a successful career that now included award-winning performances, recordings, publications, television, radio, and Jazzmo-bile, and even with the new audiences we were beginning to attract, there remained for me a nagging awareness of the work ahead, although I could not say with specificity what that work entailed. I only knew that the time for resting on my laurels would come far into the future, if it ever came at all.

There were many times in my career when some life-altering op-portunity seemed almost coincidental, an accident of synchronicity, the result of my being in the right place at the right time. Or perhaps it was simply that I'd learned well the lesson afforded me that day when I missed the chance to speak to Fats Waller. The painful sting of that experience taught me that some opportunities came only once in a life-time, and so it became my habit to seize every one that I could. And I found that even what seemed like dead-ends could sometimes lead to exciting new vistas. One such apparent dead-end led to my work on the *David Frost Show*.

David Frost was a big star who already had his own show in Great Britain. He was a political satirist who had been in the media in one way or another since the early 1960s, and his reputation had spread to the United States. In the early 1960s, Frost did a show called *That Was the Week that Was*. Humorous, irreverent, and politically charged, the show was a huge hit in England, so much so that NBC purchased the rights to do an American version of the show in 1964. I was hired to do the music for the American pilot of the show. However, I could not stay on as musical director at that time because of my contract with WNEW. The American version of *That Was the Week that Was* ran until 1965.

In 1969, David Frost decided to do a talk show in America, and he contacted me to serve as musical director for the *David Frost Show*, which ran from 1969 to 1972. At that time, I was the only African American musical director on television. David Frost became a household name, and his show, which hosted guests including Muhammad Ali, Louis Armstrong, Richard Nixon, Lawrence Welk, and Stevie Wonder, set the tone for talk shows that were to follow. Frost was the first to dare the hourlong celebrity interview, and he had a unique talent for making his guests relax, to gently disarm them so that they were speaking perhaps more candidly than they'd ever intended. I observed that his method was often to lean in so close to his guest and to fix his gaze on him or her so intently that, before long, the celebrity lost all awareness of the audience and began speaking with surprising—and sometimes embarrassing—transparency. Needless to say, the show was a hit and was broadcast five days per week, although David himself was there for only four. With another variety show back in England, Frost flew across the Atlantic Ocean each week to do double duty. He came to the States to do the talk show on Mondays and left for England again on Thursdays.

My job as musical director for the show was particularly exciting. I assembled a racially diverse band which included some of the best names in the business. On trumpet were Jimmy Owens and Dick Hurwitz, on trombone was Morty Bullman, and on reeds were Frank Wess, Seldon Powell, and George Berg. On guitar was Richie Resnicoff, the bass player was Bob Cranshaw, the drummer was Bob Thomas, and the percussion player was Marty Grupp. We played an hourlong concert every night before the show for the studio audience. But we weren't simply a jazz band. For the actual show, we did some of everything! We played for opera singers, for country-and-western groups, for pop groups, for casts from Broadway shows, and for amateurs from the audience. We even did music for animal acts. We had the kinds of musicians who were expert and versatile enough to handle both jazz and any other style of music required by the show. Some of the singers would arrive to the rehearsal with a full orchestral score. With just a couple of hours to go before the taping of the show, we'd have to quickly distill from that score an arrangement that would work for our ensemble. These guys were such experts that there was very little that I ever had to spell out for them. I could simply ask for an ending in some key—"give me an ending in the key of F"—and it would come out sounding like an arrangement they'd rehearsed. This band was a dream.

And David was a dream of a boss. He expressed genuine confidence in me and gave me a great deal of freedom. He'd tell me what he needed, and then he'd release me to do it. One day, he called me in his office and said, "Billy, we're doing a Christmas album." I said, "Okay, what are we doing on the album?" He said, "I'm reading a poem, and you're doing the rest." So, working alongside Harold Wheeler, Howard Roberts, and Phil Ramone, I organized and rehearsed the musicians and singers. David shared anecdotes between each cut and read his poem. The result was one of the best albums I've ever done, *From David Frost and Billy Taylor: Merry Christmas*.

On one of the shows, David featured me, Duke Ellington, and Willie "the Lion" Smith performing a three-piano version of "Perdido." We were each seated at our respective pianos as David came over to greet us. Just as he was about to introduce the three of us, Duke stopped him and asked if he could do the introduction instead. David agreed, and in his characteristic, velvety-smooth way, Duke began: "Ladies and Gentlemen, Mr. David Frost presents Willie 'the Lion' Smith, and . . ."

At that instant, feigning a moment of amnesia, Duke looked over at me and pretended that he couldn't remember my name! After a few seconds of struggling, and with perfect comedic timing, he finally completed the announcement as though his memory had suddenly returned: ". . . and Billy Taylor!" The audience responded with laughter and enthusiastic applause! What the audience didn't realize, however, was that Duke was paying me back for an incident that happened earlier. I had talked Duke into being a guest on *The Subject Is Jazz*, an experience which he found embarrassing. The host of the show, Gilbert Seldes, was asking questions that Duke considered ridiculously naive, and Duke would glance over at me with an expression that said, "You're kidding me, right?" In any case, he had a sense of humor, and kidding around with me that way on the *David Frost Show* was his good-natured revenge for subjecting him to such an uncomfortable conversation with Gilbert Seldes. That was the second time Duke introduced me, and a hilarious incident that I'll never forget.

Out of all of the guests and exciting moments that came with the *David Frost Show,* one incident was especially priceless. Back in those days, the Emmy Awards were hosted at Carnegie Hall, and the *David Frost Show* won two Emmys, in 1970 and in 1971, respectively. On one of those occasions, Teddi and I were sitting in the audience near David Frost and the woman who was his girlfriend.

"And the winner is David Frost!"

As the audience applauded, I leaned over and nudged Teddi. "Watch this," I said. Instantly, the camera cut to David Frost and his girlfriend— the stunning, African American star, Diahann Carroll! There for millions of viewers coast-to-coast to see was an interracial couple, a clear— and spontaneous—signal of the changing times.

I was known to the public because of radio, but there is a certain anonymity that radio announcers get to enjoy because people don't necessarily know what they look like. The *David Frost Show* changed all of that for me. I'd go over to Sardi's for a quick bite to eat, and suddenly someone would recognize me and ask for an autograph. Then someone else would do the same, and before I knew it, I was at a standstill on 44th Street signing dozens of autographs. I didn't mind at all; it was always a privilege to connect with the fans of the show.

The *David Frost Show* completed its run at around the same time that there was yet another national incident to occupy the minds of the American public. In June of 1972, there was a report about a burglary that took place at the offices of the Democratic National Committee. The incident occurred in Washington, D.C., in the Watergate office complex. As the investigation unfolded, it became clear that these were no ordinary burglars. Instead, the intruders were connected to the executive branch of the government. Within a few years after Nixon's resignation, David Frost bought the exclusive right to interview him. That famous 1977 interview, in which Frost disarms Nixon to the point of self-incrimination, has since become the topic of many conversations.

There was a distinct and undeniable changing of the guard in the early 1970s. As happens in every family when the matriarchs and patriarchs pass on and the younger generation is born, I was forced to face this natural cycle of things in the music that I loved. I don't like talking about or even thinking about death, but I suppose this uncomfortable subject is as much a part of the story of jazz as anything else.

Louis Armstrong died in 1971. When I was a young man coming of age on 52nd street in the 1940s, I always thought that Louis Armstrong was an "Uncle Tom." His incessant grin and hyper-cheerfulness seemed to confirm the false notion that many whites had of African Americans as people who were not to be taken seriously. His antics seemed to reflect the kinds of stereotypes that black people were trying desperately to overcome, and for this reason, I found his performance style offensive, even embarrassing. But as I got older, I came to realize that I judged too quickly. When I got to know Louis, I discovered that he was a man with great dignity and character. Jazz musicians of Armstrong's day rarely spoke much about the injustices they endured, if they spoke of them at all. They kept smiling, kept working, and used their music to speak for them. By the time he died, I had come to understand and respect him a great deal. Not enough people know that Louis Armstrong was a businessman, an activist, and a philanthropist. In 1931, he partially financed a New Orleans Negro Leagues team called "Armstrong's Secret Nine." During the 1950s, he spoke out publicly against segregation. And in 1969, he established and funded the Louis Armstrong Educational Foundation. The foundation has made a significant contribution to music education by developing programs, lectures, and workshops, and by contributing to scholarships and various music education endeavors for students of all ages. The foundation also contributes to Queens College, Brandeis University, and the Schomburg Center in Harlem. These are not the achievements of an "Uncle Tom," but of a man with intelligence and dignity who cared deeply both about his people and about music. I was invited to speak at Armstrong's funeral in Queens, New York, which was attended by tens of thousands. I barely made it through my tribute, as I was overcome with emotion.

Louis Armstrong was just one of several great jazz legends who passed away during the 1970s, and each departure was a tremendous loss.

Within a couple of years after the end of the *David Frost Show*, we lost the great Duke Ellington. This elder statesman had been my idol, my mentor, and my friend, and I could not help but feel a profound sense of grief when he passed away. From his early pioneering of the big-band sound, Duke's legacy covered the entire twentieth century, extends powerfully into the present day, and will reach far into this millennium and beyond. This elegant and prolific genius wrote thousands of compositions ranging from instrumental pieces to popular songs and film scores, made hundreds of recordings, starred in theatre and film, and performed all over the world. From modest beginnings in our shared hometown of Washington, D.C., Duke Ellington transcended all boundaries and came to occupy a unique place as one of the most important and beloved composers of America's Classical Music, jazz.

There are countless important jazz artists who have faded into obscurity, their accomplishments never heralded, their names rarely spoken these days. But I was comforted knowing that Duke had made his mark in such a way that his significance was abundantly clear, as was expressed by the president of the United States. In the spring of 1969, President and Mrs. Nixon hosted a seventieth-birthday celebration for Duke Ellington at the White House. Dozens of jazz luminaries were there—Cab Calloway, Count Basie, Dizzy Gillespie, Earl "Fatha" Hines, Gerry Mulligan, Clark Terry, Dave Brubeck, and many others. The evening started with President Nixon playing "Happy Birthday" for Duke and asking us all to sing along. The president then presented Duke with the Presidential Medal of Freedom, the highest civilian honor that one can attain. At one point, the president poked fun at the political double entendre of Duke's real name.

"I see here that your name is Edward Kennedy," and with that the president paused long enough for the guests to catch the humor. After several seconds, he added the surname "... Ellington." It was a hilarious moment, and everyone loved seeing this fun-loving side of Nixon. After a dinner, several of us played a concert that lasted until nearly midnight. This was a memorable occasion for Duke, and certainly no less than what he deserved.

Duke died in New York on May 24, 1974, and was eulogized at the Cathedral of St. John the Divine before a crowd of thousands of mourners which included all of the known names in jazz. The Duke Ellington Orchestra already had dates booked even when Duke's health was failing. So, before he died, he asked me, "Billy, I want you to conduct the orchestra." He wanted me to do what he did on some occasions, where he talked about the band and did brief commentaries during the performance. He was speaking of a particular booking in Bermuda. As it happened, the date that he asked me to conduct the orchestra in Bermuda was the day after the funeral. So I played at the funeral and accompanied several people, including Ella Fitzgerald and Joe Williams. And the next day, as difficult as it was, I got on a plane and went to Bermuda to do the concert as I promised him I would.

I am honored to have had the opportunity to step in for Duke in this way, but I think the person he might have called upon, had he still been living, was his right hand, Billy Strayhorn, another largely unsung hero of jazz. On many occasions, Duke acknowledged the integral role that Strayhorn played in his own career. But still, not enough people know the real story. Strayhorn was an incredibly talented pianist, composer, and arranger, as well as someone that Ellington trusted implicitly with musical tasks that he needed done but didn't have time to do himself. Back in the early 1940s, it was Strayhorn who helped to rescue Duke financially. Because Duke was an ASCAP artist, his music, like all ASCAP music, was banned from radio due to the big licensing dispute occurring at that time. But Duke depended on royalties from radio play to pay his band. So Strayhorn, who was not a member of ASCAP, stepped in to write a whole repertoire of songs that the Ellington band could legally play on the radio, and one of the songs that Strayhorn composed for this purpose was "Take the A Train."

Strayhorn was a friend of mine, and when he passed away in 1967, I was asked to play a tribute to him at his funeral. An interesting thing happened during the memorial service. I was still seated at the piano, and Ray Nance came up and told me that he wanted to play something in honor of Billy. He wasn't officially on the program, so I said, "What are you going to play?" He said "A Train." I said okay, and so he started, but very, very slowly. And it was beautiful. I had never played it that way before, but I was moved by this particular rendition performed at Strayhorn's funeral, and I've been playing it that way ever since. Everything

Billy Strayhorn did, even "Take the A Train" and some of his faster tunes, had a lovely melody.

Duke's passing felt to me like the end of an era, but neither he, nor Armstrong, nor Tatum would have wanted any of us to waste time in idle mourning. There was too much work to be done. I have always felt that the best way to pay homage to those older lions was to carry on the work that they left behind; and opportunities to do just that were seemingly always before me.

From early in my career, I always had a sense that part of my work somehow would involve bringing attention to the many marvelous female jazz artists whose achievements failed to garner the kind of spotlight given to their male counterparts. With my own daughter becoming a woman, I was sensitive to the problem of gender bias, and the very thought of Kim being slighted in any way because she was female really infuriated me. Mary Lou Williams is one of history's most underappreciated and misunderstood jazz artists. A great pianist, bandleader, composer, and arranger, Mary was a child prodigy who first performed in public when she was only six or seven years old. By the time she was in her twenties, she started working with and writing arrangements for bands. She was in enormous demand as an arranger, and everyone from Earl "Fatha" Hines, to Tommy Dorsey, to Louis Armstrong engaged her to write. By the time she was in her thirties, she was performing in clubs everywhere around the United States and Europe. At one point, Mary Lou became very frustrated with the music scene. She spent time in Europe and, while there, decided to convert to Catholicism and to abandon performing. Her feeling was that her musical life and her religious life could not coexist. Fortunately, however, her thinking changed when some priests led her to the understanding that her musical talent was a gift from God that should be celebrated and used at every opportunity. With this inner conflict resolved, Mary Lou returned to performing. Later in her life, Mary Lou served on the faculties of the University of Massachusetts–Amherst and Duke University.

Every musician I knew had the utmost respect and highest regard for this musical genius. She was the caliber of musician who could critique even giants like Thelonious Monk and Bud Powell, and they humbly took her advice because that's the level of respect they had for her. Many people don't realize that very early on, Mary Lou was already using all of the devices that later became famous in the bebop period. She was already doing the long lines, the expanded harmonies, and the innovative rhythms that later bebop artists used in their playing.

A bizarre incident occurred in which Mary Lou was unfairly criticized by people who didn't understand just how fluent she was in every style of jazz piano music from early ragtime forward. In 1971, there was a big Scott Joplin presentation at Lincoln Center, where Bill Bolcom, Joshua Rifkin, and Mary Lou were invited to come and play Joplin's music. Nine piano works were featured, and each artist was given three pieces to perform. Bolcom and Rifkin, both of whom were classically trained, each played their pieces with great accuracy and technical skill; in fact, if you were to follow along in the score, you'd see that their performances were perfectly obedient to what was on the page. When it was Mary Lou's turn to play, however, she took the approach of one who was a real native speaker of the music. She had not only composed and played in that style, but she understood how the original ragtime artists—many of whom didn't read music—would have done it, and she wanted to bring that authenticity to her performance. So she started by playing the melody, and then she improvised on it. The problem is that the critics didn't understand what she was doing. They were following along in the printed score, and when they saw that her playing departed from what was on the page, they accused her of being unprepared and of not knowing the music, when in actuality, the exact opposite was the case! Mary Lou knew the history and dialect of ragtime perhaps better than anyone else, and she was the only performer that night secure enough in the style to leave the printed page and improvise in the manner consistent with what the original rag players would have done. It disturbed me greatly that she would receive such rebuke from critics who were so grossly misinformed. It disturbed me even more that the average music lover didn't really know much about her at all.

I had been with the *David Frost Show* for a few months when I reconnected with a man who'd studied with Mary Lou Williams, a man whom I'd actually met much earlier back in the 1950s while I was playing with my trio at Le Downbeat. During one occasion, I noticed this one fellow in the audience who was listening very intently to us play and scribbling something on a notepad as fast as he could. I was intrigued, and after the set, I went over to introduce myself to him. It turns out that this young man was a musician and he was actually transcribing—accurately, I might add—my piano solo as I played it! This very impressive gentleman was Roland Wiggins.

Some twenty years had passed since that particular incident. Roland Wiggins was now on the faculty at the University of Massachusetts–Amherst. A successful protégé of Mary Lou Williams, he had gone on to study with Vincent Persichetti and Henry Cowell at Juilliard. He had become a noted music theorist and composer. By the time we reconnected in the early 1970s, Dr. Wiggins was part of a new program at the University of Massachusetts–Amherst designed to recruit noted African Americans to earn advanced degrees. And now he had come to recruit me. Some of those who agreed to enroll in this program included Bill Cosby, Betty Shabazz, and Yusef Lateef.

My work with the *David Frost Show* alone left me with a full plate of responsibilities, so it was perhaps not the most convenient time for me to pursue a doctorate degree. But I'd already been engaged to do some adjunct teaching at Manhattan School of Music and C. W. Post College. So, despite my busy schedule, there was no way to pass up such an opportunity in good conscience. It was not only a chance for me to better myself, but also a chance to better organize my teaching materials. I remembered my own mother's early days as a teacher in the "Jim Crow" South. I remembered the teachers with doctorate degrees at Dunbar High School whose prospects were curtailed by segregation, and I remembered the elitist snubs of the educators who noted my lack of credentials while they dismissed my life experiences and my wealth of musical achievement. Most importantly, perhaps, I saw where music education in this country was headed, and I knew that a doctorate degree would only help me to argue convincingly for the rightful place of America's Classical Music in our schools and colleges.

So I accepted the invitation from Dr. Wiggins and, for the first time since my days at Virginia State, I returned to the classroom and became a student again. This was a cutting session of an entirely different kind! I committed to a grueling schedule of commutes to Amherst and late-night study sessions, much of it while serving as musical director for the *David Frost Show.*

I continued to be very concerned about the public's awareness of jazz, and so in the early 1970s, I took advantage of opportunities to invest in black radio. I partnered with some other investors to purchase WSOK in Savannah, Georgia, and also joined a partnership to purchase WLIB. At that time, most black radio stations were white-owned, and the tendency of those owners was to do their musical programming in a way that was very chart-oriented, very dependent on what was selling the most at the time. But I was interested in expanding minds, in exposing people to all kinds of information that they never seemed to be able to access. Alongside jazz, I was interested in programming black classical music, and I also wanted meaningful community forums that allowed people to call in and discuss issues and ideas. Although I did not serve as musical director for either station, I expressed my thoughts about the direction in which I believed black radio should go.

The year 1972 was a watershed in many ways. Not only did it mark the end of the *David Frost Show,* the beginning of my return to the classroom, and the start of the Watergate scandal, but it was also the year that President Nixon appointed me to a six-year term on the National Council on the Arts. By this time, I had also served on the New York State Council on the Arts and the New York City Cultural Commission, and I had been very vocal and highly critical of the federal government's lack of support for the arts. I found it very disturbing that, at that time, the state of New York was giving more funding to the arts than the federal government was giving nationwide. With Nancy Hanks as chairman, others appointed to the National Council on the Arts that year included Duke Ellington, Clint Eastwood, James Earl Jones, Judith Jamison, Gregory Peck, Beverly Sills, Maurice Abravanel, and a number of other national figures who cared deeply about the place of the arts in American education.

To initiate our work on the council, Nancy organized a sort of brainstorming session and invited all of the members to attend a retreat for this purpose in Minnesota. After the meetings were over, there was a reception, and Nancy asked if I would play the piano. Of course, I agreed, and I began to play some tunes by Duke Ellington. As I played, Maurice Abravanel, whom I'd known years earlier when he was musical director for *The Seven Lively Arts* back in the 1940s, came over to me. As he listened, he remarked that the music was interesting, and he asked, "Do you think you could write something like that for orchestra?" We were at a party and I was feeling pretty good, so without much thought, I answered, "Sure," not expecting that anything would come of it. In social settings, people ask polite, rhetorical questions all the time. A few days later, however, I was surprised to get a call from Salt Lake City. It was Maurice Abravanel.

"I'm serious," he said. "I liked what you did, and I want to commission you to write something and come out and play it with the symphony orchestra here in the Mormon Tabernacle."

I gulped and paused for a moment. Had I been holding a cup of coffee, I am sure I would have dropped it! I thought to myself, "You've gotta be kidding!" This was a bit more involved than a sixteen-bar tune on a lead sheet.

Maurice became my coach, however, and over the next several months, he nursed me through the composition of *Suite for Jazz Piano and Orchestra*. Maurice was puzzled when, just before the premiere of the work, I sent him the score with nothing written out for piano.

"Where are the piano parts?" he asked.

"There aren't any," I told him. "I'm going to improvise."

"That's fine," he said, "But I need to know what you're deviating from!" So I sent him the basic melody with a harmonic framework—something like a lead sheet—and he was satisfied with that.

This was my first effort at a large-scale symphonic work, and I was very concerned about it. Added to my fear was the fact that the premiere was very widely publicized, as there was a great deal of curiosity as to how someone best known for jazz would fare in a decidedly classical setting. To make matters worse, he billed the program as "Mahler, Bartók, and Taylor." I'm not one to get stage fright, but on the evening of January 25, 1974—the night of the premiere—I was a bundle of nerves. Fortunately, the audience was great. They were very receptive, and the performance turned out quite well. *Suite for Jazz Piano and Orchestra* has been performed several times since, and a delightful feature of the work is that, because it features improvisation, it is fresh and different each time it's played, just as jazz should be.

During 1973 and 1974, details of the Watergate scandal continued to unfold, and the now embattled President Nixon was under mounting pressure to resign. Although his political popularity was rapidly declining, my personal feelings seemed to be at odds with prevailing sentiments about the nation's leader. I've never been naive about the weakness of the human condition and the reality that at any given time, any one of us is prone to failure of one sort or another. Whether someone becomes vulnerable to drug abuse or to moral impropriety, that vulnerability is itself something that we all share. A person's failure, however, never tells the entire story. No person deserves to be summed up in terms of the stains on his life when there are so many positive things to consider. I grew up in an era when the White House was off-limits to African Americans, unless you were the maid, the butler, the gardener, or someone uniquely privileged like Mary McLeod Bethune. Although I spent most of my childhood in Washington, D.C., and lived in close physical proximity to the Capitol and the other government buildings, these centers of power generally did not welcome people like me. When I went to the White House for the first time, it was for Richard Nixon's birthday celebration for Duke Ellington in 1969. I went again in 1970 along with David Frost to perform for the president's Christmas reception. I went to the White House in 1973, again at the president's invitation, to perform for the State Dinner. Needless to say, President Richard Nixon is someone that I came to respect and admire for reasons completely separate from his politics. The fact is that he opened the doors of the White House to jazz in a way that no president before him had done. By the time Larry Ridley, Bobby Thomas, and I performed for President Ford's State Dinner in 1975, the precedent was already set for jazz to be embraced by the White House, as America's Classical Music indeed should have been. I made several visits to the White House in later years. While the rest of the world may remember him for the Watergate scandal and his resignation in 1974, I remember President Richard Nixon as someone who deserves credit for helping to elevate jazz to its rightful place in the cultural life of the nation.

During this entire time, I was still a student laboring under the watchful gaze of the faculty at the University of Massachusetts–Amherst.

Finally, in 1975, I completed my dissertation, "The History and Development of Jazz Piano: A New Perspective for Music Teachers," thus finishing my doctorate degree. I was now part of the academic club and, as "Dr. Billy Taylor," hoped to do even more for the music that had given so much to me. I was humbled and grateful to be the recipient of honorary doctorates, but there was something about having an earned doctorate that gave me a different sense of legitimacy and empowerment, not for myself, but for jazz.

Many African Americans emerged from the angst of the 1960s with a new sense of pride and assertiveness in the 1970s. This was especially apparent on television, where the African American presence was becoming more pronounced than it had ever been before, and I had the good fortune to work with one of the very important television programs from that era.

Black Journal started as a national public-affairs show in 1968 and won an Emmy Award in 1969. The profile of the show changed remarkably, however, when Tony Brown became executive director in 1970. Brown had been dean of the School of Communications at Howard University and was a well-known journalist and commentator on issues of concern to African Americans. Brown's commentaries were straightforward, sometimes controversial, but always in line with his strong belief in black self-determination. Under Brown's direction, the show was unique in that its coverage not only included issues of concern to African Americans, but also addressed news relevant to black people throughout the African Diaspora. Brown also did interviews with famous entertainers of the day, like Sammy Davis Jr., Clifton Davis, Diahann Carroll, Melba Moore, and Lena Horne. But he was not one to shy away from controversy, by any means; his guests also included people like Muslim leader Louis Farrakhan, and Dr. William Shockley, who, at the other extreme end from Farrakhan, argued that blacks were genetically inferior to whites. One very interesting show featured Dr. Shockley in a debate with Dr. Frances Cress Welsing, a black female psychologist, who skillfully challenged Shockley's views. The show was carried on PBS. Because of the show's content, which many white viewers and critics viewed to be combative, Brown was frequently the recipient of angry letters and there were occasional threats to the show's existence.

But *Black Journal* had such a loyal viewing audience that Brown could easily enlist their support to ensure that the program stayed on the air even when the odds were not in the show's favor.

By 1976, the Pepsi-Cola company provided a large grant to underwrite the show, which was now commonly known as *Tony Brown's Journal.* During this same year, I became musical director for the show and had the wonderful experience of serving as composer, arranger, and conductor of an eighteen-piece band. While I played piano on occasion, I had another pianist and spent most of my time conducting, as I wanted to be sure that Mr. Brown's expectations were met. *Tony Brown's Journal* became one of the longest-running programs on PBS. Although this was another very meaningful activity on an already overcrowded plate, it was a much-needed opportunity at that point for me to really reconnect with music.

Staying connected to the music was the major challenge for me throughout the 1970s, I think. I was so busy studying, speaking, traveling, writing, and serving on various councils that it became a challenge for me to do the thing that I love most of all—actually play the music! I've always viewed myself as essentially a pianist and a composer. All the other things that I began to do were secondary. The piano is a jealous and unforgiving taskmaster, demanding regular time and attention. In my younger days, I had the luxury of focusing entirely on the instrument for hours and hours every day. Now that I was older and had become a spokesman for jazz, there were all of these other causes competing for my attention. I knew how important it was to keep practicing, to keep playing; and I knew how important it was to teach about jazz whenever the opportunity presented itself. I was caught between these two demands in my life—doing the music versus explaining the music—and the tension was not always easy to handle. But when you care deeply, you find a way. You somehow find that twenty-fifth hour in the day even though you know there are only twenty-four.

My relationship with radio resumed when, in the mid-1970s, National Public Radio conducted a poll that indicated a need for jazz programming. When NPR invited me to host the pilot, the reception was very positive, and what developed as a result was the series *Jazz Alive!* The show premiered in October of 1977 and was heard on more than two hundred stations across the country. In New York, the show aired on WNYC on Sunday evenings from 9:30 to 11:00 PM. *Jazz Alive!* was my opportunity to introduce new recordings and to interview both new artists and more familiar ones. Some of those featured on the show included Herbie Hancock, Dexter Gordon, Keith Jarrett, Sonny Rollins, Oliver Lake, and Ella Fitzgerald, to name a few. I also had the opportunity to feature my trio. *Jazz Alive!* lasted until 1983 and earned a Peabody Award.

By the mid-1970s, Jazzmobile had come into its own. When we started back in 1964, we were giving fewer than a dozen free summer concerts. During these concerts, it was especially rewarding to watch the kids gather around the bandstand and get close enough to the musicians to ask some very specific questions. For example, after a performance, a few kids would approach Bobby Thomas about playing the drums, and he'd take the time to answer their questions, giving what amounted to a drum lesson right there on the street! It was this kind of curiosity from the kids, and this kind of gracious attention from the musicians, that spurred the remarkable growth of Jazzmobile. By 1973, Jazzmobile was active not just in the summer, but throughout the entire year. We were giving about one hundred outdoor concerts in about a hundred different locations, and we'd even gone into the public schools in all five of New York's boroughs. In Harlem, we were doing weekly clinics for emerging young musicians. Jazzmobile had even begun to find its way into other cities, including Pittsburgh and Washington, D.C.

By the start of the 1980s, Billy Taylor Productions, which included two publishing companies, was operating out of an office on 57th Street, and Teddi was an enormous help to me during that period. Duane was in San Francisco enjoying a rewarding career with Wells Fargo Bank, and Kim had recently graduated from Yale Law School and was preparing for the bar. I was still traveling, writing, touring, and performing. By this time, I was playing on lots of college campuses.

Although I was doing well, I never took my good fortune for granted. At the same time, there were many organizations in the New York arts community that were suffering from cuts in funding. It always puzzles me that government leaders often fail to see the power that music and the arts have to enhance whole communities on every level. In January of 1980, we got the news that the city was proposing a major budget cut in the Department of Cultural Affairs. This news came at the same time that we learned that the State of New York and the National Endowment for the Arts would provide less funding than they had in previous years. To protest these cuts and talk seriously about the problems we shared, hundreds of leaders from various arts organizations—music, theatre, dance, and visual arts—gathered for the first time to rally at Lincoln Center. I was there as president of Jazzmobile. We discussed ways to make our government leaders aware of the importance of keeping music and the arts alive in New York City. Having grown up immersed in the very richest of cultural fare, and having made my career and my name in New York City, it seemed unthinkable to me that we had reached a place in our history when we were forced to justify the importance of the arts. To me, this was like having to justify the importance of food or water. Jazzmobile and similar organizations were doing their part to raise arts awareness, but having to actually argue for the importance of the arts seemed to be a new problem this country was facing. That Lincoln Center rally in 1980 was historic, and it strengthened my resolve to talk and teach about jazz at every opportunity. But it was only one of many occasions in the years since that I've had to join with others to remind the powers that be of how crucial support for the arts is to this country. These sobering moments always gave me new appreciation for each opportunity that came my way.

By the 1970s, New York's jazz community was listening faithfully to WRVR-FM. Amazingly, in a city as large and historically significant as New York, this was the *only* jazz station in operation at that time. WRVR served several very important functions. This particular radio station was a means for jazz labels to promote new recordings, and it was also an important source of information for people who wanted to keep abreast of what was happening with the music in various clubs around the city. So many of us were heartbroken in 1980 when Viacom purchased the station, put WRVR's extensive library of jazz records in storage, and converted it to a country format. The demise of New York's *only* jazz station effectively severed an important line of communication between the jazz clubs and record labels and the public on whom they depended for support.

The demise of WRVR teaches us an important lesson. Music must first be heard if it is to be appreciated. Once heard and appreciated, the music attracts support from consumers who are willing to purchase it on recordings or to pay to see it in live performances. The dollars that these consumers spend help to keep the artists employed. With this support from consumers, the artists can spend their time and energy on making more great music, which again, when heard by the public, enables this whole cycle to repeat. As musicians, we must do more than just play our instruments. We must remain aware not only of how this cycle works, but of the politics and commercialism surrounding decisions about what the public hears. It all starts with marketing, with keeping the public aware of jazz. Whenever the music faced these kinds of challenges, it only strengthened my resolve—and gave me additional opportunities—to do my part.

In April of 1981, I was playing a gig with bassist Victor Gaskin at the Knickerbocker in the Village when the CBS News show *Sunday Morning* came in to do a feature piece on me. This, incidentally, was one of my favorite TV shows. Around the time that the feature was aired, the musical director of the show had to go on leave because of illness. The decision was made to hire two people to replace her. One would cover classical music, and thanks to Charles Kuralt's recommendation, I was hired to cover jazz.

As the jazz correspondent on *CBS Sunday Morning,* I had the privilege of presenting many fine artists to a broad American audience, and these artists represented the range of people that jazz had come to influence by the 1980s. Chick Corea, Carmen McRae, Dizzy Gillespie, Benny Carter, Maynard Ferguson, Peggy Lee, and a young Harry Connick Jr. were some of the guests I featured on the show. These and other artists represented a diversity of backgrounds. In addition, I wanted to use that platform to teach something about the breadth of who we were as African Americans. One of my stories in 1988 was on Julius Williams, then an emerging African American conductor, composer, and jazz artist. Maestro Williams has achieved high acclaim as a classical artist and has performed and recorded around the world and has had his compositions premiered by the New York Philharmonic, the Detroit Symphony, and other prestigious groups.

One of the more interesting moments on *CBS Sunday Morning* came during a show I did on Bobby McFerrin, the vocalist whose most popular tune in the late 1980s was "Don't Worry, Be Happy." I also had a chance to feature his father, Robert McFerrin, who was a noted opera singer—in fact, the first African American man to perform in major roles at the Metropolitan Opera. I was intrigued by the contrast in their music styles and wanted to know what the classically trained father thought of his pop-artist son: "Well," he answered, "I don't like the way he dresses. He looks like a worker who's been sent on the stage to move the piano."

During the course of my time with *CBS Sunday Morning,* I was privileged to do profiles on more than 250 artists, some quite famous, some unknown, and these encounters were as much of a learning experience for me as I hope they were for the television audience.

Thanks to the mentorship of Maurice Abravanel on *Suite for Jazz Piano and Orchestra,* I had stepped out of my comfort zone to take on the composition of a large-scale work. In the early 1980s, I had that opportunity again when I was commissioned by the Atlanta Symphony to do an orchestral piece. I was asked specifically to write a work that conveyed my feelings about Dr. King, and since Dr. King was from Atlanta, I was very honored to take on this task. The result was *Peaceful Warrior,* which premiered in 1984.

I wrote both the music and the text, and the text was based upon things that I actually heard Dr. King say in private conversation back in the 1960s. I had occasion to overhear these conversations because I was the musical director for Mr. and Mrs. Jackie Robinson, who would hold picnics and various gatherings at their home in Connecticut to get their neighbors and friends involved in the fight for civil rights. Reverend King was often present. On one particular occasion, we were doing a benefit for the Southern Christian Leadership Conference. The Robinsons had a very large piece of property where they could invite several hundred guests. My role at these events was to coordinate the music and get the various performers on- and offstage as guests were mingling and eating. Reverend King was there, and I remember overhearing a sharp young man attempt to impress a young lady he was with by putting Dr. King on the spot with what he believed was a difficult question. He asked, "How do you feel when someone my age tells you that he prefers Malcolm X to your nonviolent approach?"

I listened in because I was very curious as to how Reverend King would respond. The young man had asked the question loudly enough for several standing nearby to hear.

Dr. King was unfazed and answered very quietly, "Son, it should be a matter of pride for you to know and understand who you support and why. If you prefer Malcolm X, you should say that with confidence and you should be able to say why you feel that way. It doesn't matter what anyone else thinks." This statement, "It's a Matter of Pride," provided the inspiration and title for the first movement of *Peaceful Warrior.*

On the same occasion at the Robinson home, one of the guests there approached Dr. King to express how much she would love to travel with him as he went to various places in the South to work for equality. But she said that her family obligations made it difficult for her to leave her home and children in Connecticut. She wondered how she could be of use to the movement.

Dr. King said to her, "Thanks for your interest. But if you are really concerned, then show it. Show it right here. There are things you can do to make a difference right where you are, and we need all the help we can get in Connecticut." This statement, "If You Are Really Concerned, Then Show It," became the title for the third movement of *Peaceful Warrior.* For the middle movement of the piece, I developed the text from the phrase "His Name Was Martin."

Along with the Atlanta Symphony, the premiere featured my trio with Chip Jackson on bass and Steve Johns on drums, as well as a chorus of 130 voices including singers from Morehouse College, Spelman College, and the Atlanta Center Community Choir, conducted by Robert Shaw.

The February 2, 1984, premiere of *Peaceful Warrior* was part of an effort started by the Atlanta Symphony called the "American Music Project." The purpose of this project was to expose audiences to contemporary music by American composers. I was one of thirteen composers invited to participate. Others included Karel Husa, Henry Brant, and Tyler White.

The honor of writing *Peaceful Warrior* came at about the time that I was beginning to express some thoughts about American music—specifically jazz—and the music industry. In 1985, my trio and I were invited to participate in a very exciting gala concert at the Hungarian State Opera House in Budapest. Thirty-five nations were invited to be a part of this concert, and my trio had the honor of representing the United States. The concert was simulcast on Hungary's national television and radio networks and was viewed by millions of people all over Eastern Europe. The purpose of the concert was to demonstrate the use of the arts and technology for bringing about unity between diverse groups of people. The audience of millions had the chance to hear a wide variety of music, including classical pieces, folk music, and, of course, jazz. The European audience's reaction to jazz was so overwhelmingly positive and enthusiastic that it brought home to me the fact that the American music industry was really overlooking a very valuable national treasure. In the same way that Europe's classical music had come to America centuries ago, now America's Classical Music was finding an enthusiastic reception with international audiences. It seemed deeply unfortunate to me that our own music industry right here at home did not seem to share this enthusiasm. The industry seemed focused on marketing music entirely for profit, while one of our most important cultural treasures—jazz—was left to wane. In the late 1980s, someone asked me if jazz had trouble competing with rap. My answer was, "Of course!" Each generation has the right to the entertainment of its day. But in working with Jazzmobile, I've had kids come to me countless times and say, "This is my first time ever even hearing jazz." When a kid in New York City—the site of Minton's, and the Apollo, and 52nd Street—says to me that their first and only exposure to jazz was through Jazzmobile, it's an indication of how much work we have left to do.

For this reason, it was with mixed feelings that I accepted *Down Beat's* Lifetime Achievement Award in 1984. It was my strong belief that every American child should have access to and appreciation for the music of his or her own native land. I was delighted to speak and work with young people at schools all over the country. I was especially excited to help found the "Jazz in July" summer program along with Max Roach and Dr. Frederick Tillis at my alma mater, the University of Massachu-setts–Amherst. This program has connected me to thousands of serious young players over the years. While very rewarding, however, the irony is that each of these school visits, lectures, workshops, and summer pro-grams reminded me that we still had so much further to go in educating our young people about jazz.

I had only reached my early sixties and rejected the notion that my work was somehow over, as "lifetime achievement" might imply. Yet I was coming to the realization that it was time for me to begin to rethink my activities and prioritize the things that were most important. By the late 1980s, Jazzmobile had flourished to the point that I was convinced that it could stand entirely on its own. Despite the fact that it was now a multifaceted and widely recognized institution, its heartbeat remained in Harlem. The thought of resigning as president of Jazzmobile was bit-tersweet. Daphne's idea had gone much, much further than either of us could have ever imagined. But it was time for me to step aside and allow the band on wheels to travel down the road of its own future. Under new leadership, Jazzmobile would be in good hands.

SEVEN

Reflections

I LISTEN TO THOSE OLD RECORDS and I can't believe that there was a time that I could play that fast! I miss the dexterity of my youth. And I miss those old days, that affirming sense of camaraderie we had when jazz was our gathering place. I even miss those smoke-filled, hot, and crowded clubs, the happy sounds of chattering people, clinking glasses, toasting the night that always seemed young, people that were there to hear us, to actually stop and *listen* to the band play. I have never been a smoker, and I've always hated the smell of cigarette smoke even though I've played in many different places, in various kinds of atmospheres. But somehow, whenever I was in the moment, whenever I played, the music made me forget about the nicotine. Music sometimes induces a temporary amnesia that I welcome. It makes me forget that I'm supposedly a senior citizen and that each day now I need a few minutes to steady myself when I get out of bed in the morning. Sometimes I misplace things and need help finding my glasses or keeping track of my schedule. But whenever I sit down and place my fingers on the piano keys—whether on a shiny, well-maintained Steinway, or on a less-than-pristine instrument with a key or two sticking or missing—somehow, music answers me, meets me right where I am, enlivens and rejuvenates me. There is a love affair there that always makes me forget what is wrong and draws my attention to all that is right. A few years ago, I started using more of my left hand than I ever did in my earlier days. I had to do that out of necessity. Music didn't scold me, question me, or ask me to explain; it just welcomed the change and said, "Here, I've got some marvelous things for your left hand to do." I think my right hand became envious!!

The music made us forget that society said people should be separate, made us forget—temporarily, at least—the threatening and divisive signs that labeled us and confined us to places that were either "White Only" or "Colored Only." Long before there were marches and sit-ins, protests and demonstrations, long before there were people yelling and screaming and shooting and killing each other because of their differences, there we were, united around our music, stomping at the Savoy, at the Apollo, at Small's Paradise, dancing and swaying to America's Classical Music, jazz! We were a democracy offering equal rights to all who could swing. That was the question—the only question—*Can you swing?* It didn't matter if you were as white as Carl Kress on guitar, or Al Haig on piano, or Marty Marsala on trumpet, or as Cuban as Candido on percussion, or as African American as one of us; it didn't matter if your skin was light or dark, or if your lips were thick or thin, or if your hair was straight or curly or kinky; didn't matter whether you spoke with an accent or talked jive; didn't even matter whether you could read music, or if you played only by ear. Didn't matter which part of the bus you rode on or which side of the street you walked on or who you loved when you left the club or who was beside you when you woke up in the morning. Jazz made those differences irrelevant, pushed all of that nonsense to the background. The only thing that mattered was the sound and the feel you produced, what happened when you placed your fingers on the piano, or your mouth on your horn, or when you plucked the string on your upright bass. *Can you swing?* That's all anyone wanted to know, whether you were young or old, whether you were a woman or a man. Women never got their fair shake in jazz, and we are still working to correct that inequity. But despite that unfairness, there were women who could hold their own, who could swing so powerfully that they shamed the men into conceding defeat. While the music played, your *swing* was all that mattered.

Music can teach us a lot about getting along with each other. Jazz is a perfect expression of the democracy, the equality, the freedom, and the individualism that this country values. Jazz is what America is supposed to be. If only we could live the way that jazz sounds, blending our different melodies, creating new lines and improvising new ways to harmonize, offering everybody a chance to take a solo. . . . That would be a beautiful thing.

Americans are often unaware of the treasure we have in jazz, in our own classical music. The naiveté about jazz that typifies many viewpoints came home to me during an interview that I did, along with Dick Wellstood, on PBS's *Firing Line* back in December of 1980. William F. Buckley Jr. was the host, and he started with a few questions that gave me and Dick the opportunity to explain some fundamental things about the history of the music, how Gershwin and Glen Miller fit into jazz, the way improvisation works, and so forth. The conversation was amicable at first, and I appreciated the opportunity to begin with topics that I felt were substantive and meaningful for the listening audience. The tone of the conversation began to change, however, when he started asking things which, to me, seemed to subtly question the value of jazz: "Well, Mr. Taylor, if jazz is such a distinctive part of American culture, then why has it been so slow in crossing international boundaries as compared with rock music, which seems to have gone around the world at the speed of light?"

This gave me a chance to explain the important link between the marketing of rock music with the assistance of mass media, like television, radio, recordings, and movies. Not only did technology aid in the rapid dissemination of rock music around the world, but the music business had also developed the savvy to target a specific market of consumers that simply did not exist during the 1930s and 1940s when jazz was in its heyday: teenagers. I also pointed out to him that the Captain and Tennille and Sonny and Cher had their own television shows, while some of the greatest names in jazz, like Ella Fitzgerald and Duke Ellington, never did. More sophisticated marketing and advances in technology developed in tandem with the emergence of rock music, and the music business really exploited this situation to sell to as many young consumers as possible.

I then explained to him that, despite all of this, jazz has, indeed, found a very welcoming international audience. A few months prior to that interview, we'd done some very successful performances in Budapest. I explained to him that in many places throughout Europe, you could find jazz festivals from May to October, and I pointed out to him the number of Europeans who were not only playing jazz, but were also composing the music.

He then took the conversation to a place that really irritated me. In fact, he hit such a nerve that I really had to remind myself to maintain my composure.

Buckley asked this most ridiculous question loaded with ignorant assumptions: "Why can't classical musicians ever have a drink before they play, but people who play jazz, like Art Tatum, for instance, seemed to have no difficulty drinking and playing? Is it because you're always playing by ear, and under the circumstances, your fingers just pretty much go where you want them to?"

If ever there was a moment I might have been inclined to lose it on the air, this was it. Not only did he insult my mentor, but he referenced that old stereotype that jazz and substance abuse somehow go hand in hand. His question also seemed to imply that jazz, as compared to classical performance, was somehow lacking in discipline and rigor, since, after all, jazz is just playing by ear anyway.

I contained myself and answered from my own personal experience. I said to him, "I'm amazed that anyone can do that. I can't. When I was young, I learned that if I drink and try to play, it goes straight to my fingers."

I then explained to him my relationship with Billie Holiday and Charlie Parker, two jazz greats who both had chronic drug problems. And despite the unfortunate association that is perceived between jazz and alcohol and drugs, I know from having worked with artists who struggled with addiction that their performances were never as good when they were high as when they were sober. Charlie Parker knew that kids were trying to emulate not just his music, but also his habits, and he tried very hard to dissuade them and get them to understand that the drugs were a liability.

That interview with Buckley was not my favorite, but at least it gave me the chance to try and dispel some misinformation about jazz. And Dick and I got to play some music, which helped to lighten things up a bit.

It always fascinates me that people from other countries have an enormous appreciation for jazz, and they recognize its power both aesthetically and socially, much more readily than we tend to do here at home. In 1995, I had the pleasure of doing a concert for the Asia Society's "Cross Overs" Festival and shared the stage with the Jon Jang Sextet. This performance was intended to link the sounds of American jazz with sounds of the East. It seems that our neighbors around the world have a keen awareness of the power of jazz to forge connections across cultural lines, and it is always rewarding when we reach out to each other through the music and communicate across the barriers that would otherwise separate us.

As Americans, we sometimes tend to become distracted and led astray by fads, sensationalism, quick thrills, and tabloid headlines. Back in 1998, I was invited to the White House to participate in one part of a series of discussions on jazz. This happened to be during the time that the press was having a field day with President Clinton and the Monica Lewinsky affair. At that time, there was talk of impeaching the president, so the journalists who were supposedly covering the jazz series were distracted by that. About a hundred people attended the lecture, including my friends Marian McPartland, Wynton Marsalis, and Wayne Shorter. The audience also included several dignitaries, among them the president of Czechoslovakia, Vaclav Havel. The session was broadcast on C-Span and featured the president's own comments about how jazz had influenced him personally. After I and others spoke and played various excerpts to demonstrate our points, the floor was opened for comments and questions. Suddenly, President Havel, who was quite advanced in age, struggled to his feet and reminded us all of what was really important. He described how, in his country's history, jazz had been driven underground, first by the Nazis and then by the Communists. He spoke passionately about how dangerous the music was considered to be by these oppressive regimes, precisely because jazz was such a powerful symbol of freedom. At a time when the journalists were focused on finding something in the glances and subtle gestures between Mr. and Mrs. Clinton, President Havel reminded us that jazz was now an international treasure that had very deep meaning for people around the world, people who did not have the luxury of taking their freedom for granted.

Most people fail to realize that not so very long ago people in other countries were fined or arrested and put in jail for playing or enjoying jazz. As a matter of fact, at the very same time that I was finishing college at Virginia State and preparing to make my way to New York, there was an assault on creative expression in Germany, the likes of which we have never seen here in the United States. These were the World War II years, and Hitler banned jazz on the radio, which he considered "enemy" music. Those who have experienced censorship have a very genuine and heartfelt appreciation for the privilege of enjoying good music.

Although we still have a long way to go in learning to fully appreciate and embrace our own classical music, this country has made great strides in other ways. Having grown up during segregation, I never thought I'd see an African American president in my lifetime. I never even imagined it as a possibility, and I think it's incredible. But I have not enjoyed the campaign. The debates, the political ads, the accusations all remind us that there are still some ugly feelings we must work together to overcome. It's all been too vicious. Even in 2008, there are many people who are simply not ready to call an African American "Mr. President." I can tell you now they'll give that young man a hard time. Barack Obama is sharp and optimistic and seems to really care about education, about the people. And I admire his courage. But I'm concerned about him. He'll have a hard way to go. It's always like that with anyone who blazes the trail. He has big ambitions, but there are some sobering moments ahead.

I've had the privilege of going to the White House on several occasions during my career. During some of those visits, the president was a Democrat, and during other visits, the president was a Republican. Regardless of the party affiliation, however, every invitation to the White House was extended to me by someone who cared about jazz. My purpose in accepting each of those invitations was simply to share the music which we value so deeply. Labels can be limiting and divisive, but music inspires, instructs, and unifies us.

I'm very concerned about education in this country, especially where music and the arts are concerned. Some of my most rewarding experiences as a musician have been those times when I've been before an audience of schoolchildren, youngsters who are innocent, and open, and eager to learn. I've visited many schools and spoken to thousands of students and have always marveled at the wide-eyed wonder that children have for jazz the first time they hear it. I tell young people that if they want to get good at playing, they must practice. And I'm honest with them. I tell them that sometimes it's hard. I was playing once at a school in Philadelphia and one of the kids watching my hands remarked that what I was doing seemed painful. I told him that it was. I don't have very large hands, so there are some things that are a stretch for me; I just have to work at it.

And there are some marvelous young people who've done just that. They've worked at it and paid their dues, and now they really deserve to be heard and given the credit they've earned. If anyone has any doubts about the reservoir of talent among our youth, look at Christian Sands. I first encountered Christian at our annual "Jazz in July" camp at my alma mater, the University of Massachusetts–Amherst. He not only has the work ethic and the technique, but he understands and communicates the language of jazz both in his playing and in his very articulate speaking. Look at Eldar Djangirov, the young pianist from the former Soviet Union. I met him at a Charlie Parker Symposium in Kansas City back around 2000 and was so amazed by this young man that we featured him as soon as we could on *CBS Sunday Morning*. These are just two of many young artists who are poised to do a great deal to keep jazz alive.

In the early 1990s, the Kennedy Center asked me to be their jazz advisor. I've always thought that women in jazz were the single overlooked and ill-used resource in America's Classical Music. When I was a kid, I would often hear, "She plays nice for a girl," an unfair assessment that resulted as much from ignorance as from gender bias. One of the first things I wanted to do at the Kennedy Center was the "Mary Lou Williams Women in Jazz Festival." When I told the Kennedy Center administration what I wanted to do, they asked me, "Can you find enough women to participate?" I came back with the names of one hundred female jazz artists. The 1996 festival featured Dee Dee Bridgewater, the Maria Schneider Jazz Orchestra, the Uptown String Quartet, Renee Rosnes Quartet, the Geri Allen Trio, the Shirley Horn Trio, Dorothy Donegan, Toshiko Akiyoshi, the Eliane Elias Trio, Marian McPartland, and all-star ensembles that included Terri Lynn Carrington, Carol Chaikin, Carmen Lundy, Elisa Pruett, Patrice Rushen, Lynee Arriale, Dottie Dodgion, Rebecca Coupe Franks, Debbie Keefe, and Mary Anne

McSweeney. Festivals after 1996 featured the Valerie Capers Trio, the Regina Carter Quintet, the Jane Bunnett Sextet, Ann Patterson's Maiden Voyage, the Vanessa Rubin Quartet, Jazzberry Jam, and many, many other artists that the world has been waiting to hear, women who are every bit the equal of their better-known male counterparts.

After starting the Mary Lou Williams Festival, I tried to find other ways to give female artists the recognition they deserve. I am especially proud of a segment I did on *CBS Sunday Morning* in January of 2001 on the all-girl jazz bands that were formed while the men were away fighting during World War II. Just as women stepped up to fill the vacancies in factories left by the men who were away for military service, women also filled the musical gap left by their male counterparts who were fighting overseas. There were nearly one hundred of these bands formed, including the International Sweethearts of Rhythm, Ina Ray Hutton's Melodears, and Rita Rio and her All-Girl Orchestra. The most famous of the groups was the International Sweethearts. Though predominantly African American, they were the first integrated all-female jazz band. In addition to African Americans, there were Asian American, Native American, and white musicians in the group. The band was originally started in 1937 to raise funds for Piney Woods School in Mississippi. They traveled in a bus built by the Piney Woods students and did one-nighters all over the country and became a national sensation, facing both sexism and racism, especially in the segregated South. Once the war ended, the International Sweethearts, like other female jazz groups, struggled to find opportunities to perform. They disbanded in 1949. I was thrilled to use my platform on *CBS Sunday Morning* to bring this important piece of forgotten American history to the public.

These efforts to give women musicians their long-overdue time in the spotlight are only a start. Women in jazz have been overlooked for nearly a century, so we still have a lot of catching up to do.

I wanted to do programs at the Kennedy Center that highlighted some special people. For example, we did a piano series called the "Art Tatum Piano Panorama Series" where five great pianists performed beneath a picture of Art Tatum looking down benignly upon them. I asked one of the pianists if Tatum's picture was intimidating. He responded that the image of the great master was inspirational.

For all the work we've done, sometimes I feel that we've gone back-ward in some ways. I caught a glimpse of a popular television show re-cently that raises serious questions for me about what we are teaching children to value. Contestants who had no musical talent whatsoever were auditioning for spots in a nationally televised singing competition. I could not find it entertaining. I found it shocking and sad, as it made me feel as though we have really lost sight of the importance of music education in this country.

Back when I was growing up, we were surrounded by good music and good teachers who invested a great deal in making sure that we learned to sing properly, to play properly. Whether it was classical music, or popular music, or jazz, didn't matter. What mattered was that there was a standard that we all seemed to recognize, a standard of quality that we all tried to attain. Sure, not everyone was destined to be a Roland Hayes or a Duke Ellington, but we recognized what sounded right and what didn't. We had music in our schools. In fact, there was never any question at all about the place of music and the arts in our schools. It was just a given. The arts were understood to be an indispensable part of a decent education. It really irritates me when I hear people talking about going back to basics. Music is basic. It is something that everyone can do. Everyone can sing and listen to music, even if they can't necessarily play an instrument.

Even today, we know that the kids who are getting into trouble are not the kids who are singing in the choir or playing in the band or in the orchestra or the kids who are in the school plays and musicals. The kids who are delinquent, those who stay in trouble, are the ones that have nothing to do. They are bored. They are the ones that are just sort of floating from one curiosity to the next, the ones that have never learned the discipline and satisfaction of working hard on a beautiful piece of music, or the joy and the teamwork that come from being in a band and learning to cooperate with the group in order to make something wonderful happen. The kids who are doing the shootings are not the kids who are learning to compose, or to write, or to act, or to improvise in a jazz band. The arts give children a sense of self-worth. The arts are a compass. The arts teach children how to create, how to solve problems, how to channel their ideas and frustrations in positive ways. This is not rocket science. It should be obvious to those who make policy decisions. Show me a kid who is always in trouble, and I can guarantee you that the arts are deficient in that youngster's life. Children are open, curious, and ready to receive what we're willing to teach them. I see it every time I speak at schools or give a concert where young people are present. They are intelligent. It's our job to teach them. Will we fail, or will we succeed?

I am encouraged about jazz. It excites me that right now, in the continental United States alone, there are some forty thousand jazz bands in schools around the country. If you figure that each one of those bands has about twenty people participating, and if you consider that each one of those young musicians has three or four friends or family members who may come to hear them perform, that's a large number of people who are connected to this music. I just hope that the International Association of Jazz Educators (IAJE), currently reorganized as Jazz Education Network (JEN), and some of the other groups that have been established to promote jazz will take advantage of the potential we have to really work toward improving the quality of musicianship in this country.

I'm very encouraged about what's become of Jazzmobile. It's now the longest-running summer jazz festival in New York. Over the past forty-plus years, it's grown to reach over a hundred thousand people each year, and while it remains deeply invested in the community, its reach has become international. The influence of Jazzmobile has reached many far-away places, Europe, Tokyo, Australia, the Philippines, and Canada, to name a few. The magic of Jazzmobile has always been the very immediate and practical way that it connects America's Classical Music directly to the people.

I enjoy working with the youth of this country, but I am also very sensitive to the people who are now around my age, fine musicians, many of them very accomplished players that we've allowed to simply slip away. Many of them haven't been able to get work and they are struggling. I saw the beginning of this problem when the clubs were dying out. At the same time that I was musical director for the *David Frost Show,* many great jazz musicians that I knew were unable to find work. I was very fortunate to be on television, and even more fortunate to be able to hand-pick musicians for the band, several of them African American. But I didn't pick these musicians because they were black; I

hired them because they were good. And there were scores of other superb African American musicians who were neither on television nor on
radio, and their sources of income dried up when the clubs went away. In
many cases, they were literally left with nothing to do. Understandably,
they were very frustrated because they felt that African American musicians were shut out of network broadcasting. So they decided to form
an organization called the Jazz and People's Movement (JPM), and they
launched a protest interrupting the taping of several talk shows, including the *Merv Griffin Show* and the *Dick Cavett Show.* This was in 1970.
I was the only African American musical director on television at that
time, so quite naturally, people wanted to know what I thought about
this. The fact that I was the *only* one on television should have answered
their curiosity. Whether or not people agreed with their methods, the
JPM was successful in bringing attention to the problem, which alerted
the networks to the need to hire more African American musicians.

Today, many of the older musicians who once found steady work
in clubs in the 1940s and 1950s are struggling. Some of them were rou-
tinely paid in cash, and others had money taken out of their paychecks
for Social Security and a union pension. But even for the latter group,
this income often falls short. And with age, you lose the facility and the
stamina that you once had. You can't play like you did when you were
twenty-five or thirty. But these musicians still have value and relevance.
They shouldn't be allowed to just sit and atrophy. I see this as another way
that Jazzmobile has significance and meaning, because it has provided a
way for older musicians to stay involved with young people and remain
visible in the community. Roy Eldridge, for example, couldn't hit the
same stratospheric notes that he once could when he was young, but he
was still of great value to the community as a musician. Jazzmobile gave
him an outlet for sharing his music and his story with youngsters who
might not otherwise know about him.

Funding for the arts in general, and for jazz in particular, has been
an ongoing battle, and it will continue to be a fight. The young artists
coming up today need to understand that they must be advocates of
what is important to us as musicians. They must be willing to influence
the policies that determine the quality of education our young people
will receive. Beginning in the 1960s, I spent many hours working on

councils and committees and going to meetings in order to argue for the importance of jazz. At the time, I knew that my involvement in these various efforts took away the precious hours that I would have liked to spend writing songs and playing the piano. Looking back, however, I have no regrets. It has been said that to whom much is given, much is required. I received incredible gifts from Elmira Streets, from Fats Waller, from Uncle Bob, from Henry Grant, from Roland Hayes, Paul Robeson, Marian Anderson, Mary Lou Williams, Duke Ellington, Dizzy Gillespie, and Art Tatum, and I have carried those gifts with me to all of the wonderful places that God has enabled me to go in this life. I've taken their gifts of faith, creativity, courage, and tenacity with me to every club, to every performance, to every council meeting, and to every radio broadcast. And I've tried to share those gifts with the children in Harlem running alongside the music of the Jazzmobile, as well as with the students gathered in assembly at public schools around the nation. For me, the burning desire to play has gone hand in hand with the need to teach about America's Classical Music, about what makes it special, what makes it worth playing, and loving, and preserving for the next, the next, and the next generation.

I am grateful for each opportunity I've had to pay homage to those who paved the way. In 1979, an hourlong PBS television special was produced titled *Memories of Eubie.* At the time, the veteran pianist and composer Eubie Blake was ninety-six years young. As sprightly and charming as ever, he performed several pieces, including "Charleston Rag," "Baltimore Buzz," "Memories of You," and a few other pieces. On that television special, it was my honor to do some brief narration of Eubie's life story and to play "Melodic Rag" and "Dixie on Seventh Avenue," all the while hoping for his approval and treasuring it when he gave it. Eubie's mind was sharp and his fingers were nimble. As I watched him play ragtime and stride piano, I time-traveled all the way back to my childhood in Washington, D.C., and my days of watching Uncle Bob play his own version of stride piano in our living room. Eubie's performances took me back through time to my all-too-brief lessons with Mr. Brown at the Howard Theatre and to all the master stride and rag players that I tried so desperately to emulate. And although spending that time with him conjured up cherished images and sentiments of decades gone by, there was a certain timelessness about Eubie Blake, a transcendence that proved to me that even in a body nearly a century old, the music can flow from the heart and through the fingers in a manner that simply defies the limitations of aging. His example inspired me then and inspires me now.

In 1995, I recorded a piece of mine called *Homage* with the Turtle Island String Quartet. The piece was done to honor those who had influenced me—Art Tatum, Jo Jones, Slam Stewart, Sid Catlett, Stuff Smith. These and others were the ones who laid the foundation for my life in jazz by passing to me what had been passed to them: the African heartbeat, the musical Mother Pulse with all of its history, its legacy, its responsibility. When I returned home from Europe back in the 1940s, many people asked me why I would choose to remain in America where my life was so restricted by segregation. Many African American artists immigrated to Europe for that reason, and people wanted to know why I wouldn't just do the same. I responded that America is my home, and I intended to stay here and live with the type of freedom that my elders and ancestors assured me would one day be possible. Their opportunities were limited, but their faith was strong and their predictions were right. We now know in ways that they could not how it feels to be free, how it feels to go not once, but several times to the marble and sandstone wonderland and play stride, swing, and bop for the president of the United States. But we mustn't forget our ancestors' struggles, their examples, their lessons, and their creativity. *Can you swing?* That is the question.

À Bientôt.

$\mathcal{D}$iscography

Track titles in italics indicate pieces composed by Dr. Billy Taylor. Pieces in italics and indicated with an asterisk (*) were composed by Teddi Castion Taylor.

DATE/LOCATION:MARCH 20, 1945, NEW YORK
Title: *Billy Taylor Trio*
Label: Savoy XP8095 / Savoy MG12008 / Savoy MG9035
Personnel: Billy Taylor, piano; Al Hall, bass; Jimmy Crawford, drums
Tracks: *"Mad Monk,"* "Solace," "Night and Day," "Alexander's Ragtime Band"

DATE/LOCATION:DECEMBER 4, 1946, PARIS
Title: *Billy Taylor, Ted Sturgis, and Buford Oliver*
Label: Swing 234 / Classics 11370
Personnel: Billy Taylor, piano; Ted Sturgis, bass; Buford Oliver, drums
Tracks: "The Very Thought of You," "Striding Down the Champs-Elysees"

DATE/LOCATION:JUNE 1947, NEW YORK
Title: *Billy Taylor Quartet*
Label: H.R.S. 1038 / H.R.S. 1039 / Mosaic MD6–187
Personnel: Billy Taylor, piano; John Collins, guitar;
John Levy, bass; Denzil Best, drums
Tracks: *"Well Taylored,"* "I Don't Ask Questions,"
"So You Think You're Cute," *"Twinkle Toes"*

DATE/LOCATION:SEPTEMBER 26, 1947, NEW YORK
Title: *Billy Taylor Quartet*
Label: H.R.S. 1048 / H.R.S. 1049 / MOSAIC MD6-187
Personnel: Billy Taylor, piano; Herman Mitchell, guitar;
John Levy, bass; Denzil Best, drums
Tracks: *"Mr. B. Bops,"* "Restricted," *"Striding Down the Champs-Elysees,"*
"Mitch's Pitch"

DATE/LOCATION:NOVEMBER 20, 1949, NEW YORK
Title: *Billy Taylor Quintet*
Label: Savoy XP8113 / Savoy MG9035 / Savoy MG 12008
Personnel: Billy Taylor, piano; John Hardee, tenor sax; Milt Page, organ;
John Simmons, bass; Joe Harris, Shadow Wilson, drums
Tracks: "Misty Morning Blues," "The Bug," "Prelude to a Kiss,"
"Take the A Train"

DATE/LOCATION:FEBRUARY 20, 1951, NEW YORK
Title: *Billy Taylor Quartet*
Label: Atlantic 676 / Atlantic LP113 / Atlantic LP1277
Personnel: Billy Taylor, piano; John Collins, guitar;
Al Hall, bass; Shadow Wilson, drums
Tracks: *"Good Groove,"* "Wrap Your Troubles in Dreams," "What Is There
to Say?," "Thou Swell," "Willow Weep for Me," "The Very Thought of You,"
"Somebody Loves Me," "If I Had You," *"Cuban Caper"* (unissued)

DATE/LOCATION:MAY 25, 1951, NEW YORK
Title: *Billy Taylor Trio*
Label: Brunswick 65025 / Brunswick EB71000
Personnel: Billy Taylor, piano; Aaron Bell, bass; Kelly Martin, drums
Tracks: "All Ears," "Darn That Dream," "My Heart Stood Still,"
"Double Duty"

DATE/LOCATION:NOVEMBER 1, 1951, NEW YORK
Title: *Billy Taylor Quintet*
Label: Roost 566 / Roost 537
Personnel: Billy Taylor, piano; Mundell Lowe, guitar; Earl May, bass;
Jo Jones, drums; Zoot Sims, maracas; Frank Conlon, conga
Tracks: *"Cuban Caper," "Cu-Blue,"* "Squeeze Me," *"Feeling Frisky"*

DATE/LOCATION:FEBRUARY 18, 1952, NEW YORK
Title: *Billy Taylor and His Orchestra*
Label: Unissued; recorded at the Royal Roost
Personnel: Billy Taylor, piano and conductor; Taft Jordan, trumpet;
George Matthews, trombone; Doc Clifford, George James, alto sax;
George Berg, Stan Getz, tenor sax; Bill Dogget, organ;
Earl May, bass; Charlie Smith, drums
Tracks: "Alone," "To Be or Not to Bop," "Lonesome and Blue," "Paradise"

DATE/LOCATION:MAY 2, 1952, NEW YORK
Title: *Billy Taylor Sextet*
Label: Roost 552
Personnel: Billy Taylor, piano; Chuck Wayne, guitar; Earl May, bass;
Charlie Smith, drums, Frank Conlon, Manny Quendo, bongos, conga
Tracks: "Cuban Nightingale," *"Titoro,"* "Makin' Whoopee,"
"Moonlight Saving Time"

DATE/LOCATION:JULY 11, 1952
Title: *Billy Taylor Quartet*
Label: Brunswick 80215
Personnel: Billy Taylor, piano; Chuck Wayne, guitar; George Duvivier, bass;
Sid Bulkin, drums; Oscar Pettiford, cello
Tracks: "Three Little Words," "Oscar Rides Again"

DATE/LOCATION:AUTUMN 1952, STORYVILLE CLUB, BOSTON
Title: *Billy Taylor Trio: George Wein Presents Jazz at Storyville*
Label: Roost LP406
Personnel: Billy Taylor, piano; Charlie Mingus, bass; Marquis Foster, drums
Tracks: "Laura," "Ladybird," "All the Things You Are," "I'm Beginning
to See the Light," "What Is This Thing Called Love?"

DATE/LOCATION:NOVEMBER 18, 1952, NEW YORK
Title: *Billy Taylor Trio*
Label: Prestige 796 / Prestige 797 / Prestige 24154
Personnel: Billy Taylor, piano; Earl May, bass; Charlie Smith, drums
Tracks: "They Can't Take That Away from Me," "All Too Soon,"
"Accent on Youth," "Give Me the Simple Life"

DATE/LOCATION:DECEMBER 10, 1952, NEW YORK
Title: *Billy Taylor Trio*
Label: Prestige 822 / Prestige 849 / Prestige 24154
/ Prestige PRLP 139 / Prestige LP16-2
Personnel: Billy Taylor, piano; Earl May, bass; Charlie Smith, drums
Tracks: "Little Girl Blue," "The Man with a Horn,"
"Let's Get Away from It All," "Lover"

DATE/LOCATION:MAY 7, 1953, NEW YORK
Title: *Billy Taylor Sextet*
Label: Prestige 869 / Prestige 870 / Prestige PRLP 7071
Personnel: Billy Taylor, piano; Earl May, bass; Charlie Smith, drums;
Chico Guerrero, Jose Mangual, Ubaldo Nieto, bongos, conga
Tracks: *"I Love the Mambo," "Candido," "Early Morning Mambo,"
"Mambo Azul"*

DATE/LOCATION:NOVEMBER 2, 1953, NEW YORK
Title: *Billy Taylor Trio*
Label: Prestige 888 / Prestige 895 / Prestige 900 / Prestige
24154 / Prestige PREP 1333 / Prestige PREP 1335
Personnel: Billy Taylor, piano; Earl May, bass; Charlie Smith, drums
Tracks: *"Cool and Caressing,"* "Who Can I Turn To?,"
"My One and Only Love," "Tenderly," "I've Got the World on a String,"
"Bird Watcher," "B.T.'s D.T.'s," "Hey Lock"

DATE/LOCATION: DECEMBER 9, 1953, NEW YORK
Title: *Joe Holiday–Billy Taylor Septet*
Label: Prestige 883 / Prestige 878 / Prestige 887
Personnel: Joe Holiday, tenor sax; Billy Taylor, piano, organ;
Earl May, bass; Charlie Smith, drums and conga; Jose Mangual,
bongos; Ubaldo Nieto, timbales; Machito, maracas
Tracks: "Sleep," "Besame Mucho," "I Don't Want to Walk without You," "Fiesta"

DATE/LOCATION: DECEMBER 29, 1953, NEW YORK
Title: *Billy Taylor Trio*
Label: Prestige 888 / Prestige 892 / Prestige PREP 1334
Personnel: Billy Taylor, piano; Earl May, bass; Charlie Smith, drums
Tracks: "That's All," "The Little Things," "Nice Work if You
Can Get It," "Surrey with the Fringe on Top"

DATE/LOCATION: JULY 30, 1954, RUDY VAN GELDER STUDIO,
HACKENSACK, NEW JERSEY
Title: *Billy Taylor Trio*
Label: Prestige 904 / Prestige PRLP 184
Personnel: Billy Taylor, piano; Earl May, bass; Charlie Smith, drums
Tracks: *"Tune for Tex,"* "Moonlight in Vermont," "I'll Be Around,"
"Biddy's Beat," "Eddie's Tune," "Mood for Mendes," "Goodbye,"
"Lullaby of Birdland"

DATE/LOCATION: AUGUST 25, 1954, NEW YORK
Title: *Joe Holiday–Billy Taylor Quartet*
Label: Prestige PRLP 171 / Prestige 897 / Prestige 901
Personnel: Joe Holiday, tenor sax; Billy Taylor, piano;
Earl May, bass; Charlie Smith, drums
Tracks: "I Love You Much," "Chasin' the Bongo,"
"It Might as Well Be Spring"

DATE/LOCATION: SEPTEMBER 7, 1954, RUDY VAN GELDER STUDIO,
HACKENSACK, NEW JERSEY
Title: *Billy Taylor Trio with Candido*
Label: Prestige EP1344 / Prestige PRLP188 / Prestige PRLP 7051
Personnel: Billy Taylor, piano; Earl May, bass; Charlie
Smith, drums; Candido Camero, conga
Tracks: *"Declivity," "A Live One,"* "Mambo Inn," *"Bit of Bedlam,"*
"Different Bells," "Love for Sale"

DATE/LOCATION: DECEMBER 17, 1954, TOWN HALL, NEW YORK
Title: *Billy Taylor Trio*
Label: Prestige PRLP 194 / Prestige PRLP 7093
Personnel: Billy Taylor, piano; Earl May, bass; Percy Brice, drums
Tracks: "A Foggy Day," "I'll Remember April," "Sweet Georgia Brown,"
"Theodora," "How High the Moon"

DATE/LOCATION:APRIL 10, 1955, RUDY VAN GELDER STUDIO,
HACKENSACK, NEW JERSEY
Title: *A Touch of Taylor*
Label: Prestige PRLP 7001 / Prestige 24285
Personnel: Billy Taylor, piano; Earl May, bass; Percy Brice, drums
Tracks: *"Early Bird," "À Bientôt," "Memories of Spring," "Ever So Easy,"*
"Day Dreaming," "Radioactivity," "Purple Mood," *"Long Tom," "It's a*
Grand Night for Swinging," "Blue Clouds," "Live It Up," "Daddy-O"

DATE/LOCATION:JANUARY 1 AND 2, 1956, NEW YORK
Title: *"Evergreens" Billy Taylor Trio*
Label: ABC-Paramount ABC 112
Personnel: Billy Taylor, piano; Earl May, bass; Percy Brice, drums
Tracks: "But Not for Me," "All the Things You Are," "Cheek to Cheek,"
"Between the Devil and the Deep Blue Sea," "I Only Have Eyes for
You," "It's Too Late Now," "More than You Know," "Satin Doll,"
"Then I'll Be Tired of You," "You Don't Know What Love Is"

DATE/LOCATION:JANUARY 22, 1956, CHICAGO,
THE LONDON HOUSE
Title: *Billy Taylor Trio at the London House*
Label: ABC-Paramount ABC 134
Personnel: Billy Taylor, piano; Earl May, bass; Percy Brice, drums
Tracks: "Gone with the Wind," "I Cover the Waterfront,"
"It Might as Well Be Spring," "Our Love Is Here to Stay,"
"The London House," "Midnight Piano," "Stella by Starlight"

DATE/LOCATION:MARCH 1, 1956, NEW YORK
Title: *Know Your Jazz*
Label: ABC-Paramount ABC 115
Personnel: This album demonstrates the various styles of jazz and
includes eleven different artists. The Billy Taylor Trio on this
project includes Billy Taylor, piano; George Duvivier, bass; and
Percy Brice, drums.
Tracks: "Indiana" (the only tune on the album performed by
Taylor Trio.)

DATE/LOCATION:NOVEMBER, 1956, NEW YORK (?)
Title: *Billy Taylor Trio Introduces Ira Sullivan*
Label: ABC Paramount ABC-162
Personnel: Ira Sullivan, trumpet, alto sax, tenor sax;
Billy Taylor, piano; Earl May, bass; Ed Thigpen, drums
Tracks: "So in Love," "Imagination," "Strollin',"
"They Can't Take That Away from Me," "Leslie's Gauge,"
"In a Mellow Tone," "You Don't Know What Love Is"

DATE/LOCATION: JANUARY 8, JANUARY 22,
AND FEBRUARY 5, 1957, NEW YORK
Title: *My Fair Lady Loves Jazz: Billy Taylor Trio with Quincy Jones*
Label: ABC Paramount ABC-177/GRD 141
Personnel: (All personnel for entire project) Billy Taylor, piano; Earl May, bass;
Ed Thigpen, drums; Ernie Royal, trumpet; Don Elliott, trumpet, mellophone,
vibraphone, bongos; Jimmy Cleveland, trombone; Jim Buffington, French horn;
Don Butterfield, tuba; Tony Ortega, alto sax and tenor sax; Charlie Fowlkes,
Gerry Mulligan, baritone sax; Al Casamenti, guitar; Jay McAllister, tuba;
baritone sax; Quincy Jones, conductor
Tracks: "Show Me," "I've Grown Accustomed to Her Face," "With a Little Bit of
Luck," "The Rain in Spain," "Get Me to the Church on Time," "Wouldn't It Be
Lovely?," "I Could Have Danced All Night," "On the Street Where You Live"

DATE/LOCATION: AUGUST 8, 1957, NEW YORK
Title: *Billy Taylor Trio* Label: Atlantic unissued
Personnel: Billy Taylor, piano; unknown, bass; unknown, piano
Tracks: "You Make Me Feel So Young," "Can't You Tell?,"
"Blues," "I Get a Kick Out of You"

DATE/LOCATION: OCTOBER 25, 1957, NEW YORK
Title: *The New Billy Taylor Trio*
Label: ABC Paramount ABC(S) 226
Personnel: Billy Taylor, piano; Earl May, bass; Ed Thigpen, drums
Tracks: "Small Hotel," "The More I See You"

DATE/LOCATION: OCTOBER 28, 1957, NEW YORK
Title: *The New Billy Taylor Trio* (aka "*The Billy Taylor Touch*")
Label: Atlantic LP1277
Personnel: Billy Taylor, piano; Earl May, bass; Ed Thigpen, drums
Tracks: "*Can You Tell by Looking at Me?*," "You Make Me Feel
So Young," "I Get a Kick Out of You," "*Earl May*"

DATE/LOCATION: NOVEMBER 17, 1957, CHICAGO
Title: *Billy Taylor and His Orchestra* (also released as *Taylor-Made Jazz,* 1959)
Label: Argo LP(S) 650
Personnel: Billy Taylor, piano and conductor; Earl May, bass; Ed Thigpen, drums;
Willie Cook and Clark Terry, trumpet; Britt Woodman, trombone; Johnny Hodges,
alto sax; Paul Gonsalves, tenor sax; Harry Carney, baritone sax
Tracks: "*Biddy's Beat,*" "*Theodora,*" "*Mood for Mendes,*" "*Daddy-O,*"
"*Cu-Blue,*" "*Day Dreaming,*" "Can You Tell?," "Tune Up!"

DATE/LOCATION: DECEMBER 16 AND 17, 1957, NEW YORK
Title: *Billy Taylor Trio*
Label: ABC Paramount ABC(S) 226
Personnel: Billy Taylor, piano; Earl May, bass; Ed Thigpen, drums
Tracks: "'Round Midnight," "I Never Get Enough," "*Sounds in the Night,*"
"Will You Still Be Mine," "*Titoro,*" "There'll Never Be Another You"

DATE/LOCATION:JUNE 24, 1959, NEW YORK
Title: *Billy Taylor Trio*
Label: Atlantic LP (SD) 1329
Personnel: Billy Taylor, piano; Earl May, bass; Kenny Dennis, drums
Tracks: "Summertime," *"One for Fun," "That's for Sure,"*
"A Little Southside Soul," "Blue Moon," "Poinciana,"
"At Long Last Love," "When Lights Are Low"

DATE/LOCATION:JULY 20 AND JULY 24, 1959, NEW YORK
Title: *Billy Taylor with Four Flutes*
Label: Riverside RLP306 (reissued on Original Jazz Classics)
Personnel (all personnel for both dates): Billy Taylor, piano;
Tom Williams, bass; Dave Bailey, Al Heath, drums; Chino Pozo,
conga; Phil Bodner, Herbie Mann, Frank Wess, Jerome Richardson,
Bill Slapin, Jerry Sanfino, Seldon Powell, flute
Tracks: "The Song Is Ended," *"Back Home," "One for the Woofer,"*
"Kool Bongos," *"Blue Shutters,"* "St. Thomas," "Oh Lady Be Good,"
"How About You?," *"No Parking"*

DATE/LOCATION:FEBRUARY 4, 1960, PRELUDE CLUB, NEW YORK
Title: *Billy Taylor Trio* (see also *"Billy Taylor Uptown Live"*)
Label: Riverside RLP 319 / Original Jazz Classics 1901
Personnel: Billy Taylor, piano; Henry Grimes, bass; Ray Mosca, drums
Tracks: "La Petite Mambo," "Jordu," *"Just the Thought of You,"*
"Soul Sister," "Moanin'," *"S'Wonderful,"* "Warm Blue Stream,"
"Biddy's Beat," "Cu-Blue"

DATE/LOCATION:MARCH 26, 1960, NEW YORK
Title: *Billy Taylor Trio*
Label: Riverside RLP 12–339 (see also *Custom-Taylored—*
Sesac 3001 and Fresh Sound 205)
Personnel: Billy Taylor, piano; Henry Grimes, bass; Ray Mosca, drums
Tracks: *"Warming Up,"* *"Easy Like,"* *"That's Where It Is,"*
"Coffee Break," "Native Dancer," *"Afterthoughts," "Easy Walker,"*
"Lonesome Lover," "Don't Bug Me," "You Know What I Mean,"
"Uncle Fuzzy," "No Aftertaste"

**DATE/LOCATION: JANUARY 3, 1961, RUDY VAN GELDER STUDIO,
ENGLEWOOD CLIFFS, NEW JERSEY**
Title: *Billy Taylor—Interlude*
Label: Moodsville MVLP 16
Personnel: Billy Taylor, piano; Doug Watkins, bass; Ray Mosca, drums
Tracks: *"You Tempt Me,"* "Did You Dream Too?," *"You're All that*
Matters," *"Interlude," "You're Mine,"* "My Heart Sings," *"I Sigh,"*
"Here Today," "Gone Tomorrow Love," *"All Alone"*

DATE/LOCATION:SEPTEMBER 12 AND 13, 1961
Title: *Original Jazz Score of Kwamina Featuring the Billy Taylor Orchestra*
Label: Mercury MG 20654
Personnel: Billy Taylor, piano; George Duvivier, bass; Osie Johnson, drums;
Clark Terry, trumpet and flugelhorn; Jimmy Cleveland, trombone; Julius Watkins,
French horn; Jay McAllister, tuba; Phil Woods, alto sax; Frank Wess, tenor sax;
Jerome Richardson, baritone sax; Les Spann, guitar; Jimmy Jones, arranger, conductor
Tracks: "Something Big," "I See Rainbows," "Ordinary People,"
"The Cocoa Bean Song," "What's Wrong with Me," "Nothing
More to Look Forward To," "Another Time, Another Place,"
"Happy Is the Cricket," "Sun Is Beginning to Crow"

DATE/LOCATION:MAY 8, 9, AND 10, 1962, NEW YORK
Title: *Billy Taylor Impromptu*
Label: Mercury MG20722/Mercury 60722
Personnel: Billy Taylor, piano; Jim Hall, guitar; Bob
Cranshaw, bass; Walter Perkins, drums
Tracks: *"Don't Go South," "Empty Ballroom," "Impromptu," "Muffle Guffle,"*
"Paraphrase," "At La Carrousel," "Capricious," "Free and Oozy"

DATE/LOCATION:1962–1963, NEW YORK
Title: *Right Here, Right Now! Billy Taylor with Trio and Oliver Nelson*
Label: Capitol (S) T2039
Personnel (all sessions): Billy Taylor, piano; Ben Tucker, bass; Grady Tate, drums;
John Bello, Snooky Young, Joe Newman, Thad Jones, Ernie Royal, Doc Severinsen,
Clark Terry, trumpet; Wayne Andre, Britt Woodman, Quentin Jackson,
Tony Studd, Urbie Green, trombone; Phil Woods, Jerome Richardson,
Romeo Penque, Stanley Webb, Danny Bank, saxophones;
Oliver Nelson, arranger and conductor
Tracks:*"That's Where It Is," *"Lot of Livin' to Do," "Right Here, Right Now,"
"I Believe in You," *"Easy Walker,"* *"Afterthoughts,"* "Stolen Moments,"
"Give Me the Simple Life," *"Something Always Happens," "Soul Sister,"*
"Freedom," "I Wish I Knew (How It Would Feel to Be Free)"

DATE/LOCATION:OCTOBER 12, 13, AND 14, 1964
Title: *Midnight Piano*
Label: Capitol ST-2302
Personnel (all sessions): Billy Taylor, piano; Robert Northern, percussion;
Romeo Penque, Robert Ashton, Jerome Richardson, reeds; Joseph Singer,
Richard Berg, horn; Tony Studd, Quentin Jackson, Jimmy Cleveland,
Urbie Green, trombone; Ben Tucker, bass; Phil Woods, alto sax; Snooky Young,
Clark Terry, Joe Newman, Joe Wilder, trumpet; Ray Alonge, horn; Barry
Galbraith, guitar; Julius Held, percussion and reeds; GradyTate, drums
Tracks: *"Midnight Piano,"* "You Came a Long Way from St. Louis,"
"Just the Thought of You," *"A Secret," "My Romance,"* *"It's a Grand Night*
for Swinging," "You Tempt Me," *"Don't Ever Say that We're Through,"*
"Days of Wine and Roses," "Miss Fine," "This Is All I Ask," "Love for Sale"

DATE/LOCATION:APRIL 1969, NEW YORK
Title: *Billy Taylor Today* (See also Billy Taylor Trio, *Sleeping Bee*")
Label: Prestige 7762
Personnel: Billy Taylor, piano; Ben Tucker, bass; Grady Tate, drums
Tracks: "La Petite Mambo," *"Theodora," "Paraphrase,"*
"Bye Y'all," "Don't Go Down South," "Brother, Where Are You?,"
"There Will Never Be Another You," "A Sleeping Bee"

DATE/LOCATION:1970, NEW YORK
Title: *OK Billy!*
Label: Bell Records 6049
Personnel: Billy Taylor, piano; Jimmy Owens, Dick Hurwitz, trumpet;
Morty Bullman, trombone; Frank Wess, alto sax and flute; George Berg,
Al Gibbons, saxophone; Bob Cranshaw, electric bass;
Barry Galbraith, guitar; Bobby Thomas, drums
Tracks: "By George—It's the David Frost Theme," *"OK Billy!,"*
"Somewhere Soon," "Tell Me Why," "Dirty Ole Man," *"If You Really Are*
Concerned, Then Show It," "Break Away," "After Love Emptiness"

DATE/LOCATION:1970, NEW YORK
Title: *From David Frost and Billy Taylor, Merry Christmas*
Label: Bell 6053
Personnel: Billy Taylor, piano and conductor; Jimmy Owens and
Dick Hurwitz, trumpet; Morty Bullman, trombone; Frank Wess,
Seldon Powell, and George Berg, reeds; Richie Resnicoff, guitar;
Bob Cranshaw, bass; Bob Thomas, drums; Marty Grupp, percussion
Tracks: "Joy to the World," "Rise Up Shepherd," *"We Need Peace and*
We Need Love," "Wexford Carole," *"Bright Star in the East,"* "Away in a Manger,"
"Stable Down the Road," "Merry Christmas," "Christmas Song," "Go Tell It on
the Mountain," "The House of Christmas," "Go Tell It on the Mountain (reprise)"

DATE/LOCATION:JUNE 21 1977, RECORDED LIVE AT
THE UNIVERSITY OF TEXAS AT AUSTIN
Title: *Jazz Alive*
Label: Monmouth Evergreen Mes 7089
Personnel: Billy Taylor, piano; Victor Gaskin, bass; Freddie Waits, drums
Tracks(recorded premiere of *Suite for Jazz Piano and Orchestra*): *Duane* (first
movement of the *Suite*), *Well It's Been So Long* (second movement of the *Suite*),
Côte d'Ivoire (third movement of the *Suite*), "Solitude," "In a Mellow Tone,"
"Drop Me Off at Harlem," "Caravan," "Come Sunday," "Satin Doll"

DATE/LOCATION:DECEMBER 2 AND 3, 1977, NEW YORK
Title: *Live at Storyville*
Label: West 54 8008
Personnel: Billy Taylor, piano; Victor Gaskin, bass; Grady Tate, drums
Tracks: "Misty," "A Night in Tunisia," "My Heart Sings," "Naima,"
"Bird Watcher," "Lush Life," *"I Wish I Knew How It Would Feel to Be Free"*

DATE/LOCATION:JANUARY 1, 1978
Title: *The Billy Taylor Trio in Live Performance*
Label: Monmouth MES 7098
Personnel: No information available
Tracks:No information available

DATE/LOCATION:1981
Title: *Where've You Been?*
Label: Concord Jazz CJ 145
Personnel: Billy Taylor, piano; Victor Gaskin, bass;
Keith Copeland, drums; Joe Kennedy, violin
Tracks: *"Where've You Been?," "Night Coming Tenderly,"*
"Ray's Tune," "Antoinette," "I'm in Love with You,"
"All Alone," "I Think of You," "Capricious"

DATE/LOCATION:JUNE 24, 1985
Title: *You Tempt Me*
Label: Taylor Made 1004
Personnel: Billy Taylor, piano; Victor Gaskin, bass; Curtis Boyd, drums
Tracks: "Take the A Train," *"Tom, Vaguely," "You Tempt Me," "Let Us Make*
a Joyful Noise," "Rejoice," "Prayer," "Celebrate," "Walking in the Light"

DATE/LOCATION:JUNE 14 AND 15, 1988
Title: *White Nights and Jazz in Leningrad*
Label: Taylor Made T 1001
Personnel: Billy Taylor, piano; Victor Gaskin, bass; Bobby Thomas, drums
Tracks: "Secret Love," "Pensativa," "A Child Is Born," "C-A-G, " "I
Remember You," *"Your Smile," "My Romance," "Jingles," "Morning"*

DATE/LOCATION:AUGUST 1 AND 2, 1988, NEW YORK
Title: *Billy Taylor Solo*
Label: Taylor Made T 1002
Personnel: Billy Taylor, piano
Tracks: "All the Things You Are," *"À Bientôt," "Handle with Care,"*
"Old Folks," *"A Tune for Howard to Improvise Upon," "Cool and Caressing,"*
"I Didn't Know What Time It Was," "Yesterdays," "More than You Know,"
"A Bit of Bedlam," "For Undine," "Billy's Beat," "Gone with the Wind"

DATE/LOCATION:APRIL 5 AND 6, 1989, NEW YORK
Title: *The Jazzmobile Allstars*
Label: Taylor Made T-1003
Personnel: Billy Taylor, piano; Victor Gaskin, bass; Bobby Thomas, drums;
Ted Dunbar, guitar; Jimmy Owens, flugelhorn and trumpet;
Frank Wess, saxophone and flute
Tracks: *"Bird Watcher," "Ceora," "Is This the Blues?," "Solo for Flugelhorn,"*
"Same Old Seven," "Fanfare for Soprano Sax," "Valse," "Turnaround,"
"Ballade," "Sketch"

DATE/LOCATION:1993, NEW YORK
Title: *Billy Taylor, "Dr. T" Featuring Gerry Mulligan*
Label: GRP 9692
Personnel: Billy Taylor, piano; Victor Gaskin, bass;
Bobby Thomas, drums; Gerry Mulligan, baritone sax
Tracks: "I'll Remember April," "'Round Midnight," "Line for Lyons,"
"Cubano Chant," "Lush Life," "Who Can I Turn To?," "Laurentide
Waltz," *"You're Mine," "Just the Thought of You,"* "Rico Apollo"

DATE/LOCATION:1993, NEW YORK
Title: *It's a Matter of Pride*
Label: GRP GRD 9753
Personnel: Billy Taylor, piano; Christian McBride, bass; Marvin Smith, drums;
Stanley Turrentine, tenor saxophone; Grady Tate, vocals; Ray Mantilla, conga
Tracks: *"At La Carousel," "Picture This," "It's a Matter of Pride,"*
"His Name Was Martin," "Titoro," "Back Home," "Lookin' Up,"
"Paraphrase," "I'm a Lover," "If You Really Are Concerned"

**DATE/LOCATION:OCTOBER 10 AND 11, 1994, CLINTON
RECORDING STUDIOS, NEW YORK**
Title: *Homage*
Label: GRP GRD 9806
Personnel: Billy Taylor, piano; Chip Jackson, bass; Steve Johns, drum;
Jim Saparito, percussion; and the Turtle Island String Quartet, including
Darol Anger and Tracy Silverman, violin; Danny Seidenberg, viola;
Mark Summer, cello
Tracks: *"Homage,"* Parts I, II, and III; Step into My Dream: *"Step into My Dream,"*
"Billy and Dave," "On this Lean Mean Street," "Barbados Beauty," "Kim's Song,"
"Hope and Hostility," "Uncle Bob," "Two Shades of Blue," "Dave and Billy,"
"Back to My Dream"; "It Happens All the Time," "One for Fun"

DATE/LOCATION:AUGUST 6, 7, AND 8, 1996, NEW YORK
Title: *Music Keeps Us Young*
Label: Arkadia Jazz 71601
Personnel: Billy Taylor, piano; Chip Jackson, bass; Steve Johns, drums
Tracks: "Wouldn't It Be Loverly," "Lover Come Back to Me," *"I Wish I Knew
How It Would Feel to Be Free,"* "Body and Soul," *"One for the Woofer," "Ballade,"*
"Naima," "Up Jumped Spring," *"Caravan," "Interlude," "Arkadia Blues"*

DATE/LOCATION:1999, NEW YORK
Title: *Ten Fingers One Voice*
Label: Arkadia Jazz 71602
Personnel: Billy Taylor, piano
Tracks: "Wrap Your Troubles in Dreams," "In a Sentimental Mood,"
"Joy Spring," "Laura," *"Easy Like,"* "Night and Day,"
"Can You Tell by Looking at Me," "Early Bird," "Tea for Two,"
"Solo," "My Heart Stood Still"

DATE/LOCATION: NOVEMBER 13 AND DECEMBER 9, 2000,
MANHATTAN CENTER STUDIOS, NEW YORK
Title: *Urban Griot*
Label: Soundpost Records SP-3050-2
Personnel: Billy Taylor, piano; Chip Jackson, bass; Winard Harper, drums
Tracks: *"Local Color / Can You Dig it?," "Reclamation," "Gracious Chucho,"*
"Etude," "Conversion," "Spoken," "In Loving Memory," "Like a Heartbeat,"
"Invention / Looking for Another Theme," "Transformation," "A Duke-ish Blues"

DATE/LOCATION:JANUARY 13, 2001,
29TH ANNUAL IAJE CONFERENCE, NEW YORK
Title: *Live at IAJE*
Label: Soundpost Records SP 5090-2
Personnel: Billy Taylor, piano; Chip Jackson, bass; Winard Harper, drums
Tracks: "Introduction by Dr. Ron McCurdy," *"Impromptu,"*
"Body and Soul," *"Conversion," "Titoro," "Côte d'Ivoire"*

Selected Publications Authored

BY DR. BILLY TAYLOR

1949. *Billy Taylor's Basic Bebop Instruction for Piano*. New York: C. H. Hansen Music Company.

1950. *Ragtime Piano Solos and How to Play Them*. New York: C. H. Hansen Music Company.

1953. *Modern Jazz Piano Solos*. New York: C. H. Hansen Music Company.

1954. *Combo Arranging: How to Arrange for Jazz Trios, Quartets, and Quintets*. New York: C. H. Hansen Music Company.

1955. *Touch of Taylor: Four Modern Piano Solos*. New York: C. H. Hansen Music Corporation.

1982. *Jazz Piano: History and Development*. Dubuque: W. C. Brown.

1999. *The Billy Taylor Collection*. Milwaukee: Hal Leonard Corporation.

2004. *Billy Taylor's Taylor Made Piano*. New York: Duane Music.

2007. *Billy Taylor Piano Styles: A Practical Approach to Playing Piano in Various Styles*. Milwaukee: Hal Leonard Corporation.

Index

Page numbers in *italics* indicate photographs.

DR. BILLY TAYLOR (1921–2010) served as the Duke Ellington Fellow at Yale University, Artistic Advisor for Jazz to the Kennedy Center for the Performing Arts, and Board Member on the National Council for the Arts. A lifelong spokesperson for jazz, he hosted radio shows in New York, on National Public Radio, and became the jazz correspondent on *CBS Sunday Morning*. With over 23 honorary doctoral degrees, Dr. Billy Taylor is also the recipient of two Peabody Awards, an Emmy, a Grammy, and a host of prestigious and highly coveted prizes, such as the National Medal of Arts, the Tiffany Award, a Lifetime Achievement Award from *Downbeat Magazine*, and election to the Hall of Fame for the International Association for Jazz Education.

TERESA L. REED is director of the School of Music at the University of Tulsa, where she teaches music theory and African American music.